Sexual Harassment

Other Books in the Current Controversies Series:

Sexual Harassment

Louise I. Gerdes, *Book Editor*

David Bender, *Publisher*
Bruno Leone, *Executive Editor*

Bonnie Szumski, *Editorial Director*
David M. Haugen, *Managing Editor*

CURRENT CONTROVERSIES

Cover photo: © Tony Stone Images/David Oliver

Library of Congress Cataloging-in-Publication Data

Sexual harassment / Louise I. Gerdes, book editor.
     p. cm. — (Current controversies)
    Includes bibliographical references (p.   ) and index.
    ISBN 0-7377-0067-X (lib. : alk. paper). — ISBN 0-7377-0066-1
(pbk. : alk. paper)
    1. Sexual harassment of women—United States. 2. Sexual harassment of men—United States. 3. Sexual harassment—Law and legislation—United States. I. Gerdes, Louise I. II. Series.
HQ1206.S454   1999
305.3—dc21   98-56191
                                          CIP

Contents

Chapter 1: Is Sexual Harassment a Serious Problem?

Yes: Sexual Harassment Is a Serious Problem

No: Sexual Harassment Is Not a Serious Problem

Chapter 2 : What Causes Sexual Harassment?

Chapter 3: How Can Sexual Harassment Be Reduced?

Chapter 4: Are Legal Definitions of Sexual Harassment Useful?

Yes: Legal Definitions of Sexual Harassment Are Useful

of privacy, defamation, and violation of due process and free speech rights. Unless the discipline was clearly improper, courts usually support employers and their interpretation of sexual harassment law.

No: Legal Definitions of Sexual Harassment Are Harmful

Foreword

By definition, controversies are "discussions of questions in which opposing opinions clash" (Webster's Twentieth Century Dictionary Unabridged). Few would deny that controversies are a pervasive part of the human condition and exist on virtually every level of human enterprise. Controversies transpire between individuals and among groups, within nations and between nations. Controversies supply the grist necessary for progress by providing challenges and challengers to the status quo. They also create atmospheres where strife and warfare can flourish. A world without controversies would be a peaceful world; but it also would be, by and large, static and prosaic.

The Series' Purpose

The purpose of the Current Controversies series is to explore many of the social, political, and economic controversies dominating the national and international scenes today. Titles selected for inclusion in the series are highly focused and specific. For example, from the larger category of criminal justice, Current Controversies deals with specific topics such as police brutality, gun control, white collar crime, and others. The debates in Current Controversies also are presented in a useful, timeless fashion. Articles and book excerpts included in each title are selected if they contribute valuable, long-range ideas to the overall debate. And wherever possible, current information is enhanced with historical documents and other relevant materials. Thus, while individual titles are current in focus, every effort is made to ensure that they will not become quickly outdated. Books in the Current Controversies series will remain important resources for librarians, teachers, and students for many years.

In addition to keeping the titles focused and specific, great care is taken in the editorial format of each book in the series. Book introductions and chapter prefaces are offered to provide background material for readers. Chapters are organized around several key questions that are answered with diverse opinions representing all points on the political spectrum. Materials in each chapter include opinions in which authors clearly disagree as well as alternative opinions in which authors may agree on a broader issue but disagree on the possible solutions. In this way, the content of each volume in Current Controversies mirrors the mosaic of opinions encountered in society. Readers will quickly realize that there are many viable answers to these complex issues. By questioning each author's conclusions, students and casual readers can begin to develop the critical thinking skills so important to evaluating opinionated material.

Current Controversies is also ideal for controlled research. Each anthology in the series is composed of primary sources taken from a wide gamut of informational categories including periodicals, newspapers, books, United States and foreign government documents, and the publications of private and public organizations. Readers will find factual support for reports, debates, and research papers covering all areas of important issues. In addition, an annotated table of contents, an index, a book and periodical bibliography, and a list of organizations to contact are included in each book to expedite further research.

Perhaps more than ever before in history, people are confronted with diverse and contradictory information. During the Persian Gulf War, for example, the public was not only treated to minute-to-minute coverage of the war, it was also inundated with critiques of the coverage and countless analyses of the factors motivating U.S. involvement. Being able to sort through the plethora of opinions accompanying today's major issues, and to draw one's own conclusions, can be a complicated and frustrating struggle. It is the editors' hope that Current Controversies will help readers with this struggle.

Greenhaven Press anthologies primarily consist of previously published material taken from a variety of sources, including periodicals, books, scholarly journals, newspapers, government documents, and position papers from private and public organizations. These original sources are often edited for length and to ensure their accessibility for a young adult audience. The anthology editors also change the original titles of these works in order to clearly present the main thesis of each viewpoint and to explicitly indicate the opinion presented in the viewpoint. These alterations are made in consideration of both the reading and comprehension levels of a young adult audience. Every effort is made to ensure that Greenhaven Press accurately reflects the original intent of the authors included in this anthology.

"Some authorities argue that the definition of hostile environment sexual harassment is too vague, while others argue that a broad definition is necessary to protect victims of sexual harassment."

Introduction

Although the public has recognized sexual harassment as a serious issue, there is still no widely agreed upon definition of the concept. Anne Fischer, who answers reader questions about conduct in the workplace in her "Ask Annie" column in *Fortune* magazine, revealed that after publishing one letter from a reader who was confused about sexual harassment, she received "a torrent of e-mails pretty clearly demonstrating that on this subject, lots of folks are utterly clueless."

Initially, the courts only recognized sexual harassment cases in which women were compelled to trade sexual favors for professional survival. This is known as *quid pro quo* or "this for that" sexual harassment, and it occurs when employment decisions on hiring, promotion, transfer, discipline, or termination are made on the basis of submission to or rejection of unwelcome sexual conduct. For example, in July of 1994, the Pittsburgh branch of the Federal Reserve Bank paid more than $200,000 to Arlene Spirko, who was demoted and then fired by her supervisor after she rejected his unwanted advances.

In 1986, in *Meritor Savings Bank v. Vinson*, the Supreme Court upheld the Equal Employment Opportunity Commission (EEOC) definition of sexual harassment, which treats such conduct as sex-based discrimination in violation of Title VII of the 1964 Civil Rights Act. The Court ruled that employees have the right to work in environments free from discriminatory intimidation, ridicule, and insult. With this ruling, the Court recognized what has become known as "hostile environment" sexual harassment.

However, interpretation of the "hostile environment" clause of the EEOC guidelines has been the source of much of the debate over sexual harassment. According to the guidelines, "Unwelcome sexual advances, requests for sexual favors, and other verbal or physical conduct of a sexual nature constitutes sexual harassment when . . . such conduct has the purpose or effect of unreasonably interfering with an individual's work performance or creating an intimidating, hostile, or offensive working environment." Because this broad definition can be interpreted in a variety of ways, it has created ambiguity both in and out of the courts. Some authorities argue that the definition of hostile-environment sexual harassment is too vague, while others argue that a broad definition is necessary to protect victims of sexual harassment.

Some of those who think the definition is vague argue that because organizations do not know how to interpret the guidelines, they often respond with strict policies that can have absurd and costly outcomes. These authorities point to cases in which people who have been punished by overly strict policies have filed successful reverse-harassment lawsuits. For example, Jerold Mackenzie was fired by the Miller Brewing Company after recounting a scene from the situation comedy *Seinfeld*. In the episode, Jerry Seinfeld knew only that his date's name rhymed with a female body part; he remembers her name in the final scene, yelling "Dolores!" To explain the punch line, Mackenzie showed co-worker Patricia Best a dictionary definition of the word clitoris. Best was offended and reported Mackenzie's conduct, and the company concluded that his behavior violated its sexual harassment policy. However, a jury of ten women and two men in Milwaukee, Wisconsin, did not believe Mackenzie's behavior violated the legal standard for hostile-environment sexual harassment and ordered the Miller Brewing Company, as well as the woman who filed the sexual harassment claim against Mackenzie, to pay him a total of $26 million.

Other authorities note that many colleges and universities have also been accused of overreacting to the EEOC guidelines and restricting any conduct that might create a hostile or offensive learning environment. Some legal scholars are concerned that these rigid policies inhibit free speech. "If you have actual sexual extortion going on, then something should be done," argues Eugene Volokh, who teaches at the UCLA School of Law. "What's really problematic is when you're talking about imposing liability for speech." An example in which a professor's speech was interpreted as harassment occurred in 1992 at San Bernardino Valley College, in professor Dean Cohen's remedial English class. Anita Murillo, a student in the class, was offended by Cohen's focus on topics of a sexual nature, his use of profanity, and comments she believed were directed at her and other female students. When Cohen asked the students to write essays defining pornography, Murillo asked Cohen to provide her with an alternative assignment. Cohen refused, and Murillo stopped attending the class, ultimately failing the course. The college found Cohen guilty of violating its sexual harassment policy, but the California Court of Appeals held that the college's policy was unconstitutionally vague.

Defenders of the EEOC definition maintain that it is not vague, arguing instead that its broad scope is necessary to protect victims from this type of sexual harassment. These experts claim that definitions which require judges and juries to make subjective judgments on the social and psychological context of behavior are not uncommon in the law. According to sexual harassment training specialist Barry Spodak, "Charges of murder, assault, rape and obstruction of justice are just a few of the criminal areas where context plays a crucial role in determining guilt. Yet nobody says that these crimes are undefined." Although these authorities admit that the definition has resulted in a few ludicrous lawsuits and verdicts, they believe most judges and juries have reacted reasonably to complaints.

Some proponents of a broad definition of sexual harassment argue that media focus on the rare, absurd cases gives support to those who oppose any advances for women. According to Judith Vladeck, a prominent sexual harassment plaintiff's attorney, "A lot of the confusion is deliberate. People who are against any kind of feminist advance in the workplace spread these absurd rumors, like, 'Oh, if you even tell someone you like the blouse they're wearing, they can sue you.' It's arrant nonsense, yet people believe it." She claims that determining what is and is not sexual harassment is easy. "Even the most thickheaded people will suddenly 'get it' if you ask them, Would you like someone to treat your daughter this way?"

Although many agree with Vladeck's belief that identifying hostile-environment sexual harassment ought to be easy, others remain convinced that reverse-harassment suits are a sign that the definition is too vague. The issue remains a subject of debate, one of the many difficult questions that surround the problem of sexual harassment. The authors of the viewpoints in *Sexual Harassment: Current Controversies* examine this and other social, legal, educational, and ethical issues raised by the sexual harassment debate.

Chapter 1

Is Sexual Harassment a Serious Problem?

Sexual Harassment: An Overview

by Sarah Glazer

About the author: *Sarah Glazer is a freelance writer from New York who specializes in health and social policy issues.*

Peggy Kimzey, a Wal-Mart shipping clerk in Warsaw, Mo., was bending over a package when she heard the store manager and another male employee snickering behind her. Kimzey stood up and asked what they were doing. "Well," the manager smirked, "I just found someplace to put my screwdriver." When Kimzey asked him to stop the crude remarks, he replied, "You don't know, you might like it."

That may have been the most offensive comment directed at Kimzey during her four years at Wal-Mart, but it was far from all she endured, according to her attorneys. Toward the end of her employment, Kimzey says, female employees were subjected almost daily to kicks and degrading remarks.

Controversial Damage Awards

Kimzey quit her job in April 1993 and a year later sued Wal-Mart for sexual harassment, claiming that the company never responded to her complaints about harassment. In June 1995, a jury ordered the huge retailer to pay her more than $50 million—the largest damage award ever in a sexual harassment case.

Some observers see the jury's award as an example of the sexual harassment litigation wave run amok. *Forbes* magazine recently cited the case as an example of lawyers going after companies "with the deepest pockets" for trivial slights.

We have denied that much of the [alleged] activity occurred, and what activity occurred [Kimzey] didn't complain about," says Wal-Mart spokeswoman Betsy Reithmeyer. The company's position is that Kimzey "wasn't offended by it because she didn't complain about it," Reithmeyer adds.

The case is [as of July 1996] under a two pronged appeal. Wal-Mart is challenging the verdict itself, and Kimzey is appealing the judge's decision to reduce the $50 million award for punitive damages to $5 million. "Fifty million

Excerpted from Sarah Glazer, "Crackdown on Sexual Harassment," *CQ Researcher*, July 19, 1996. Reprinted by permission of Congressional Quarterly, Inc.

sounds like a lot," says Carla Holste, one of Kimzey's lawyers, "but when compared with Wal-Mart's $32 billion in assets, even they admit it's not enough to bankrupt them. I think the jury felt like $50 million is enough to deter [Wal-Mart] from doing it again. Five million is nothing; they'll make it up in a day."

The Kimzey case is a reminder that sexual harassment cases are rarely simple. As Americans learned during the October 1991 Supreme Court confirmation hearings for Clarence Thomas, every story has two sides, and it is often difficult to discern the truth.

In the five years since University of Oklahoma law Professor Anita Hill charged Thomas with sexual harassment, men and women alike have become much more aware of the issue.

The Thomas hearings gave Americans a "crash course" in sexual harassment, says Helen Norton, director of equal opportunity programs at the Women's Legal Defense Fund. Although many Americans didn't believe Hill, Norton says the hearings opened women's eyes. "Women saw there was a legal name for what they had experienced—and it was illegal," she says. "It emboldened them to come forward."

Since the hearings, sexual harassment complaints filed with the federal Equal Employment Opportunity Commission (EEOC) have more than doubled, and monetary awards have more than tripled. "A lot of us forget how recently sexual harassment has been accepted as a violation of the law," says EEOC Legal Counsel Ellen Vargyas. "It's been only 10 years since it was accepted as a viable legal theory" by the Supreme Court.

Prosecutions Continue

Yet new cases continue to touch raw nerves, years after some experts had predicted that sexual harassment would die away with the growing acceptance of women in the workplace. On April 9, 1996, the EEOC sued Mitsubishi Motor Manufacturing of America Inc. in what could become the largest sexual harassment suit ever prosecuted.

The class-action suit alleges that sexual harassment has been rampant at the Japanese automaker's Normal, Ill., plant since at least 1990. The agency says that if it wins, the victims could number in the hundreds, the damages in the tens of millions.

> *"Every story has two sides, and it is often difficult to discern the truth."*

The alleged harassment ranged from sexual graffiti to making women's acquiescence in sexual relationships a condition of their employment. Women complainants have said that male workers circulated photographs of sex parties with naked women, drew obscene pictures on the assembly line and grabbed women's breasts and genitals.

Mitsubishi's initial defiance surprised the business community. *The Wall Street Journal* called the company's denial of all charges and hardball tactics a "risky" strategy. On April 11, 1996, shortly after the suit was filed, Mitsubishi sponsored an all-expenses-paid trip for employees and their families to protest the suit in front of the EEOC's Chicago offices. Afterwards, a female worker who had complained of sexual harassment said she received an anonymous death threat—a scrawled note in her locker with the words, "Die Bitch! You'll be Sorry."

> *"Lawsuits, usually long and costly, can become Pyrrhic victories even if they're successful."*

The business community has rarely reacted to sexual harassment charges with "the kind of in-your-face challenge to the EEOC" that Mitsubishi initially exhibited, says Peter Eide, manager of labor relations at the U.S. Chamber of Commerce. Mitsubishi's conciliatory step in May 1996, when it hired former Labor Secretary Lynn Martin to review the company's policies and practices, was "more indicative of what companies are doing," Eide says. "Most employers, I think, understand the need to take complaints seriously."

By comparison, the Swedish pharmaceutical company Astra USA Inc. responded swiftly when it was thrown on the defensive. On April 29, 1996, just days before *Business Week* published the results of a six-month investigation reporting wide-ranging sexual harassment, the company quickly suspended its U.S. chief executive and two top lieutenants.

Authorities Disagree over Remedy

Women's-rights groups credit passage of the sweeping Civil Rights Act of 1991 for the increase in sexual harassment litigation. By giving women alleging sexual harassment the right to jury trials and the right to sue for compensatory and punitive damages, the act led to much larger monetary awards. Previously, the law only allowed women to win reinstatement in their old job and back pay.

But some critics believe the nation overreacted in its determination to respond to sexual harassment complaints. The Independent Women's Forum was founded in 1992 by a group of politically conservative women, some of whom had been active in Thomas' defense. "We don't deny sexual harassment exists," says Anita Blair, executive vice president and general counsel of the Arlington, Va.-based organization, "but we do not think it should be trivialized. Unfortunately, a lot of times real, serious harassment is overlooked in favor of things that are really more a case of people not getting along together in the workplace."

In the same vein, *Forbes* assailed the trend toward million-dollar sexual harassment suits as Washington's attempt "to stamp out sex in the workplace." The magazine calculated that the EEOC's suit against Mitsubishi could result in damages of up to $210 million—if every female employee receives the maximum $300,000 allowed under the 1991 civil rights law. "[D]oes the punishment truly fit the crime? Do we really want lawyers and bureaucrats dictating personal behavior?" the authors [Alexander Alger and William G. Flanagan] asked.

Lawsuits, usually long and costly, can become Pyrrhic victories even if they're successful. Alice W. Ballard, an employment-rights lawyer in Philadelphia, warns clients to be prepared to lose their jobs if they sue. "It's likely you'll get fired or life will get so unpleasant you will have to leave," she says.

Most women don't face the kind of retaliation reported at Mitsubishi. "The more common thing is the person just loses position," Ballard says. "They don't get anything important to do; they're put in an uncomfortable workspace; they're left out of meetings; their messages get lost; there's more and more petty harassment."

Employers trying to avoid costly lawsuits tend to invest in employee training, consultants and strongly worded policies. But conservatives charge that these efforts mainly create unnecessary paranoia and tension between men and women. "Men are retreating to the safety of their offices, avoiding private contact with female co-workers and carefully censoring their speech," wrote Harsh K. Luthar and Anthony Townsend in the conservative *National Review*.

"Every insult, joke and dirty picture shouldn't be a federal case," agrees Ellen Frankel Paul, professor of political science at Bowling Green State University in Ohio and a longstanding critic of current trends in sexual harassment law. Her advice to women is to "cool it" before reacting to unpleasant incidents or remarks. These days, she complains, things have gotten so bad that men have to think twice about everything. "Should I be saying, 'You look nice today?' If someone is upset, do you put your arm around them and say, 'Is something wrong?' Everything is under a fine microscope, which I don't think is good for men and women."

> *"Employers trying to avoid costly lawsuits tend to invest in employee training, consultants and strongly worded policies."*

But San Francisco psychiatrist Peter Rutter, author of the 1996 book *Sex, Power and Boundaries: Understanding and Preventing Sexual Harassment*, sees the new tension as an inevitable consequence of changes in what is socially acceptable. "Society has taken a stand" against sexual harassment, he says, "that creates a new standard for people to meet in daily life." This stage may be awkward, he adds, but it can also be educational.

Indeed, although women are still more likely than men to see certain kinds of workplace behavior as sexual harassment, surveys show the differences in perception between the sexes are narrowing. But differences still remain.

"It's very clear that men have been raised to think they should push against boundaries at least until they've been told 'No'—then maybe a little bit after they've been told 'No,'" Rutter says. . . .

Are Sexual Harassment Penalties Excessive?

In one of the nation's first sexual harassment cases, an Environmental Protection Agency employee alleged in 1974 that her job was abolished after she refused to sleep with the boss. She charged it was a case of discrimination based on her sex. A federal district court dismissed the case because, it said, the discrimination was based not on the fact that the plaintiff was a woman but that she refused to have sex with her supervisor.

Three years later, the decision was reversed on appeal, and the woman was awarded $18,000 in back pay. The U.S. Court of Appeals for the District of Columbia ruled, in *Barnes v. Costle*, that sexual harassment is a form of discrimination in employment, which is illegal under Title VII of the 1964 Civil Rights Act. It was the first federal court to do so.

Women's rights activists often cite the *Barnes* case in spotlighting past deficiencies in the old legal system, when sexual harassment was not yet widely recognized as a form of discrimination. Even once it was recognized, women still could not receive much in damages.

"A lot of harassment victims were just made miserable—they couldn't leave their job because they needed to pay the rent," says Norton at the Women's Legal Defense Fund. "You saw cases where the woman proved the case but because she hadn't lost her job, the judge said, 'There's no remedy for you' and ordered her to pay her employer's court costs."

> *"The 1991 Civil Rights Act gave women the right not only to collect 'compensatory damages' for the abuse they suffered but also 'punitive damages' aimed at punishing the employer."*

The 1991 Civil Rights Act gave women the right not only to collect "compensatory damages" for the abuse they suffered but also "punitive damages" aimed at punishing the employer. President George Bush, who had opposed an earlier version of the bill, agreed to a compromise that limited the damages an employee could recover to $300,000, depending on the number of employees in the company. The bill also permitted sexual harassment cases to go before juries, a provision opposed by business lobbyists because juries tend to be more sympathetic than judges to plaintiffs.

In the bill's wake, some critics say, juries are awarding verdicts far out of proportion to the offense. The most heavily publicized verdicts far exceed the $300,000 federal cap because lawyers often invoke state employment-discrimination laws that allow higher money damages or they bring additional legal actions for personal injuries—known as torts—on such grounds as intentional infliction of emotional distress.

The Punitive Damages Controversy

Writing in the quarterly journal of the Independent Women's Forum, California business analyst Elizabeth Larson recently compared Barnes' $18,000 award in 1977 to the $50 million Wal-Mart was ordered to pay Kimzey. "How did the courts come to regard a tasteless remark as nearly three thousand times more serious than a woman losing her job for refusing sex with her boss?" Larson asked. The answer, she suggested, lies in a legal system that "has gone from punishing behavior that is objectively wrong to that which is subjectively offensive."

Forbes, too, singled out the Wal-Mart award as a case of money-hungry lawyers suing wealthy companies for trivial slights. "Consider the plight of Wal-Mart with 630,000 employees and sales last year of $94 billion," the article said. "Since punitive damages are allowed in sexual harassment cases, companies with the deepest pockets are hit hardest."

"The punitive damages are based on an amount that is supposed to deter the company from doing that again," counters Kenneth Kowalski, who teaches employment law at Cleveland State University's Marshall College of Law. "To have a big company like Wal-Mart sit up and take notice, it's going to take a lot of money. Ten thousand dollars is nothing to Wal-Mart."

The perception that big awards go to women overreacting to trivial remarks or crude jokes is inaccurate, women's-rights groups maintain. According to the U.S. Merit System Protection Board's 1995 survey, *Sexual Harassment in the Federal Workplace,* only 6 percent of those who experience sexual harassment take formal action. That suggests that only the most egregious behavior leads to lawsuits, the groups contend.

"It's inaccurate to say companies pay millions of dollars because someone told an off-color joke," says Ellen Bravo, executive director of 9 to 5, the National Association of Working Women, based in Milwaukee, Wis. "No one has ever called our hotline to say, 'My manager calls me Honey or says I looked nice today.' People call to say, 'So and so is groping me, came to my hotel room with only a shirt on, insists on telling me about sexual exploits, raped me.' They are unable to make it stop even though they've tried."

Some conservative critics charge that employers get hit with lawsuits no matter how they handle harassment complaints. Employers who act promptly—as the EEOC urges—and fire the alleged harasser may get hit with countersuits on such grounds as defamation or unjust dismissal. On the other hand, if the company does a thorough investigation, more harassment may occur in the meantime, worsening the employer's position if the complaining employee later sues.

"Critics charge that employers get hit with lawsuits no matter how they handle harassment complaints."

"It's this type of Catch-22 situation that I think is going to be a big problem as these lawsuits proliferate," says Timothy Lynch, assistant director of the Center for Constitutional Studies at the libertarian Cato Institute.

Indeed, some critics say, it's not the size of jury awards that is the problem with sexual harassment cases but rather the prospect of paying lawyers' fees to fight or settle a suit.

"We all know there are way too many lawyers, and there's harassment value in a bad case," says Michael Weiss, an adjunct professor at the University of Houston School of Law. "There's a lot of frivolous threats brought and money paid by companies" in settlements that amount to blackmail, he says. "You say to the company, 'I'm going to sue and it will cost you $8,000 [in legal fees to fight it]. Pay us $8,000' " to settle. . . .

Are Companies Doing Enough?

Most large companies now have policies against sexual harassment, and a growing number train employees in an effort to head it off. According to a June 1996 survey by the American Management Association (AMA), 89 percent of the 456 mid-size and large companies polled have formal policies or procedures for dealing with sexual harassment and 65 percent provide training. Nonetheless, women's-rights groups note, many smaller firms don't have training programs or written policies.

The growth in training has tracked the rise in companies that have experienced allegations of sexual harassment. Between 1991 and 1996, the percentage of companies that reported at least one claim grew from 52 percent to 72 percent, according to the AMA. In 1991, only 40 percent of the firms surveyed offered training on the issue.

Eric Rolfe Greenberg, director of management studies for the association, says "companies tend to be reactive rather than proactive. They wait for a second claim [before they] develop a policy." But he also notes

> *"Predictably, there has been enormous growth in consultants offering sexual-harassment training."*

that companies that already had training programs were less likely to see claims develop into lawsuits. Eight percent of companies with training were sued as opposed to 12 percent of those with no training.

"If a company puts in a training program," Greenberg says, "it may find an increase in reported incidents because of heightened awareness among victims of what constitutes sexual harassment and of the company's policy saying it's not acceptable. The good news is [complaints are] less likely to rise to the level of a legal claim."

For the most part, employers are not bucking the trend toward taking sexual harassment seriously, business groups say. "No business benefits from sexual harassment," says Eide at the Chamber of Commerce. "It decreases productivity. Most enlightened employers don't want it." The key to avoiding expensive lawsuits, Eide says, is a preventive approach: having a written policy against sexual harassment and well-publicized procedures for investigating complaints.

Women's-rights activists say that while more companies have policies against sexual harassment than five years ago, problems remain, such as retaliation against women who complain, supervisors who tolerate harassment and lack of neutral investigations. The death threats that were reported in the Mitsubishi case are a grim reminder that harassment victims face a "double whammy," Norton says. "When [women] complain about it, they face retaliation, additional harassment or they're fired." Moreover, a woman who files a complaint with the EEOC can wait months or more for a resolution.

Protection or Promotion

Predictably, there has been enormous growth in consultants offering sexual-harassment training. The growth has been fueled in part by new state laws, such as California's requirement that employers take reasonable steps to prevent sexual harassment and Maine's that employers provide sexual-harassment seminars for new employees.

But some critics say all this activity actually fuels claims rather than prevents them. "Employers may think they are hiring consultants to protect them from lawsuits," Larson wrote, "but what is actually being taught is a very different lesson: A wink or a leer can be money in the bank."

Management Professor Anthony Townsend of the University of Nevada, Las Vegas, criticizes training videos used by corporations for generally portraying men as harassers and women as victims. The message, he says, is "Men are bad." It "doesn't leave open to men the possibility that they may be victims, too. And that possibility is very real as more and more women are put in charge of men."

In fact, a backlash has been quietly developing, not just in the pages of conservative journals but also among a growing number of men who say they were unfairly accused of sexual harassment and who counter-sue.

John Kirsch was publisher of the *South Florida Business Journal* in 1992 when, he said, he told Advertising Director Karen Van Der Eems that she would either have to quit or be demoted because of poor sales. As a "face-saving" way to explain the demotion, Kirsch said he suggested that Van Der Eems say she wanted to devote more time to her marriage. In response, Van Der Eems sent Kirsch a memo implying, he recalls, that her marriage "was something I couldn't emotionally stand and I was firing her because of that." The next week Kirsch was fired.

> *"The rights of innocent men could be trampled in the stampede by employers eager to show they are doing something about sexual harassment."*

Kirsch sued for defamation. His lawyer argued that Kirsch had been forced to defame himself by admitting in job interviews that he had been fired for sexual harassment. Kirsch says the company never investigated the charges. He also says that contrary to the memo's implication, he never had a romantic relationship with Van Der Eems.

In an out-of-court settlement in 1993, the newspaper's parent company, American City Business Journals, paid Kirsch $40,000. Kirsch says he also received a letter from Van Der Eems saying he had not sexually harassed her.

Innocent Men Lose Their Rights

"The reality today is that the easiest person to get rid of, the person that will cost you the least to fire, is a middle-aged white male," Kirsch says. Kirsch's lawyer, Donna M. Ballman of North Miami Beach, says, "The company thought it's easier to fire someone than do the right thing by both parties." Ballman says the case shows that companies should do thorough investigations when charges arise.

Critics of current trends in sexual harassment law say cases like Kirsch's stand as warnings that the rights of innocent men could be trampled in the stampede by employers eager to show they are doing something about sexual harassment.

> *"The differing perceptions among men and women of what constitutes sexual harassment can put employers in a difficult position."*

Under federal guidelines, the main way employers can avoid liability after being sued for sexual harassment is by showing they took prompt action to remedy the situation.

"There's a possibility of sexual harassment [charges being used] in organizational or political power struggles," says Harsh K. Luthar, assistant professor of management at Bryant College in Smithfield, R.I. "If it's decided a manager has to be gotten rid of, it's a nice pretext to hide behind." In a 1994 article, Luthar calls for more research on the extent of "baseless accusations of sexual harassment made against males."

About 19 percent of male federal workers surveyed in 1994 reported experiencing sexually harassing behaviors during the preceding two years, up from 14 percent in 1987.

Townsend cites a lawsuit filed by an air traffic controller against the Federal Aviation Administration in connection with a sexual harassment training workshop. Controller Douglas Hartman charged he was forced to walk through a crowd of female co-workers who grabbed his body and commented derisively on his attributes in an exercise aimed at making men sensitive to the harassment experienced by women in control towers.

What men and women have to look out for is real discrimination," Townsend says. "I think [corporate training] has gone overboard with political correctness. There isn't a direct relationship between someone having a foul mouth in the office and someone not getting a job." Adds political science Professor Paul, also a critic of such training, "It's made people second-guess their behavior."

Barbara Spyridon Pope, a Bethesda, Md., training consultant, says she hears men say "they are afraid to have normal work relations. They're afraid that someone may sue them when they do performance appraisals."

Using professional actors in skits and simulated game shows, Spyridon demonstrates that the difference between friendliness and harassment can be as subtle as the length of a touch or a look. "Two seconds is OK; 10 seconds is too long," Pope says. "When you see it, you know exactly."

Do Men and Women See Harassment Differently?

Ironically, when employees watching the training sessions are asked to say when the lingering touch or look becomes sexual harassment, men tend to call it harassment before the women do, she says. "Some of that comes from paranoia about where the boundaries are."

Some consultants acknowledge the criticisms of training programs that bad-mouth men. "With high-quality training, that's the last thing you do, because that is divisive," says Susan L. Webb, president of Pacific Resource Development Group in Seattle, Wash.

Alan McEvoy, a professor of sociology at Wittenburg University in Springfield, Ohio, compares the nervousness around sexual harassment to the heightened awareness of child abuse in recent years and the overreaction of teachers who avoid any physical intimacy with children. "One of the prices we pay for heightened awareness is paranoia and fear," McEvoy says. "But by the same token, I don't know that we have an alternative. The alternative of ignoring it and pretending it doesn't exist and allowing it to persist is worse."

Though women are more likely than men to define certain behaviors as harassment, they have more areas of agreement than disagreement, surveys show. The most recent surveys show that if the majority of women think something is harassment, the majority of men tend to agree, though by a smaller margin.

> *"Some men argue that as females gain more power, males are being discriminated against, too."*

Men and women are most likely to agree when it comes to the starkest kind of harassment, such as pressure for sexual favors from a supervisor, says John Pryor, a professor of psychology at Illinois State University in Normal, Ill. "Where you see the larger differences are in the more gray areas," Pryor says, such as sexual joking among co-workers. It is these grayer areas, which come under the umbrella of "hostile environment" harassment, that are the most common form of sexual harassment, according to the American Psychological Association.

Over time, the gap in perception between man and women has been closing, says Barbara A. Gutek, a psychologist at the University of Arizona. In her oft-cited 1980–81 study of 1,200 working men and women in Los Angeles, Gutek researched the reactions of men and women to a sexual proposition from a co-worker. Sixty-seven percent of the men but only 17 percent of the women said they would be flattered by a proposition.

In a more recent unpublished survey of faculty, staff and students at the University of Arizona, "Fewer men say they would be flattered by such overtures," Gutek says. Why the change? "I think it was an issue men hadn't thought about very much [in 1980]," she says. "The sensitization to sexual harassment in the workplace [has made them aware] there can be strings attached."

25

When federal workers were surveyed in 1987, less than half the men considered a co-worker's sexual teasing, jokes or remarks to be sexual harassment while 64 percent of the women did. When the survey was repeated in 1994, the percentage of men who considered such remarks harassment had risen to 64 percent; among women the proportion had risen to 77 percent.

Employers Are Caught in the Middle

The differing perceptions among men and women of what constitutes sexual harassment can put employers in a difficult position. "What you're often faced with as a practical matter is two people, one of whom says an event occurred and another who denies it," says Eide. "The employer is judge and jury as to whether a situation occurred. We're no better than anyone else at [determining] what happened. If you discharge the alleged harasser, you're subject to a suit for defamation or wrongful dismissal.". . .

Some men argue that as females gain more power, males are being discriminated against, too. Townsend questions surveys showing that 40–60 percent of working women have been sexually harassed but less than 20 percent of men. "If men were subjected to the same kind of cultural exposure to this notion," he says, "I think we would see very similar numbers for men."

Townsend still remembers the female teacher in graduate school who called him a "typical anal-retentive male." He said the comment made him worry she would mark his papers down.

When Townsend asks students how many have heard a female faculty member make disparaging jokes about men, about 60 percent of the males raise their hands. But only a handful say they've suffered sexual harassment.

"Men really are experiencing this stuff; it's just that they're not sensitized to potential damage on their education and careers," Townsend says. "Men like to think, 'I can overcome this problem.' But women are tough, and if they have power they have to be stopped from [harassing people] just like men."

Sexual Harassment Is a Serious Problem

by Kathryn Quina

About the author: *Kathryn Quina is on the faculty in the psychology department at the University of Rhode Island.*

In the comic strip "Beetle Bailey," common forms of sexual harassment are carried out by harmless characters whom we are supposed to love, or at least feel a kind of charitable forgiveness toward. General Halftrack is the archetypical older gentleman whose dowdy wife starves him for affection. His secretary Miss Buxley—who can't type—drives him wild with her sexy figure and short skirts. "Killer" (short for *lady-killer*, a curiously violent name) is always whistling at "chicks" (who love it), accompanied by Beetle, who is equally aggressive but not as successful. Zero just stares at women's bodies.

Sexual Harassment Is Not a Joke

Played out in the real world, these scenarios are not funny. The similarity of a university department to a comic strip seems especially incongruous, yet many of us have had to cope with Generals, Killers, Beetles, and Zeros in our professional as well as personal lives. In my first five years as an academic, I experienced an older professor literally chase me around a desk, similar-aged colleagues determined to bed me, and a dean who simply could not stop staring at my chest (and I'm not Miss Buxley!). Sadly, I am not the only one to relate these experiences. In most of the instances described above, I learned about other victims of the same offenders; in my research on sexual harassment and rape, I have met many more victims of other offenders.

The striking thing about sexual harassment is that it is also not harmless. I will argue that all forms of sexual harassment share important commonalities with rape. While harassment is usually less physically intrusive and less violent or life-threatening, it is not substantially different structurally or socially from rape. This conceptual framework defines rape and harassment as sexual assaults lying on a continuum of sexual exploitation, varying in degree of physical intru-

Reprinted from Kathryn Quina, "Sexual Harassment and Rape: A Continuation of Exploitation," in *Sexual Harassment on College Campuses*, edited by Michele A. Paludi, by permission of the State University of New York Press. Copyright ©1996, State University of New York. All rights reserved.

sion and potential physical injury to the victim. At the pole of the least physically violent, this continuum begins with verbal assaults, including sexually offensive jokes or degrading comments, also called "gender harassment." At the pole of the most violent are rape, murder, and femicide. On such a scale, sexual harassment and rape are relatively close together. In fact, many assaults now called "harassment"—those involving sexual contact—are legally the equivalent of rape.

> *"The striking thing about sexual harassment is that it is . . . not harmless."*

This continuum perspective allows us to utilize the extensive literature on rape victimization and recovery to gain insight into and understanding of the sexual harassment situation and survivor reactions. In fact, much of the recent research in sexual harassment began as an extension of research on rape offenders, attitudes toward rape victims, and the like.

Commonalities with Rape

Six major commonalities underlying this continuum are discussed here, illuminated with stories from students and colleagues and from my own life to provide a glimpse of the reality of these sexual assaults. These areas of commonality are (1) power dynamics, (2) gender roles and relationships, (3) offender characteristics, (4) cultural stereotyping, (5) emotional reactions of victims, and (6) costs to the survivor. . . .

The rapist is likely to have greater physical size and strength than the victim, or to wield a gun or knife. The sexual harasser uses age or social position, or wields economic power and authority, as weapons. In all cases, however, a power advantage is essential to the act.

Gender, age, hierarchical status, and race are important points of vulnerability to a sexual harasser's power. By far, the sexual offender is most likely to be a male: An estimated 99 percent of rapists and 75 to 90 percent of sexual harassers are men. The victim is most likely to be female and young. Minority women are more frequently asked for sexual favors or dates, and subject to more sexually offensive gestures, than nonminority women are. S.G. Bingham and L.L. Scherer found that 78 percent of the harassed academic faculty and staff women were victimized by men of greater or "equal" status (although, in academia, nontenured and tenured faculty are clearly not equal), compared to 42 percent of comparable men.

Ann was a new assistant professor, the only woman in a large department. Only one colleague had welcomed her arrival and had informally begun to mentor her. Late one night, he called her to "discuss a problem." He began talking about her future tenure decision and her need to be more "friendly." He also suggested they have dinner to discuss their relationship, since he knew it would "help her get ahead." At the same time, he warned her not to associate with students (the only other women) or the women's group on campus, because such associations would "look bad" in the eyes of her colleagues. Already isolated, she now avoided him as well as the women.

When harassment is "contrapower," that is, involves subordinates as harassers, other vulnerabilities for women emerge. Faculty women, who should be at the upper levels of the power hierarchy in universities, find themselves subjected to sexual harassment by male students in substantial numbers. Underscoring women's tenuous existence within the ivory halls, almost 9 percent of those who knew the student harassing them chose to remain silent for fear of personal or professional repercussions.

No Support at Work

Increasing attention has been paid to the work environment as a source of power for the sexual abuser. In society at large, media and other images of women create a culture that is, if not supportive, at least not opposed to sexual violence. Academic and other organizations can be characterized by their level of support for harassment victims. In nonsupportive environments, it may be assumed that the harasser can tap into the organizational "power base."

Finally, rapists and harassers gain enormous power when victims do not report the incident, or when institutions designed to protect victims do not respond to reports. It is estimated that less than 10 percent of victims of all sexual assaults report them to the police or other authorities. Among those who do report sexual harassment, fewer than a third find favorable decisions from authorities.

Beyond gender, cultural expectations of masculinity and femininity seem to be extremely important to rape and harassment. Rapists endorse, and perhaps attempt to act out, extreme versions of the cultural stereotype of masculinity as dominance over women. There is evidence that sexual harassers hold the same stereotypes and desire the same macho image. D.L. Mosher and M. Sirkin found that men with hypermasculine patterns held more callous attitudes toward women, and suggested they were more likely to harass as well as rape. On a larger level D. Jaffe and M.A. Straus's state-by-state analysis of sexual assault data revealed a relationship between higher rape rates and evidence of hypermasculine cultural gender roles (e.g., sex magazine readership).

"Much of the recent research in sexual harassment began as an extension of research on rape offenders, attitudes toward rape victims, and the like."

Women who accede to cultural demands on women to be "feminine"— that is, to be passive, submissive, helping, and nurturant—probably have an increased likelihood of being victims of rape or harassment.

For several months, Beth remained silent about her major professor's sexual comments and the way he touched her whenever they were alone. She tried to be nice, partly to avoid his wrath and partly because she didn't know what else to do. As a southern woman, she had only been taught "niceness." Meanwhile, other graduate students were beginning to tease her about him. One day, as she described it, she "freaked out." She yelled at him to get out of her office and quit bothering her. She was deeply embarrassed by her outburst, but held back her urge to apologize. Not only did his abuse stop, but the other students, who overheard the interaction, began to treat her with greater respect. Until she spoke up, they had assumed she was "using her femininity."

Characteristics of the Abuser

Rapists and child molesters are "habitual" offenders; many commit various kinds of assault, some with hundreds of victims. K. Pope has observed a high repetition (recidivism) rate among therapists who have sex with clients, an act he effectively argues is similar to rape and incest, and which structurally is similar to seduction of students by teachers.

Sexual offenders often carry out their repeated assaults in a highly stereotyped fashion, or *modus operandi*. Even those rapists who claim to be in love with their victims are likely to have a characteristic pattern of behaviors leading up to, during, and following the assault. Although data are not widely available on harassers, it is likely that many practice "personal favorite" styles.

Cindy, a student tutor, was assaulted by a client, who accused her of "exuding sexuality all over the place." She remained silent, embarrassed by the experience and frightened by the powerful message she felt she must be projecting. A month later, a co-worker filed a complaint of sexual assault against the same man, and Cindy spoke up. In the ensuing legal proceedings, another student victim came forward, and records revealed that several previously reliable tutors had resigned after working with this client.

> *"Among those who do report sexual harassment, fewer than a third find favorable decisions from authorities.*

This has important implications for any victim: Someone else probably has a similar story to tell. Unfortunately, we have a tendency to view each assault as an isolated incident, attributing the cause to the individual's character or behavior, and fail to look for a pattern. The legal implications are also important: It might be possible to identify others who have shared the experience and to pursue a group grievance.

Cultural Attitudes

S. Brownmiller provided an excellent review of the cultural mythologies surrounding rape, and the images of rape victims, extending back to biblical writings. Thanks to extensive educational efforts and the willingness of some victims to speak up, these attitudes now are less prevalent with respect to rape. Raising awareness about sexual harassment was initially difficult because offensive behaviors had never been named or defined. Increasingly, however, men and women respond similarly in making judgments about severe harassment. Studies have found that well over 90 percent of male and female college students labeled certain behaviors (sexual bribery, coercion, and assault) as harassment or rape.

Stereotypes and misinformation continue to be applied to less severe forms of sexual assault. There is considerable disagreement even among

> *"Perpetrators of rape and harassment (or both) also believe myths about women and rape."*

women over whether verbal or other gender harassment and seductive approaches constitute harassment. Gender differences are stronger for these forms of harassment; women are more likely than men to label them as harassment and less likely to attribute responsibility to the victims. Similar gender relationships in labeling and attributions of blame are found for stranger- versus date-rape scenarios. Both men and women who hold conservative attitudes about gender roles in society find harassment less serious or offensive.

Beliefs and myths about their (female) victims most likely allow sexual abuse as well. Perpetrators of rape and harassment (or both) also believe myths about women and rape. J.B. Pryor found high correlations among college men's scores on measures of likelihood to rape, likelihood to sexually harass, and related attitudes such as accepting rape myths and rejection of feminism, as well as behavioral measures of unnecessary sexual contact with women confederates in a neutral setting (a poker game). C.A. Bartling and R. Eisenman gave an extended set of measures to men and women, and confirmed these intercorrelations, though they were weaker for women. On the positive side, Mosher and R.D. Anderson showed increases in guilt, shame, and awareness among high-likelihood-to-rape college men after a guided rape fantasy.

Common Myths

The most common of the myths shared by rape and sexual harassment offenders (and other members of society) fall into the following three categories.

1. *Sexual assault is harmless and a form of seduction.* Throughout history, from ancient literature (e.g., Homer's Sirens) to our contemporary culture (e.g., Cindy's case), rape images are imbued with images of women as temptresses and men as helpless slaves to powerful sexual drives. In a study of college students' attitudes toward date rape by D.R. Holcomb et al., one in three college men agreed that women "often" provoke rape, and 14 percent disagreed that a man could "control his behavior no matter how attracted he feels toward someone." M.C. Meyer et al. advised women in the workplace to be careful about the way they dress and talk, because it could cause their co-workers to harass them. L.F. Fitzgerald et al. found that professors who dated students were more likely (than nondating professors of the same students) to perceive that women stu-

dents had approached them.

2. *Women secretly need/want to be forced into sex.* Young men are taught by peers from an early age that women like to be forced into sex and that they "say no but mean yes." Holcomb et al. found that nearly one in two college men endorsed the item "Some women ask to be raped and may enjoy it, and one in three agreed that a woman "means 'maybe' or even 'yes' when she says no." It is not surprising, then, that harassment usually continues or escalates when the victim has given no positive response or even a negative response. Harassers offer such excuses as "I know her better than she knows herself," while onlookers—like Beth's fellow graduate students—may suspect the victim really enjoyed the attention.

3. *Women do not tell the truth.* Until the 1970s, charges of rape had to be corroborated by a witness in some states, and judges' instructions to juries included a warning that rape is easy to accuse and hard to prove. Such suspicion clouds victims of sexual harassment as well. Among the forms this mistrust takes are questions of whether the victim has any grudge against the alleged offender or any other motive for complaining. R.J. Summers found more victim blame by college students if the harassed woman was described either as competing for the same job (a personal motive) or as a feminist (presumably, a political motive).

> *"It is not surprising . . . that harassment usually continues or escalates when the victim has given no positive response or even a negative response."*

At a conference I attended a few years ago, a university counsel (a woman!) recommended that any time a sexual harassment case ended in acquittal, the university should consider bringing charges of false accusation against the alleged victim.

Victim Reactions

Sexual assaults across the continuum can cause severe trauma. Even when their lives are not in danger, victims of harassment report fear, loss of control, and disruption of their lives—experiences shared with victims of more physically dangerous traumas such as rape or natural disasters. Ninety percent of the harassed graduate student women surveyed by B.E. Schneider reported negative reactions, and two thirds worried about potential and actual consequences.

"Looking back I don't know what I was afraid of," mused Deborah some years after her traumatic experience, as a student worker, of being fondled by a professor, "but I was terrified each time this man came toward me." At the end of the semester, Deborah wrote a short note about the professor's advances, gave it to her dorm advisor, and left school. She gave up her ambitions to become a scientist, and didn't retune to college for many years.

Like other sexual assaults, harassment is also a violation. Physical contact is not necessary to create intense disgust, as noted in the reactions of women who receive obscene phone calls or street harassment. Because in sexual harassment the victim usually knows the offender, a violation of trust is almost always experienced. Most survivors also report feeling degraded by the experience, "stripped" of their dignity by the abuser. In these last two dimensions, harassment bears important similarities to incest.

When a nationally known scholar asked her to participate in his research project, Ellen was thrilled. Flattered by his attentiveness and excited by promises of a letter of recommendation to top graduate schools, she worked long hours, collecting data and writing up a paper herself. Shortly before it was to be sent for publication Dr. X delivered his ultimatum: no sex, no authorship. Ellen submitted, although disgusted by him physically, because she was so invested in the project. After they had sex, he laughed at her tears. The next day, he told her he did not consider her contributions very thoughtful or important, certainly not sufficient to deserve authorship, and that he had allowed her to work on these projects only because he knew how much she wanted to be near him. Ellen lost a year of work, her chance for a good graduate placement, and two publications. More importantly, she lost her confidence. Dr. X's comments were emotionally devastating, and ultimately felt more degrading to her than the sexual acts.

Costs to the Survivor

Emotional responses to rape and sexual harassment, of course, vary widely as a function of the severity of the assault, the number of experiences with assault, personal coping style, emotional vulnerability, and the availability of social support. However, survivors of all the sexual assaults on our continuum have described long-term emotional aftereffects: grief, anger, fear, lowered self-esteem, helplessness, self-blame, shame, body image distortion, sexual dysfunction, and problems in other relationships.

Emotional reactions are compounded by social losses. Among Schneider's graduate women, 29 percent reported a loss of academic or professional opportunities, and 14 percent reported lowered grades or financial support, because of sexual harassment. Employees who file charges of sexual harassment face a range of negative responses, including being demoted or fired, lack of support or continued harassment by co-workers, and other insults. In too many cases, the survivor experiences revictimization by institutions during the complaint process, as administrators become defensive or even attack the victim. Academia has long maintained a facade of civilized, nonviolent behavior, and the disillusionment (in the value-free nature of scholarship and science, as well as the revered institution) can create emotional distress as well.

> *"Because in sexual harassment the victim usually knows the offender, a violation of trust is almost always experienced."*

Too often, survivors find little comfort and support from others after rape or harassment. Those who remain silent, like Ann, often become increasingly isolated and begin to view themselves as deviant. To those who tell, family, friends, and co-workers might respond with rejection, blame, or disbelief. These secondary betrayals increase the severity of long-term emotional reactions, and interfere with healthy resolution.

> *"Too often, survivors find little comfort and support from others after rape or harassment."*

At first, Faye didn't tell her mother about the abuse she was experiencing at work, or about the charges she had filed against the department chair. Unfortunately, a local newspaper picked up the story, and her mother learned about the case when a friend who lived near the university called her. Faye's mother, embarrassed by the publicity, accused Faye of "bringing shame upon the family," and said, "None of my friends would have gotten themselves into a mess like this—I raised you to know better!" Faye had to deal with the private anger of her family along with the public humiliation of a media-interest trial. Eventually she dropped the case, too emotionally exhausted to testify. Her family relationships continue to be strained.

Two other potential effects of sexual harassment are essential to understanding its long-term impact. First, sexual harassment can revive wounds from the survivor's past, including prior rape or incest. Past sexual abuses have been shown to increase fear of sexual harassment and to cause the survivor to reexperience the emotions of prior sexual abuse.

In addition, women who fear sexual assault tend to avoid potentially dangerous or abusive situations. As women define a wider scope of situations as abusive, they restrict their scope of activities. In academia, this can translate directly into reduced willingness to seek out mentoring or related contacts, loss of opportunities for joint projects, and ultimately career damage. The costs to the organization can also be enormous.

Sexual Harassment Is a Serious Problem Among Schoolchildren

by Erik Pitchal

About the author: *Erik Pitchal was a law student at Yale and a columnist for the* Yale Daily News *at the time this viewpoint was originally written.*

For months, LaShonda Davis suffered. The boy who sat next to her, G.F., kept trying to touch her breasts and vaginal area. He said things like, "I want to get in bed with you," and "I want to touch your boobs." He cornered her in the hallways and rubbed up against her in a sexual way.

LaShonda regularly complained to supervisors, but they did nothing. It took three months of daily requests before they agreed to reassign G.F. to another desk. The harassment had such a debilitating effect on LaShonda that she wrote a suicide note. Her tormentor eventually was charged with and pled guilty to sexual battery in a Georgia court.

Schoolchildren Are Not Protected

LaShonda Davis and G.F. were fifth-graders. If LaShonda had been a grown-up and her harassment had occurred in the workplace, her employer would have been liable. Under Title VII, a federal law prohibiting sex- and race-based discrimination on the job, businesses are responsible for ensuring that their employees work in an environment free from sexual hostility. Employers are liable whether the source of sexual harassment is a supervisor or a co-worker.

But because LaShonda was only 10 years old, and because her emotional trauma occurred at school, many judges and lawyers feel that her "supervisors"—her teacher and the school principal—were under no legal duty to pay attention to her pleas and notice the constant barrage of humiliation and sexually-inspired torture she faced every day.

Eve Bruneau, a sixth-grader in upstate New York, was also a target of vicious

Reprinted from Erik Pitchal, "Just a Little Kiss?" *Z Magazine*, December 1996, by permission of *Z Magazine*.

student-to-student sexual harassment. She and other girls in her class were referred to by some boys as "lesbian," "prostitute," "whore," and "ugly dog-face bitch." Boys also snapped the girls' bras, stuffed paper down their blouses, and cut their hair.

In a landmark 1992 decision, the Supreme Court ruled that sexual harassment of students by teachers violates Title IX, the federal law which mandates equal educational opportunities for boys and girls. But whereas Title VII covers worker-to-worker harassment, courts currently disagree about whether Title IX should be interpreted to prohibit student-to-student harassment when teachers and principals stand by and do nothing.

LaShonda Davis's principal knew what was happening to her but took no action against G.F. This is a boy who eventually pled guilty to sexual battery, but the only thing the principal could think to do was to threaten him a little bit harder. Mostly the principal wanted to know why "LaShonda was the only girl complaining. It should not matter under the law whether LaShonda's tormentor was a peer or an adult.

The Media Influence

This is the backdrop for the case of Johnathan Prevette, the 6-year-old North Carolina boy who was suspended from first grade for kissing a female classmate on the cheek. School officials at first said that Johnathan had violated the school's sexual harassment policy. The outrage in response to this story was international. "Political correctness run amok," the headlines read. "What's wrong with an innocent peck on the cheek?"

The sexual harassment policy at Johnathan's school was instituted in response to "LaShonda Davis's case and others like it. These policies are a good thing, because they serve as a constant reminder to teachers and administrators that they must take complaints of sexual harassment from students very seriously.

Sexual harassment at the elementary school level is a major problem. A study by the Minnesota Attorney General's office reported that in the 1992–93 academic year, there were over 2,200 reports of sexual harassment in 720 elementary schools. There were an additional 377 reports of sexual violence.

> *"Willful blindness to the disgusting reality of student-on-student sexual harassment is a grave injustice."*

I do not doubt that the officials at Johnathan Prevette's school overreacted when they applied their policy to his behavior. Most likely this 6-year-old did not intend any malice towards his classmate—according to his parents, he is a very affectionate boy. Kissing in class is inappropriate, and this should have been explained to him the same way most first grade rule violations are. But this case pales in comparison to the wretched pattern of harassment suffered by LaShonda Davis and Eve Bruneau.

The Backlash Is Dangerous

Some conservative commentators insist that the worst thing that can happen in elementary schools these days is still catching the cooties. I fear that the Prevette case will lead to a nationwide backlash against strong policies to root out sexual harassment among students. The enormous media exposure this case received may have been the first salvo in a coordinated backlash campaign. It is no surprise that the major sources quoted in the front-page *USA Today* story were Camille Paglia and Rush Limbaugh. Meanwhile, the U.S. Department of Education's Office of Civil Rights is about to release long-awaited guidelines on peer harassment. [The guidelines were published in March 1997.]

> *"What happened to LaShonda Davis was not a little kiss. What happened to LaShonda Davis was a nightmare."*

What happened to Johnathan Prevette was too bad. School officials have now admitted that they erred and have apologized. But willful blindness to the disgusting reality of student-on-student sexual harassment is a grave injustice. What happened to LaShonda Davis was not a little kiss. What happened to LaShonda Davis was a nightmare.

Sexual Harassment Is a Serious Problem for Asian American Women

by Tamina Davar

About the author: *Tamina Davar is a contributing editor to* A. Magazine: Inside Asian America.

"Susan," a Filipina American salesperson, had been working at a well-known national fashion designer's retail store in New York for four months when, according to Susan, Regional Manager "Sam" told her over the phone that he had a white male friend with a fetish for Filipina women. Ordering her not to tell her coworkers, he pressured Susan to perform a sexual favor for this friend, saying he'd get in trouble if she didn't comply.

He offered Susan money, adding that another Asian woman had previously complied with this request. "I was in shock this was happening," Susan recalls. "I thought if I could just convince him to leave me alone, that would be it. I was scared. I was thinking if I didn't cooperate with this guy, he could do something to me."

Afraid and Without Support

Susan told her immediate supervisor what had happened. Then, she says, Sam called Susan at home and threatened her. "He knew I needed this job to survive. And he was really scaring me." As a result, Susan, fearing the loss of her job, and believing his promise that he would stop harassing her, unwillingly complied with his demands.

But they didn't stop. Meanwhile, Susan had been told she'd soon be transferred to Sam's store. "I told myself there's no way I'd go there, where he could harass me all he wanted to." Her supervisor was unable to do anything—the company had not made employees aware of their rights or options. So Susan quit, and took a much lower-paying job. But that wasn't the end of it. Sam kept

Reprinted, with permission, from Tamina Davar, "Indecent Proposals," *A. Magazine: Inside Asian America*, October/November 1996 (revised by the author).

calling her at home. She reported his actions to the police. Previously, on a friend's suggestion, she had filed an Equal Employment Opportunity Commission (EEOC) charge. But now, like many women who cannot afford to hire a lawyer, it seems that Susan is no closer to justice. Sam is still on the payroll. But Susan's life has been turned upside-down.

Susan had moved to New York to pursue her dream of designing accessories—and since her former employer is a leader in the industry, she felt it was the ideal place to start work. A growing corporation with stores around the country, the company's slick ads are marketed to the independent '90's woman.

Susan could have put the entire painful episode behind her. But instead, she started to fight back.

Help for Asian American Women

Susan located the Committee Against Anti-Asian Violence (CAAAV), a grassroots racial justice organization in New York City, which has since begun working with her and a coalition of Asian American community groups to seek legal recourse for Susan, organize a boycott of her former employer's products, and call much-needed public attention to Asian American women's experiences of sexual harassment, and to the workplaces that tolerate it.

"Women are harassed because of stereotypes," says Irene Natividad, chair of the National Commission on Working Women and executive director of the Philippine American Foundation. "And when it comes to women of color, clearly the stereotypes about each particular ethnic group become exacerbated."

Since Anita Hill focused the nation's attention on sexual harassment in 1991, charges filed with the EEOC have shot up from 6,883 in 1991, to 15,549 in 1995, an increase of over 100 percent. [In October 1991, law professor Hill charged U.S. Supreme Court nominee Clarence Thomas with sexual harassment. Despite the allegations, Thomas was confirmed.] Over 90 percent of complainants are women. But the experiences of women of color, including racialized sexual harassment—as Susan experienced— have yet to be adequately dealt with

> *"The experiences of women of color . . . have yet to be adequately dealt with in the research, media coverage, public dialogue, and legal responses."*

in the research, media coverage, public dialogue, and legal responses surrounding the debate.

According to a 1995 national survey of over 400 Asian American women compiled by the Pennsylvania-based business development consulting firm BTB-Quality Solutions, over one-third of the women had experienced sexual harassment, and almost two-thirds knew other Asian American women who'd been harassed. Lawyer Kimberly Miyazawa, Senior Project Manager at J.B. Reid & Associates, a Cincinnati-based management consulting firm, finds that when dealing with women who've experienced sexual harassment, "any time it's a woman of color, there are racial implications." Yet, women like Susan—who finally located CAAAV after many dead ends—finds that neither women's nor people of color organizations are able to fully address their issues.

Stereotypes of Submissiveness

Social messages to women and minorities "perpetuate that women can be objectified, particularly the Asian woman," explains Mary Ann Wong, an external consultant to corporations on diversity. "There's a difference between being a sexual being, which we all are, and being sexually objectified. When you dehumanize a person this way," says Wong, "it's easier than to abuse someone." In fact, racial harassment and violence toward Asian Americans reflect strikingly similar patterns of abuse to those of general sexual harassment and violence—where, based on stereotypes of submissiveness, the perpetrator uses their position of power to verbally or physically degrade and humiliate the victim.

Experts point out that when women of color experience sexual harassment, race plays out in ways which are distinct from those of white women—no matter what the race of the harasser. In particular, two main experiences for women of color emerge. If the harasser is of a different race, especially white, "there are sexualized stereotypes of women of color that don't apply to white women, or men of the same race" that particularize

> *"Experts point out that when women of color experience sexual harassment, race plays out in ways which are distinct from those of white women."*

his harassing behavior, says Verna Williams, senior counsel at the National Women's Law Center in Washington, D.C. And if he has a fetish towards women of a particular ethnicity, as Susan's harasser did, it can isolate his target from others who aren't affected.

But if the harasser is a man of one's own ethnic background, as Anita Hill found when she brought out Clarence Thomas's harassment, women of color are often pressured by men and women of their own community to remain silent for the sake of not "betraying racial unity." When "the gender issue gets subsumed," says Wong, "it gives license for minority men to be sexist, and to harass without fear of retribution." It also further victimizes Asian American women, who are reminded how society already vilifies or emasculates men of their race, and ultimately feel that they must choose "allegiance." Both these aspects of harassment significantly hinder women of color from dealing with their experiences in an empowering way.

A History of Exploitation

Sexual—and racial—harassment and violence are about demonstrating one's dominance over an individual or class of people. As white women climb the rungs of the professional world, some say that white men are reacting to this perceived assault on their power by dominating those who seem to have less power—and that means women of color. And if they perceive Asian women as the most submissive of them all, it isn't a surprise, given that sexualized stereotypes of Asian women have long offered white men license to exploit Asian women as exotic, subhuman, and sexually servile. In particular, the U.S. military's continued presence in Asian countries, where poor women are given few options for economic survival other than

> *"Sexualized stereotypes of Asian women have long offered white men license to exploit Asian women as exotic, subhuman, and sexually servile."*

selling their bodies in and surrounding military towns, has ensured that millions of American men see Asian women as sex workers—or as wives they can order straight from a catalog.

This connection was particularly resonant for Susan, because her harasser implied that being of Filipina origin, she should comply with his threats to do the sexual favor. And it's equally resonant for Irene Natividad. She relates that in her travels around the country for work, "frequently, a man will come up to me and say, 'are you Filipino?' and I'll say 'yes.' And he will say 'Oh, I was there during the war.' And I know what's coming." Be it as master-slave or GI-prostitute, as Judy Scales-Trent pointed out in one of the first articles on sexual harassment and race in 1981, these harassing behaviors often directly reference a historical or current situation where it was condoned and encouraged for white men to sexually exploit women of color. While these assumptions about the unquestioning sexual availability of Asian women were engendered decades ago during World War II and the Korean and Vietnam wars, they continue today in the sex industries created during those periods. And from the experiences of Asian American women around the country, these misperceptions are as vivid in the imaginations of American men as if all three wars had just ended yesterday.

Speaking Up

According to Kim Miyazawa, a harasser assumes "that you're going to be subservient, that you're not going to expose him"—especially if you're Asian. But while age, immigrant status, and culture are factors in whether women fight back against sexual harassment, in general, Asian Americans seem no less likely to come forward than other women of color.

Of all EEOC charges filed by Asian Americans in 1995, 6.6 percent were sexual harassment charges—a percentage slightly lower than that of Latinos and slightly higher than African Americans—but all of which were lower than the percentage of charges filed by whites. A current study on sexual harassment by the Women of Color Resource Center in San Francisco also sees trends of underreporting by women of color across the board. "It's just really difficult to speak out, whether you're Asian or not," says one young Korean American woman. "I'm usually a pretty sharp person. But when I felt violated, it was humiliating, degrading, and frustrating to the point where you just want to forget it."

All women who are targets of sexual harassment in the workplace fear losing their jobs. But it has a sharper resonance, says Irene Natividad, for women of color, who "have a harder time with this issue, because they tend to be at the lower rungs of the economic ladder, and they're very afraid of getting fired." Citing not the glass ceiling, but "sticky floors," Natividad continues that "if the person harassing you is the one who decides if you get out from the bottom" or controls the workplace grievance procedure, your options are limited. Options also depend on other complexities, including the type of workplace or school; whether a union, or minority employee network exists; and differences in Asian American women's ethnicities, generation, and language abilities. Natividad adds that the growing number of immigrant Asian women workers who are more vulnerable to sexual harassment are often the ones less able to take action.

Fighting Back

Once a victim recognizes that she has a right to stand up against harassment, women's advocacy groups warn that she must take the initiative and become her own advocate. Which means trying to exhaust all existing options before going the legal route, starting with calling the harasser on his action—not an easy task, especially when his response may be retaliation.

But in the "ideal" workplace, recourse may look like this: an employer, not wanting to risk publicity as a bad place for women of color to work, will have strong anti-harassment policies, and widely disseminated information about employee rights and procedures. It will offer several confidential reporting options to a superior, who is required to take all complaints through a specific course of action. Results may be specific to the situation; or if the problem seems larger, may lead to evaluation and solution strategies for the entire workplace. And there will be strong Asian American and women's employee groups to support you.

> *"Harassing behaviors often directly reference a historical or current situation where it was condoned and encouraged for white men to sexually exploit women of color."*

However Yasmin, who worked in a racially diverse marketing department, learned the hard way that even when such structures exist, they don't always work and can even be adversarial for Asian Americans.

When Yasmin's white supervisor learned she was South Asian, "he said he'd read in the *Kama Sutra* about all the sexual tricks 'my people' could do," she says. "At first, I told him 'I'm Moslem, I wouldn't know,' and tried to shrug it off."

But he began cornering Yasmin and comparing her to photos of Hindu goddess carvings which lined his office—as if they were pornographic. The personnel department told Yasmin she was overreacting to his "multicultural interest." After he made Yasmin's attendance at a marketing conference dependent on giving him "a lesson," she confronted him.

> *"The growing number of immigrant Asian women workers who are more vulnerable to sexual harassment are often the ones less able to take action."*

"He tried to convince me there was nothing unusual about his threat, adding that 'you Asian women are all too uptight.'" After the mostly male Asian American employee group balked, Yasmin approached the Black employee network's leader, a woman, who immediately gathered a group of women of color to go straight to the company president. He refused to fire the harasser, moving him to another department. Meanwhile, Yasmin found she couldn't deal with his continuing presence, and quit. "It made me sick how he used Asian culture to degrade and threaten me," she says.

If going through the workplace for recourse is not useful or possible—and this is especially true of small businesses—the next step is to file a charge with your state human rights division (for workplaces of less than 15), or with the EEOC. But be wary: despite the EEOC's brand-new way of processing charges, based on priority, and a reduced backlog, it can still take over a year before a decision is made to investigate or drop a case. Meanwhile, women can also request a "right-to-sue" letter from the EEOC, which enables her to pursue legal action. But if a lawyer isn't affordable, many women, like Susan, are faced with the choice of staying and enduring harassment, or quitting and risking economic consequences.

The Double Discrimination Debate

Women of color who've experienced sexual harassment have long known that there is a relationship between racial and sexual harassment. Both race and sex discrimination (which harassment falls under) are both violations under Title VII of the 1964 Civil Rights Act. The problem is that they've been legally treated as two different entities. Women of color in the legal arena say that despite a growing body of legal writing on "intersectionality" of race and sex discrimination (primarily by African American women in academia), and a growing exploration of its legal implications by the EEOC and within courts, intersectionality remains an "emerging area" of the law.

If you go the legal route, observes Yolanda Wu, staff attorney at the National Organization for Women (NOW) Legal Defense and Education Fund in New York, currently there are no hard and fast rules on how charges involving more than one basis of discrimination play out in court, although many now allow "aggregating" claims of racial and sexual harassment. So far, there's only been a handful of cases where courts implicitly recognize intersectional discrimination. "It's been an ongoing debate and question—what to do with this—that courts struggle with," says Wu.

Paul Igasaki, vice chair of the EEOC, says that exploring the intersectional implications of race and gender discrimination is among the priorities of the EEOC's recently adopted National Enforcement Plan. So far they've been gathering input from civil rights and community leaders, but are looking to develop a holistic policy. Cases the EEOC actually litigates, he says, will "send a message that the government considers this an area that needs to be focused on."

But how will this actually impact individual Asian American women filing a charge with the EEOC? Since sexual harassment, as a general rule, and intersectional issues particularly are prioritized, you will see greater sensitivity," he adds. "We're hoping that people will know that an Asian American woman who is harassed in both a racial and a sexual way won't be forgotten or lost in the system."

Alternative Solutions

There's a long way to go in implementing culturally appropriate workplace solutions—even with the issue of sexual harassment gaining visibility in the workplace, it's still presented as a white issue, and racial harassment as an entirely separate issue. Serious change is needed—in trainings, materials, and language—so employees are better equipped to talk about connections of race and sex.

"If a lawyer isn't affordable, many women . . . are faced with the choice of staying and enduring harassment, or quitting and risking economic consequences."

Irene Natividad believes that solutions to sexual harassment do not lie only in the reactive work taken on by government agencies and the legal arena: "In the end, workplaces must take responsibility for this problem, and should be institutionalizing practices." Training and education are not enough, she says. What's also needed is "an objective evaluation program by the employer to examine any charges of sexual harassment, that maintains privacy of the employees, that doesn't ostracize the complainant and that actually works—and that they're serious about." Natividad feels it's critical to share tried-and-true sexual harassment prevention strategies across industries. And leaders must set the tone.

Accountability becomes harder, says Natividad, in smaller or decentralized workplaces, like the store Susan worked in. "But the last thing a company should want is a sexual harassment suit as part of their image," she says, "especially now that they recognize that women are a large customer base. And that's where our strength lies."

In fact Paul Igasaki, acknowledging limitations of the EEOC and legal avenues, cites instance where the Asian American community "has pitched in and created an atmosphere of pressure on a particular employer" around an incident or issue. This especially occurs in scenarios that revolve around "an employer people feel is getting benefits from the Asian American community." In Susan's case, that's exactly what CAAAV's community campaign hopes to achieve. Janice Pono, one of the case coordinators, explains. "We want to show that Asian Americans are not passive consumers, but we are fighters."

But permanent, stable support systems and infrastructures to address Asian American women who are sexually harassed—especially those who are economically disadvantaged—have not yet been built in our communities, say many Asian Americans who work on these issues. Without them, they say, grassroots justice campaigns around individual cases like Susan's will only achieve short-term solutions. They also point to the fact that high-profile sexual harassment cases involving Asian American women have been rare, perpetuating a lack of dialogue in Asian American media, and among men and women in our communities. As for resources, most Asian American legal and racial justice organizations readily acknowledge their limited ability to address sexual harassment. And while strong Asian American networks around domestic violence do exist, they say their resources, too, cannot extend to that area. But everyone agrees on one point: that only coalition work connecting Asian American legal, women's, and community organizations working on these issues can ensure that a strong—and necessary—Asian American voice on sexual harassment emerges.

> *"Serious change is needed–in trainings, materials, and language–so employees are better equipped to talk about connections of race and sex."*

And that communication is beginning. One arena with the potential to create change is the women of color legal community, observes Claudia Withers, executive director of The Fair Employment Council. In Washington, D.C., she says, "there's a very active 'caucus' of us who touch bases across racial lines." And an existing coalition model is the National Network for African American Women and the Law, which, Verna Williams says, enables its members to "bring our resources to bear to address our own particularized set of discrimination issues." Asian Americans working on sexual harassment say it's crucial to promote more documentation and dialogue—and to then make it more public and accessible.

"Until then," warns Miyazawa, "it will be one-woman battles and private fights."

Sisters Helping Sisters

Miyazawa advises that "Asian American women need to know we have the right to explore" new options for recourse "where you don't have to go the public route." These include professional arbitration, and for-profit consulting firms which may well take on pro-bono cases.

Jean Ishibashi was supported by a community coalition when she sued the

American Friends Service Committee for sexual harassment several years ago. Ishibashi says that asking for help and finding support from coworkers, friends, or community groups "is critically important for the health of the individual, but also of the whole community."

Some Asian Americans say that in order to speak out against sexual harassment, we must struggle against silence, as if it were some inherent Asian trait. Yet, as M. Evelina Galang relates in her short story on sexual harassment, "Filming Sausage" (from *Her Wild American Self*), you may be surprised by what your grandmother has to say:

> Last night your lola told you to sue the man. "Where we come from young ladies don't let men act this way."
>
> "Lola, it's not like I'm encouraging this," you cried to her.
>
> "Then you should speak up, hija, you should speak up."

Same-Sex Sexual Harassment Is a Serious Problem

by Anne-Marie Harris

About the author: *Anne-Marie Harris teaches law and government part time at Bentley College in Waltham, Massachusetts.*

Jody Oncale, who worked on an oil rig for Sundowner Offshore Services, told company officials of "being restrained by two co-workers, while the supervisor placed his penis on my neck, on one occasion, and on my arm, on another occasion; threats of rape by the supervisor and a co-worker; and the use of force by the supervisor to push a bar of soap into my anus while a co-worker held me." These complaints of sexual harassment fell on deaf ears.

How could any self-respecting 1990s manager fail to identify Jody's experiences as sexual harassment? The answer? Jody Oncale is a man.

During the 1990s, employers have experienced a rise in the numbers of complaints and successful lawsuits by employees alleging sexual harassment at work. In January 1998, Reuters reported that "companies are spending as much as $100,000 a year in premiums for employment-practices liability insurance, the type of policy that covers sexual harassment lawsuits."

If we have become so knowledgeable about the abuse of power that manifests itself as sexual harassment, why was Jody Oncale forced to put up with such egregious behavior when women in this country are protected against such abuses of power? How could his claim be dismissed without even an examination of the facts?

Courts Examine Same-Sex Cases

Until *Oncale v. Sundowner Offshore Services, et al.,* the Supreme Court had never been called upon to determine whether Title VII protects individuals against sexual harassment by members of the same sex. Some lower courts had held that same-sex harassment was not illegal under our civil rights laws. They found it repugnant and childish, but mere "horseplay." But March 4, 1998, the Supreme Court unanimously declared that, despite Jody's sex—or, perhaps more precisely, "because of his sex"—he has articulated a valid claim of sexual harassment.

Under the Supreme Court's direction, the 5th U.S. Circuit Court of Appeals must now re-examine *Oncale* to determine whether the plaintiff was, in fact, a victim of illegal sexual harassment. The lower court may now decide to adopt the rule that has emerged from the majority of federal appeals courts since 1993.

As noted by Justice Antonin Scalia, who wrote the court's opinion in *Oncale,* there has been a "bewildering variety of stances" among the many federal and state courts that had previously considered the issue of same-sex harassment.

Some situations are easier to identify as sexual harassment despite their same-sex context. For example, in *Wrightson v. Pizza Hut of America,* 1996, the plaintiff, a heterosexual male, alleged that his homosexual male supervisor sexually harassed him when he "graphically described homosexual sex and repeatedly touched the plaintiff in sexually provocative ways including pull[ing] out plaintiff's pants in order to look into them," among other conduct.

Here, the "predatory" homosexual harasser is treating the heterosexual victim in the same way as a "typical" heterosexual male harasser behaves in the paradigm opposite-sex harassment case. Thus, the 4th Circuit did not hesitate to declare that Title VII protects heterosexual victims from this type of same-sex harassment.

In grappling with the difficult issue of same-sex harassment, several circuits have determined that the applicability of Title VII depends on the sexual orientation of the alleged harasser. Only homosexuals who harass heterosexuals of the same sex can be liable under Title VII, they decided—the implication being that actionability attaches solely if the presumed motive is sexual attraction.

Although the Supreme Court stated in *Oncale* that "harassing behavior need not be motivated by sexual desire to support an inference of discrimination on the basis of sex," it did not directly address the question of the parties' sexual orientation in same-sex harassment cases. Therefore, it is still possible that the 5th Circuit will follow the reasoning developed by the 4th, 6th and 11th circuits. Such an outcome would be a grave error.

> *"Why should the harasser's sexual orientation become determinative of the outcome in same-sex harassment?"*

When a male harasser threatens his female victim with job loss unless she performs sexual favors, the law does not require an inquiry into the sexual orientation of the alleged harasser. Why should the harasser's sexual orientation become determinative of the outcome in same-sex harassment?

The only possible usefulness would be to identify motive. This reasoning is based on the assumption that an individual harasses another because he or she is sexually attracted to the victim. However, it is generally agreed that the motivation can arise from a variety of sources, ranging from sexual attraction, to the assertion of power, to puerility, perversity and even self-loathing.

Motives Should Be Irrelevant

The 5th Circuit must decide that the harasser's motives are irrelevant to establish illegal same-sex harassment. To reason otherwise, an alleged harasser would violate Title VII only if sexual attraction was involved. Puerility, perversity and the desire to control others would serve as legitimate defenses.

In the 1996 same-sex harassment case *Quick v. Donaldson*, Phil Quick alleged that co-workers at the Donaldson Co. engaged in a game they called "bagging," which consisted of "the intentional grabbing and squeezing of another person's testicles." Mr. Quick testified that 12 heterosexual male co-workers had "bagged" him approximately 100 times during a two-year period. Must the federal courts make determinations of fact with respect to the motivations behind such a game?

Furthermore, if same-sex harassment is only actionable under Title VII when the harasser is homosexual, then a "homosexual defense" ought to exist in cases in which harasser and victim are of the opposite sex.

> *"In all such cases, the defendant's motive should be irrelevant to a determination of liability."*

Are we also prepared to ask our federal courts to make determinations of fact with respect to the sexual orientation of the parties before them?

One hopes these scenarios are far-fetched and beg the conclusion that, in all sexual harassment cases, the inquiry focuses on the effect of the harassing behavior on the victim. In all such cases, the defendant's motive should be irrelevant to a determination of liability.

As the Supreme Court concluded in *Oncale,* "Common sense, and an appropriate sensitivity to social context, will enable courts and juries to distinguish between simple teasing or roughhousing among members of the same sex, and conduct which a reasonable person in the plaintiff's position would find severely hostile or abusive."

Perhaps a dose of common sense is exactly what the Supreme Court needed to inject into the ongoing struggle toward friendly and peaceful work environments for all.

The Extent of Sexual Harassment Is Exaggerated

by Marianne M. Jennings

About the author: *Marianne M. Jennings is a professor of legal and ethical studies in the College of Business at Arizona State University and director of the university's Lincoln Center for Applied Ethics.*

Nearly 30 years in the workplace, and not once have I been sexually harassed. I suppose I'm grateful, but given the action other working women seem to be getting, part of me wonders: Exactly what's wrong with me? It's not as if I haven't been in high-risk environments. I began my legal career as an intern for the federal government. Yet I haven't had so much as a compliment from a male co-worker since the Reagan administration. After the Anita Hill spectacle in 1991, I noticed men averting their eyes.

Court Decisions Make Women Appear Helpless

But what I resent more than the lack of attention is the assumption underlying the rules and court decisions governing sexual harassment: that I am incapable of handling unwanted sexual suggestion. My employer trusts me with budgeting, lobbying, fund-raising and shaping the minds of the next generation, but is forced by the Equal Employment Opportunity Commission and the courts to conclude that I can't handle the advances of knuckleheads.

I resent the women who bring sexual harassment suits and convince courts that we are as helpless and victimized as Melanie Wilkes in *Gone With the Wind.* I come from a long line of unharassed women who taught me that the best defense against offensive male behavior is a good offense. The female arm has an appendage created for dealing with cads. Women in the 1940s used said appendage quite effectively to administer a slap in the face and thereby deter drunken sailors. And yet working women today can't handle a boor in wing tips and bifocals without the help of the Supreme Court?

The court's rulings on harassment make it easier to win damages against a company even if it is unaware that a supervisor is harassing an employee, and even if the plaintiff suffered no career damage. The likely result: Companies will redouble their already vigorous efforts aimed at preventing harassment.

But who's harassing whom when I'm forced to attend "sensitivity training" seminars and reveal my personal feelings to co-workers with whom I don't even exchange recipes? At one Fortune 500 company, a sensitivity consultant instructed employees to conduct the following "group exercise": "I want all of the men to sit down on the floor in the center of the room. You are not allowed to speak while sitting down. The women are to stand around the men in a circle and begin to whistle and make sexist comments about the appearance and anatomy of the men." What if I don't *want* to talk about my colleagues' anatomy?

Victims Are Not Innocent

How innocent are the victims of harassment anyway? *Dateline NBC* ran a story on women who claimed they were harassed while working on the production lines at a Ford plant in Chicago. They tearfully told of sleeping with supervisors to keep their jobs and of being hospitalized for stress. These women defined their ethical dilemma as most people who make poor decisions do: Either I stay here and get harassed, or I leave and take another job for less pay but keep my sanity and virtue. To put it another way, the supervisors' brutish behavior was awful, but for $22 an hour the employees were willing to put up with it. Similarly, if you believe Anita Hill's story, she tolerated Clarence Thomas's misbehavior for years because riding to a career pinnacle on the tails of a shooting star was worth it.

Like tenants who claim "constructive eviction" due to horrible living conditions yet remain on the leased premises, the legal claim of women that their working environment is hostile doesn't jibe with their own decision to remain. Women define what's repulsive, stay in it and then file and win multimillion-dollar verdicts, which in many cases exceed the amounts awarded to children crippled in horrific accidents. The courtroom playing field reflects academic theories such as the following, touted in the *Journal of Business Ethics:* "Sexual harassment signifies

> *"Working women today can't handle a boor in wing tips and bifocals without the help of the Supreme Court?"*

to women that their presence is threatening to the dominant patriarchal order, that they are unwelcome, and works to maintain gender stratification." The guys at the Ford plant were interested in "gender stratification"? Sounds to me like they were just after a roll in the hay.

Laws Make Men Afraid

The most damaging result of sexual-harassment law is the chilling effect it has on men in the workplace. Mentoring, which I had from decent and honorable men and without which I would not have survived 30 years ago, is a lost art. Men who hold the keys and skills for advancement hesitate to involve themselves in one-on-one counseling of female employees. Men fear closing the office door during meetings with women. At the University of Nebraska, a graduate student was even ordered to remove a picture of his bikini-clad wife from his desk after two colleagues complained.

> *"The most damaging result of sexual-harassment law is the chilling effect it has on men in the workplace."*

I see a fear in my male colleagues' eyes that they will unwittingly offend someone and will be the subject of a career-derailing investigation. The fear is justified. An accused rapist, after all, receives better treatment than an accused harasser. The rape defendant is entitled to due process, the presumption of innocence and his day in court. When a man is charged with sexual harassment, the employer's response will be swift, decisive and one-sided.

I resent that men in my office feel they must cast their eyes downward. It's not their sexual appetites they're holding back. It's candor. It's friendliness. It's lunch together. They're certainly not harassers, but they can no longer risk being my friends or mentors. Feminists claimed victory with these latest decisions because liability for sexual harassment now rests squarely with those responsible—employers. That's wrong. Employers don't cause sexual harassment. Women have defined it, capitalized on it and exacerbated it. We also possess the tools for handling it, without a federal judge or bureaucracy. Dear sisters, we have met the enemy and she is us.

The Exaggeration of Sexual Harassment Is Costly to Business

by Elizabeth Larson

About the author: *Elizabeth Larson writes on business issues for various magazines, including* Investor's Business Daily *and* American Enterprise.

Sexual harassment is "subtle rape," or so says psychologist John Gottman. Judging from the millions of dollars U.S. companies are being forced to spend to combat sexual harassment, American men have apparently become subtle rapists and sexual predators on a scale unimaginable even to the most vocal feminists of a decade or two ago.

A New Industry

Sexual harassment lawsuits such as the ones brought about by the Del Laboratories secretaries and employees of Mitsubishi make headlines nationwide, but too many companies and organizations still think "that can't happen to us." But it can—and an entire industry has sprung up since the early 1990s to help businesses avoid the nightmare of a sexual harassment lawsuit.

Unfortunately, though, this army of experts may in fact be fostering sexual harassment complaints even as it seeks to prevent them. Like the college twentysomethings persuaded by their feminist sisters that they were in fact raped, today's young businesswomen are being taught that behavior they would have once considered boorish or inappropriate should be rendering them victimized and helpless—and in desperate need of huge financial compensation.

Like the concept of "date rape," the term "sexual harassment" didn't even exist two decades ago. It joined the American lexicon with the publication of Lin Farley's *Sexual Shakedown: The Sexual Harassment of Women on the Job* (1978) and Catharine MacKinnon's *Sexual Harassment of Working Women* (1979). MacKinnon, the well known feminist law professor, was largely re-

Reprinted from Elizabeth Larson, "The Economic Costs of Sexual Harassment," *The Freeman*, August 1996, by permission of *The Freeman*.

sponsible for convincing the legal community and social theorists that sexual harassment is a form of sex discrimination—thus implying it is as reprehensible a crime as racism.

A Surge in Complaints

Complaints began to arrive at the Equal Employment Opportunity Commission slowly. Women filed a total of 3,661 charges in 1981, and that figure rose gradually throughout the decade, reaching 5,623 in 1989. With the nineties, however, came an explosion. From 6,127 cases in 1990, the numbers skyrocketed to 14,420 in 1994. Evidence from state agencies mirrors the surge at the EEOC. The Kansas Human Rights Commission received only 75 complaints of sexual harassment in 1991, for example. That figure jumped 261 percent by fiscal year 1995 to reach a record 271 reports of alleged harassment.

Lawyers point to several reasons for the increase in complaints filed. In the 1986 case *Meritor Savings Bank v. Vinson,* the hostile-environment argument [the claim that unwelcome verbal or physical conduct creates an intimidating, hostile or offensive work environment] was upheld for the first time. This dramatically increased an employer's liability: the plaintiff was no longer required to prove she had been subjected to a *quid pro quo* situation (e.g., "have an affair with me or you're fired"). As the hostile-environment argument caught on, complaints that would once have been considered frivolous were suddenly accorded legal merit. Then came 1991 and Anita Hill. [Hill charged U.S. Supreme Court nominee Clarence Thomas with sexual harassment. Despite the allegations, Thomas was confirmed.] In the three weeks after the Clarence Thomas hearings, the EEOC saw a 23 percent surge in complaints of sexual harassment filed with its offices. The 9 to 5 National Association of Working Women received 200 calls in the average week before Anita Hill stepped forth; after Hill's allegations, they were fielding 200 calls a day.

> *"Unfortunately . . . this army of experts may in fact be fostering sexual harassment complaints even as it seeks to prevent them."*

That year was a banner one for sexual harassment lawyers and radical feminists for other reasons as well. The "reasonable woman" standard was created in *Ellison v. Brady* (the standard was affirmed by the U.S. Supreme Court in 1993), and the *Jacksonville Shipyards* case resulted in the inclusion of workplace pinups as proof of a hostile environment.

Potential Litigation

The high and continually rising numbers of complaints of sexual harassment filed means that the potential for litigation is serious for U.S. businesses, especially since the compensatory and punitive damages awarded to complainants have also risen sharply in recent years. A quick look at cases over the last two decades shows the steep climb in awards.

In what is considered the first sexual harassment case, *Barnes v. Train* in 1974, a woman working as the administrative assistant to the director of the Environmental Protection Agency's Equal Opportunities Division filed suit alleging that her position was abolished after she refused to engage in an "after-hours affair" with the director. The District Court dismissed the case because, although Barnes was discriminated against, the discrimination was based not on the fact that she was a woman but that she refused to engage in sexual relations with her boss. The decision was reversed on appeal. Barnes was awarded just $18,000 in back pay as damages for lost promotions.

> *"Like the concept of 'date rape,' the term 'sexual harassment' didn't even exist two decades ago."*

The rise in awards over the years that followed seems directly proportional to the decline in seriousness of the complainants' charges. The 1990 settlement in *Bihun v. AT&T Information Systems,* for example, was for $2 million. This small fortune was awarded to a personnel manager who suffered mental distress after receiving unwelcome advances from her supervisor, taking time off from work to recover, and finding her job eliminated when she returned. Today, Wal-Mart Stores is appealing a 1995 court ruling that awarded $50 million in punitive damages to a receiving department worker who charged that her supervisor was verbally abusive and liked to joke about her figure.

The transition from an "after-hours affair" to "verbally abusive" behavior as the definition of what constitutes sexual harassment mirrors a shift in our moral worldview. As Ellen Frankel Paul has noted, we have gone from punishing behavior that is objectively wrong to that which is subjectively offensive. As the courts' sensitivity to super-sensitive women has expanded, the average amount being awarded to plaintiffs has skyrocketed to reach $250,000. The $18,000 awarded to Ms. Barnes, whose treatment few would not consider genuine sexual harassment, is pocket change by comparison.

The Cost to Business

While relatively few women filing complaints actually get a shot at this legal lottery (the EEOC ended up litigating just 50 cases in 1990), the numbers available regarding how much all of this alleged harassment costs companies in terms other than court awards and legal fees are staggering indeed. Of the women who feel they have been sexually harassed, more than 25 percent use leave time to avoid the situation. At least 15 percent leave their jobs. Nearly half of them try to ignore the harassing behavior and suffer a 10 percent drop in productivity as a result (moreover, their friends who are aware of the situation suffer a 2 percent drop in productivity as well). One estimate puts the grand total to U.S. businesses for sexual harassment at $6.7 million annually in absenteeism, employee turnover, low morale, and low productivity. A 1988 study, however, found that sexual harassment in federal offices cost the government about $267 million in turnover and lost productivity over two years. Clearly such costs are difficult to quantify, but even the more conservative estimates available are extremely high.

And attempts at pinning down the vague costs of things like productivity are just the beginning of what U.S. businesses are paying for the thousands of sexual harassment claims filed every year. A 1992 study, for instance, found that 21 federal departments paid $139 million simply *to process* the 6,883 complaints filed with the EEOC the previous year.

> *"The rise in awards over the years . . . seems directly proportional to the decline in seriousness of the complainants' charges."*

Faced with the surge in sexual harassment cases nationwide, employers are adopting a two-pronged approach to the problem. Their offensive strategy is to "re-educate" their employees so that the sexism and thoughtlessness that results in sexual harassment in the workplace is eliminated. Their defensive approach is to line up legal experts to review their companies' harassment policies in preparation for the inevitable harassment charge and, more recently, to purchase a new type of business insurance designed to help them through a sexual harassment case without being financially destroyed.

A New Type of Liability Insurance

Thanks to the overall rise in employment discrimination cases (up 2,200 percent in the last two decades), sales of general employment-practices liability insurance have been on the rise in recent years. But companies ranging in size from a dozen workers to more than 10,000 employees are now purchasing sexual harassment liability insurance. Invented in the aftermath of Anita Hill's allegations against Clarence Thomas, such policies have only started catching on very recently. Although President Bill Clinton's policy was a personal rather than corporate one, the information released in the spring of 1996 about his use of $900,000 in liability insurance to cover the costs of Paula Jones's sexual harassment case against him will undoubtedly boost the sales of such policies for businesses.

Premiums for this new type of business liability insurance range from $1,500 to $25,000 annually, depending on many factors including turnover rates and whether the company has faced sexual harassment charges before. Coverage ranges from $250,000 to $25 million and includes court awards and defense costs—although not necessarily punitive damages.

The first to introduce liability policies to cover sexual harassment specifically was Lexington Insurance, in March 1992. Chubb Insurance Company followed suit, but until as recently as 1994 the two had the field pretty much to themselves. By the middle of that year, sales of the policies had risen 25 percent, and companies like Reliance National and New Hampshire Insurance were joining the trend. Company officials will not reveal exactly how many of the sexual harassment policies have been sold, but Chubb has said its business has been at least doubling every year. Business is certainly good enough that today there are about a dozen insurance companies jockeying for their share of clients. Although less than half of the Fortune 500 companies now have sexual harassment coverage, insurance company officials predict it will become a standard part of most business insurance portfolios.

> *"We have gone from punishing behavior that is objectively wrong to that which is subjectively offensive."*

Sexual harassment liability insurance does have its critics, though—many of them from the corps of experts in prevention and re-education who believe that the best way for a company to protect itself is by hiring them to stop sexual harassment from occurring in the first place.

The Cost of a Defense

But try telling that to someone like Bill Buckingham. "I'll get even," were the last words the president of Buckingham Computer Services Inc. heard when he fired a female employee for not doing her job. He and his company, a computer consulting business with some 40 employees, were sued for sexual harassment and wrongful discharge.

"Her comment was that I touched her on the back, which I had," Buckingham told *Inc.* magazine at the time. "We're a pretty close-knit company, and there was no question that I had patted people on the back. Nothing sexual. I'd tell people they were looking sharp today, ask if that was a new dress, stuff like that. That's basically what the suit was based on."

The ex-employee demanded more than $100,000 to settle the case. Since that figure represented a year's profit to his company, Buckingham tried to fight. He gave up after a year-and-a-half battle and $25,000 in legal costs. The most vigorous of prevention programs would not have saved Buckingham from such a suit, but sexual harassment liability insurance would have been a financial lifesaver.

There is no national clearinghouse for information on the sexual harassment industry, but sampling some of the different items these entrepreneurial experts offer gives a good extent of the enormous, and growing, business they have on their hands. Because many consultants combine sexual harassment training with their entire "diversity training" programs, the numbers for sexual harassment programs, as high as they are, are still conservative.

Sexual harassment prevention consultants provide a myriad of services to the business, small or large, seeking to minimize workplace problems. They will write a sexual harassment policy and the procedure for enforcing it tailored to specific companies' needs. They provide general staff seminars on what sexual harassment is, how to avoid a sexual harasser, and what to do if you feel you have been sexually harassed. They provide seminars specifically geared to the management personnel who are responsible for investigating and dealing with harassment charges. And they offer additional training for management so they themselves can conduct future workshops within their company.

Such seminars range from four or so hours to two days and cost upwards of several thousands of dollars each time. And that's just the beginning. As the *9 to 5 Guide to Combating Sexual Harassment* suggests: "Training should be *ongoing,* not a one-time session, and presented *on paid time." Sexual Harassment on the Job,* another guide for employers, recommends that companies serious about combating sexual harassment have employees complete a Sexual Harassment Survey every six months. And don't forget that every new employee—especially in management—must go through the awareness and prevention program if the company wants to minimize its risk.

For the smaller companies that cannot afford real-life consultants, there are numerous books, manuals, and videotapes to help them. Videotapes can range from $50 to $200 for a 24-hour rental. The Seattle-based Pacific Resource Development Group, one of the best known in the business, offers audiocassettes beginning at about $13.00; a videotape, *Shades of Grey,* for about $1,500; and a monthly newsletter for $120 annually. The company's annual sales exceed half a million, and its director, Susan Webb, has trained about a dozen other folks (at $5,000 a head) to go into the harassment-prevention consulting business themselves.

> *"Employers are required to almost assist employees in their claims against them."*

Lawyers Join the New Industry

Consulting firms aren't the only ones getting in on the action. Law firms are also expanding their programs to include sexual harassment prevention. The San Francisco-based firm of Littler, Mendelson, Fastiff, Tichy & Mathiason, one of the largest employment law firms in the nation, has gotten into the business of helping companies avoid sexual harassment lawsuits. A typical one-day seminar for 30 or so people costs from $1,500 to $3,000. With the majority of Littler's cases now relating to sexual harassment, this one firm alone has a tremendous market for its prevention seminars.

An excerpt from one sexual harassment guide indicates the extent to which these legions of experts are advising companies to go:

> To maximize options for the complainant, the policy must allow for *several different channels.* The procedure should not require the complainant to report the problem to her supervisor, since that person may be the harasser. At least

one option should be to complain to an employee through an affirmative action committee, women's committee, or other committee. If feasible, designate an ombudsperson to counsel victims. . . . Management should designate one or more specially trained employees who will carry out investigations. . . . Follow-up should also be done with harassers—even if they are asked to resign—to make sure they understand what was wrong with their behavior.

As these recommendations indicate, an aggressive program requires the employer not just to support the sexual harassment industry directly but to create actual salaried positions for in-house harassment experts. Yet the threat of lawsuits is so great that, according to the Society for Human Resource Management, three-quarters of the companies in a recent poll had implemented some form of the many costly prevention steps now being recommended. Among the major corporations known for their "enlightened" sexual harassment programs are AT&T, Coca Cola, Avon, Texas Industries, and Harley-Davidson. DuPont company maintains a toll-free sexual harassment hotline. Four staff members trained in sexual harassment and rape prevention are assigned to the hotline and carry beepers 24 hours a day. The company assigns one man and one woman to investigate each case. Corning Inc. picks up the tab for employees who wish to speak with a confidential outside consultant.

The Government Intervenes

In some areas of the country, the burgeoning sexual harassment industry has not been getting a boost simply from plaintiff-friendly juries, but from state legislatures as well. Since 1993 California has required all employers—regardless of size—to notify employees that sexual harassment is unlawful. The employer must provide examples of what constitutes sexual harassment and clearly explain how harassed employees can get in touch with the appropriate government agencies. As one California lawyer who conducts prevention seminars said, "Employers are required to almost assist employees in their claims against them." Connecticut employers with more than 50 employees have been required since 1992 to conduct at least two hours of sexual harassment training for all management; if an employer has more than three workers, posters about sexual harassment must be prominently posted in the workplace. Other states have considered similar legislation in recent years.

> *"This rapid growth of the sexual harassment industry is nothing less than liberalism's tax on the business world.*

This rapid growth of the sexual harassment industry is nothing less than liberalism's tax on the business world. The culture of victimization is becoming so embedded in the courts and, increasingly, the state legislatures, that a handful of sexual harassment lawsuits are now seen as representative of the average working woman's lot—and both working women and their employers are paying the very high cost. The continual rise in sexual harassment claims, even as women are poised to take over the reins at 50 percent of the small and mid-sized businesses in one recent survey (to use just one example), suggests that the sexual harassment industry itself is in large part to blame for this phantom epidemic that has employers so scared.

Rather than limiting themselves to explanations of the law, the experts are teaching women to spot lechery and lasciviousness behind every friendly smile. In such a world, where every man is considered a potential rapist (subtle though he may be), sexual harassment lawsuits easily become a tool for revenge. Of course, there is certainly boorish behavior going on in workplaces all across America, but for much of that, too, we can thank liberalism. The degradation of manners and proper social behavior that is the legacy of the anything-goes Sixties merely compounds workplace situations in which women are encouraged to go to the courts for every little slight.

> *"Rather than limiting themselves to explanations of the law, the experts are teaching women to spot lechery and lasciviousness behind every friendly smile."*

A More Reasonable Approach

It's time to inject a little reasonableness into workplace relationships. And ironically enough, the feminist *9 to 5 Guide* offers some genuine common sense in its guidelines for "How Not to Harass." First: "Until you learn otherwise, assume that a woman you don't know will *not* enjoy off-color jokes or sexual advances at work." Second: "Sharpen your listening skills. If a woman's response, whether verbal or physical, seems negative, trust that it is. Does she avert her eyes or turn away? Assume that no means no." And third: "If you're not sure whether your workplace behavior is acceptable, ask yourself how you'd feel if your wife, daughter, or sister were witnessing your words and actions or were on the receiving end of such behavior."

Yet what this feminist manual is offering are basically rules for how any civilized, courteous group of people would interact. In other words, mind your manners! It is a sad commentary on social mores when we have to turn to a workplace manual to be told how proper people behave—once upon a time such behavior was learned at home.

As with so many other liberal causes—date rape, domestic abuse, child abuse—the expansion of the crime's definition serves only to obscure genuine instances of it. When we look back at cases such as *Barnes*, there is little doubt that spotlighting the role of women in the workplace, as the women's movement certainly did, has served to curtail such abuses of power. But teaching today's young women to find harassment and slights on every rung of the workplace ladder hurts everyone in the long run—most of all women.

The more inroads women make into the workplace the more they will have to deal with office curmudgeons and critics, louts and loudmouths, backstabbers, brutes, and, yes, boors—as working men have always had to do. Unpleasant personalities can never be legislated away. But when a woman is cast in with a colleague from the last of these categories, the best advice for handling him comes not from any high-priced sexual harassment expert but from the pages of literature. As Cervantes once said, "The woman who is resolved to be respected can make herself so even amidst an army of soldiers."

Frivolous Sexual Harassment Charges Impair Academic Freedom

by Clay Reynolds

About the author: *Clay Reynolds is a freelance writer who lives in Denton, Texas.*

Editor's Note: The author wishes the reader to note that most, if not all, of the cases mentioned in this article as "ongoing" in 1995 have since been resolved.

Scene: Administrative conference room at a major university. Five grim-faced faculty members sit around a long table and stare at The Accused, who sits at one end, apart and alone. He is well dressed, young middle-aged, nice looking but not particularly handsome. Each member of the Committee has in front of him or her a thick sheaf of papers, which they all consult from time to time. Just to the side, a woman sits apart from the committee. She is the Federal Affirmative Action Officer. At the head of the table, the Provost studies his papers briefly, then begins to speak. Provost (rises; to everyone): "This hearing is to inquire into allegations stemming from specific complaints against a faculty member of this university. Everyone is advised that the proceedings are to be conducted in a fair and professional manner." (He sits, opens a file folder, reads briefly, and then says to the Accused) "So, Professor Bookbinder, when, precisely, did you start harassing women?"

Not Isolated Accusations

As farcical as the above opening may appear, it is a drama that is being played out with increasing frequency across university and college campuses and even in some public school board rooms throughout the United States. For a while, such Star Chamber inquiries were held in secret (the preferred term is

Reprinted from Clay Reynolds, "Sexual Harassment and the Academy," *Chronicles: A Magazine of American Culture*, May 1995, by permission of the author.

"in confidence"), but now their results are appearing in daily newspapers and professional tabloids.

For a time, such inquiries concerned isolated accusations of impropriety on the part of a male faculty member or administrator by female students or workers. Now, however, they seem to be coming in bunches. At one university in Texas, for example, four faculty members, including a former department head, stand accused of displaying "gender bias," one of the several euphemisms being used by administrators to avoid the word "sex." At another school, two faculty members have been denied tenure, they assert, on the basis of the hint of complaints of sexual harassment circulated among administrators by "secret memo." At yet another school in the Southwest, the rumor is that as many as 16 faculty in the past three years have been forced to resign quietly or face charges of sexual harassment.

> *"No proof is required. No witnesses are required. No blatant physical or even verbal abuse needs to have occurred."*

One department head in Alabama confidentially asserts that nationwide as many as a thousand faculty members were forced to resign or were denied tenure in 1992 when even the threat of sexual harassment complaints arose. He himself claims that he left his previous position at a major state university because he was told he "had a year to find another job," or else he would also be targeted for similar complaints.

An attorney in Dallas, Texas, says that he has recently or is currently representing more than 30 professors, instructors, and secondary school teachers, all of whom have been accused of sexual harassment or sexually biased discrimination. His advice to all of them is "cut the best deal you can and resign," although most of them prefer to fight what they see as nothing more than legal blackmail.

To the general public and most academics, this seems to be proper. These men have, in the parlance of our time, "hit on" women who were subordinate to them. They either threatened them with punishment if the women were not compliant or made an outright offer of better grades or job advancement in exchange for sexual favors. Or, at least, they have been accused of having done one or all of these things. If they are guilty, they should be severely punished, for women should be able to work or study without the threat of randy wolves prowling the hallways in search of vulnerable sex partners. Almost no one in the academy believes otherwise. Sexual harassment is a despicable form of intimidation that should, when it occurs, be stopped swiftly.

Policies Are Dangerous

If that was what was going on in most of these cases, there would be no real problem. Women who have been victimized in this way could come forward, file their complaints, give proof of the damages done to them, and the guilty would be confronted, judged, and punished. Unfortunately, that is not happening in many—possibly more than many—instances. Instead, something far more dangerous is afoot.

In almost all the cases receiving media publicity—and many that are not—the women bringing the complaints are invoking a clause in their schools' sexual harassment policy that has to do with the work (or study) place. If, in a woman's opinion, a male superior's behavior creates a "threatening environment" or makes her uncomfortable in any way, then she is able—indeed she is encouraged—to come forward with a complaint.

No proof is required. No witnesses are required. No blatant physical or even verbal abuse needs to have occurred. Indeed, all a woman has to do is to assert that she has developed an *impression* that her superior has sexual designs on her or even that his presence makes her uncomfortable. She might even have encouraged him, might, indeed, have been the originator of a flirtation or a solicitor of his attention. That does not matter. All that matters is that she is not happy with those attentions—real or imagined—when they are directed toward her.

Certainly, there are serious complaints. Overt propositions, requests for sexual favors, repeated badgering for dates or assignations, inappropriate comments on a woman's sexuality all constitute clear violations of propriety if not a school's stated policy. But at least some charges are, in the main, frivolous. In one instance, a woman complained that a professor "wiggled his eyebrows" at her in a suggestive way; in another, a woman claimed that a professor held a door open for her and let her pass by him so he could sneak a peek down the arm-hole of her sweater; in another, a computer operator said her superior tended to pull his chair too close to hers when he needed to read what was on her screen.

> *"There is no statute of limitations on a careless comment or thoughtless gesture, an off-color joke, or the reading aloud of published material."*

Silly as these complaints may sound, they are taken very seriously by the Office of Equal Opportunity, and they are sufficient cause for university officials to launch a full and sometimes secret investigation of a professor's or administrator's background, to interview potential witnesses, indeed to ruin the career of any academic if he has ever, at any time, made any untoward gesture or comment toward a female at the school. Instances can range back for years; there is no statute of limitations on a careless comment or thoughtless gesture, an off-color joke, or the reading aloud of published material, even great literature containing potentially offensive language.

Frivolous Accusations

Here is a list of several cases:

• An adult, married female student writes in a diary erotic fantasies about one of her professors. She and her husband separate shortly afterwards. The husband finds the diary and threatens to bring charges and/or a lawsuit against the *professor*, who has no personal relationship with the woman at all, unless the university acts against him.

• A woman approaches a university attorney about a professor she says has "bothered" her. The attorney advises her to wear a "wire" or carry a tape recorder to gather evidence. She enters the professor's office and blatantly propositions him, even describes specific sexual acts she is willing to perform for him. He agrees and is lured into suggesting a time and place. He is later confronted with the tape, *minus* her proposition and suggestions, which have been erased, and invited to resign or face charges.

• An unmarried assistant professor invites a *former* and also unmarried student on a between-semesters date to a nearby town. On their return, he blatantly propositions her, but he does not connect the proposition to any school function or activity; nor does he attempt to coerce her on the grounds that he, as a member of the university faculty, might do her harm. She refuses, and he takes her home; she files a complaint against him. He is reprimanded by his department for sexual harassment, even though the incident occurred on personal time, away from campus, between semesters, and between adults. The following fall he is advised not to put himself forward for tenure but to "start looking for another job." He is terminated in the spring.

• A professor is asked for a ride home by a student he has known since childhood. On the way, she explains that her husband is gone and invites him, in what he infers is a suggestive tone, to come inside for a drink. He immediately pulls over into a convenience store parking lot, calls her a taxi from a pay telephone, and stands in clear view of the counter attendant until the cab arrives. She files charges against him the next morning for "humiliating and sexually harassing" her.

• A female student who has consistently bragged of her "former life" as a professional prostitute and of several present "lovers" approaches a professor from whom she has never had a class. She overtly propositions him; he accepts and follows her to her apartment. She files sexual harassment charges against him the next day. He is told to face charges, although his accuser is not named, or to resign.

> *"Very few universities provide counsel or legal representation to an accused faculty member."*

• A male instructor fails a male student who has, in front of witnesses, made a provocative homosexual suggestion to him in a restaurant away from campus. The instructor rejects the advance, and when the final grades are posted, the student files a sexual harassment complaint. The instructor is suspended for two semesters "pending an investigation."

Apart from these, there are dozens, maybe hundreds of cases, where complaints are based on far *less* obvious evidence. In some cases, students have stated merely that they "felt" a professor's "eyes on them" either during class or elsewhere.

One might argue—and most university officials do—that there is a system, a process in place for the investigation of all such complaints. It is generally established by faculty handbooks to deal with matters of professional misbehavior. But these systems were designed to handle cases where hard evidence could be produced, not situations where inference, innuendo, and even intuition and hearsay become admissible evidence. The basis of most complaints is subjective in the extreme, and since an alleged action or statement may have taken place in private, it comes down most often to the word of the accuser against the word of the accused.

> *"It is particularly likely that complaints will be forthcoming when the accused is unpopular, politically controversial, or professionally threatening to his colleagues."*

Most departmental or college committees are ill-equipped to function as judiciary bodies, are often ignorant of the "rules of evidence" such as might function in a legal court, rules that do not apply in university procedures anyway. They are rarely trained in psychoanalysis, a vital tool necessary to determine whether a complainant's "fearful feelings" are the result of genuine threats and insinuations. Hence, the procedures become little more than rubber stamps for administrators who want the "problem" dealt with rapidly and quietly. The most expedient method is to get rid of the accused faculty member. After all, professors can be replaced more readily than federal grants, and liability suits filed by dissatisfied complainants can be ruinously expensive. But the administrative bureaucrats go through the motions, anyway. And matters are usually handled "by the book," even though the accused usually finds himself completely alone and without reliable advice.

Very few universities provide counsel or legal representation to an accused faculty member. It is more efficient to proceed from the point where the prima facie evidence is offered. It is a reductive process: the faculty member is male and claims he is innocent; the accuser is female and claims he is guilty; therefore, he is guilty. His options, if his university is beneficent, are equally simple: he can fight it through a lengthy and confused university process, where the "fix" is usually in, or he can resign and hope to find another position elsewhere.

A "fair hearing," relying on "due process" as it is normally understood, usually does not happen any more often than the accused is found totally innocent. The institution acts as investigator, prosecutor, judge, and jury. The only role missing in what would ordinarily be seen as a judicial process is that of defense attorney. There, the "defendant" is on his own, faced with the enormously unjust proposition of proving himself innocent in the face of presumed guilt.

Chapter 1

Gathering the Evidence

In an effort to build a strong case, most university officials will interview virtually any woman who has had contact with the professor and inform her that it is not only her right but also her obligation to report any improper behavior on the part of a superior—any superior. Sometimes pressure is applied; in at least some cases, threats of recrimination have been implied unless "the truth" is forthcoming. In at least one case, a female graduate student was told that her "continued progress toward a degree" might well depend on her "veracity." (Ironically, she was cohabitating with the accused professor at the time, although university officials were unaware of this.)

When scrupulous inquisitors undertake their inquiries, they do not divulge the name of the accused, but only a complete idiot believes that the women being summoned for interview are in the dark about what is going on or who is on the hot seat. In one case, a departmental worker was on the phone soliciting witnesses against an accused professor even before he was aware that anyone had filed a complaint or before the investigation was officially underway. Her "enthusiasm" for gathering damning evidence soon reached the accused, which

"The student's record does not matter, nor do possible personal motives."

was the first he knew he was being investigated at all. Secrecy and confidentiality are rare commodities on any university campus, particularly when a sensational cause such as sexual harassment is involved.

Such investigations almost always turn up sufficient cause to proceed with a full inquiry. It is impossible for any faculty member to teach several thousand students over a period of years and not to offend somebody. It is particularly likely that complaints will be forthcoming when the accused is unpopular, politically controversial, or professionally threatening to his colleagues. It is not unheard of for a complainant to be amorously involved with a departmental rival of the accused, and it is not unusual for that rival to apply pressure on other women to come forward and file new and totally unexpected complaints along the way. They need not fear lying—perjury is not a crime within the university committee hearing—and they can change their stories at will if the accused proves elusive or too cunning in his responses.

Proof of Innocence Is Difficult

Generally, the accused is not informed of who is being solicited for testimony or what might have been said. On the contrary, he is often warned to stay away from any woman he even suspects might speak against him. In some cases, he may be covertly given tidbits of what is being said against him, all designed to frighten him into a preemptive resignation. In one case, a faculty member was told secretly that if he did not resign forthwith, the university administration would "close ranks" against him and feed him to the press. "They'll paint you black," he was told. "Quit and save your family the embarrassment."

One might assume that if a faculty member is completely innocent, he should be able to prove that easily enough and to go back to his position, his name cleared, his reputation intact. But proof of innocence, antithetical as it is to the entire system of jurisprudence, is even harder in cases where the charges are based on inference and subjective perception. As another attorney put it, "It's not like murder, where you have to have a witness or a corpse or at least a weapon. It's not like robbery, where you have something that was stolen. The accused doesn't just have to prove he didn't do it, but he has to prove that he never *thought* about doing it, that he never looked at the accusing individual and thought, 'Hey, she's pretty.' God help him if he ever said that to anyone, even to his closest friend."

In reality, no matter how ridiculous and unfounded complaints may eventually be proved to be or how completely an individual may be cleared of any charges or wrongdoing, the faculty member is tainted. His classes will not make, his committee assignments will be restricted, his ability to function as a counselor or colleague has been impaired, and he will have to work under a cloud of suspicion that he somehow "beat the rap."

A Presumption of Guilt

As some university officials have admitted (off the record, of course), in such matters as sexual harassment, established processes are totally inadequate. Like the Spanish Inquisition, they are designed to ferret out guilt and mete out punishment, not to seek truth. Once a departmental committee meets to hear a complaint, the word has probably already come down from the higher administration, and the verdict is *pro forma*. In a sense, whatever opportunities offered to the accused faculty member for defense are predicated on the fallacy of the complex question. There is no doubt that he must have done this—for he stands accused by *a student*. The student's record does not matter, nor do possible personal motives. The only meaningful question for the committee is what to do about "the problem in the department."

No appellate committee at the college, university, or system level is likely to overturn a departmental committee's ruling. After all, if the department head and attendant committees want the guy gone, if the higher administration wants him gone as well, why should they interfere? If they buck the system too hard, they might be targeted themselves. The only true recourse an innocent party has is to endure the drumhead justice of the university and to take them to a real court. But this is more difficult than it seems, and it is marvelously expensive, usually well beyond the reach of a typical faculty salary.

> *"One faculty member was looking at more than $25,000 by the end of his university committee hearings."*

The complexities are numerous. It can take anywhere from several months to a year or more before the university procedures are exhausted and the faculty member is terminated or forced to resign. His suit, then, cannot be filed on the basis of whether or not he was guilty of sexual harassment; rather, he must attack on the basis that he was wrongfully dismissed. This can take another year or more to get to court, and even if he wins, appeals and filed motions can delay a final decision for as long as half a decade. The school

> *"Every coed is a potential Mata Hari, every colleague a potential fink."*

does not mind waiting. It has bags of money to spend on defense and all the time in the world.

Another Dallas attorney points out that most schools would far rather risk a "wrongful dismissal" suit than "take a federal hit." The former could cost the school hundreds of thousands, but the latter could run into millions of dollars and create a "domino effect" that could continue for years. The faculty member, though, who is not teaching and is not drawing a salary because he has taken the matter into a public forum, probably is not employable. Further, about all he can hope to win from his suit is restitution of back pay and restoration to his former position, full in the knowledge that everyone on the campus knows he was guilty—after all, did the university not say so?—and that his colleagues and department head resent his presence. Only then can he sue for damages and attempt to prove his innocence.

The Cost of a Defense

In the meantime, legal bills mount up. One faculty member was looking at more than $25,000 by the end of his university committee hearings. Another $15,000 was required to file suit, and yet another $10,000 would be due when the case went to court. He might not recover these costs, even if he wins, not without filing a damages suit, which will require even more up-front money with even less likelihood of a return.

It is an incredible situation. In a way, it is as if a New Inquisition has risen, wherein only the suggestion of heresy is the occasion for a full *auto-da-fé,* wherein somebody has to be pilloried to maintain the stability of a corrupt system. Perhaps a more contemporary if not more fitting analogy would be found in the early 50s, when professors were called in and grilled about the political affiliations of their youth. Now, as then, comparatively sane, logical, and intellectual administrators find themselves fearfully responding to mass hysteria. America's universities saw the ruination of many careers and the almost complete destruction of academic freedom, all to protect schools from governmental or social reprisals if they stood their ground and exercised constitutionally mandated rights.

But this is no illustration of a philosophical question about due process and fundamental democratic rights or academic freedom. It is a dangerous mania that is sweeping through the nation's universities and creating a "climate of fear" that forces individuals to be so guarded in their associations, casual comments, and even formal lectures that they begin to suspect everyone around them of being spies, ready to do them in for the most innocent of remarks or gestures if they give offense on any grounds whatsoever. Every coed is a potential Mata Hari, every colleague a potential fink.

At this writing, cases are being prepared to fight against this unbridled abridgment of individual liberty and attack on academic freedom. But in the meantime, no one knows for sure how many hundreds—or even thousands—of highly qualified and capable faculty members have quietly resigned and faded off into the darkness to avoid public scandal and personal attacks by the very schools to which they had dedicated their careers. Victims of hysterical reactions or collegial jealousy or departmental politics, some of these people have given up 20 or 30 years of tenure because unlike even an accused thief or murderer, they were not permitted to face their accusers, were denied due process, and were forced to prove their innocence in the face of abstract and often totally subjective and unproven testimony.

Thus, the dramatic opening to this essay is not so incredible at all. It may well be a fairly accurate representation of a tragedy that is being played out on some university campus every week of every semester. One dean said that he was taking early retirement rather than face another case. He believed that universities in America were entering a "dark period," where their function, their value, indeed their very existence will be called into question by a society that already sees them as general wastes of time and money, filled with myopic, oversexed professors whose interests run far too much to the philosophical and away from the pragmatic, too much toward nubile young coeds and away from solid "family values."

The Cost to Women

The current situation involving sexual harassment cases seems to underscore the correctness of this bleak vision. But regardless of what status universities may enjoy in the future, the most tragic result of this drama may be its negative impact on women's advancement in the academy. The inevitable result of the probability of unfounded accusations resulting in the ruination of a career is that men will become suspicious of any female colleague who expresses friendliness or seeks close

> *"The most tragic result of this drama may be its negative impact on women's advancement in the academy."*

professional association. Male professors will eventually become fearful of so much as speaking to female students, let alone offering them counsel and advice on matters academic. If almost any comment or aside can be deliberately misconstrued as a *double entendre* and used as a basis for complaint, why risk speaking to any woman at all? Why not draw an invisible line between men and women in the academy and establish, if need be, a separate but equal policy that prevents all contact between the sexes?

For years, women have justifiably complained that the academy is a "man's bastion" and "old boy" network; if this trend toward unjust treatment for those merely accused of sexual harassment continues, if women can bring unfounded and unproved allegations without fear of reprisals if they are demonstrated to be false or brought only for personal gain, then the very forces that set out to protect women from unwanted sexual advances may be guilty of building higher and tighter walls between males and females in the university. Collegiality cannot possibly be achieved when one gender works and lives in fear of the other; the inevitable result will be an effective barrier to opportunities for female advancement.

On the other hand, women are not necessarily impervious to this "witch hunt" mentality. At least a handful of cases involve complaints by men against their female professors who "came on" to them. Likewise, there are currently cases involving homosexual and lesbian advances on students. We might recall that the Grand Inquisitor was wonderfully multicultural in his charges.

It may be time to stop and define precisely what is meant by sexual harassment, rather than leave it to abstract interpretation and subjective impression. There is no question that it exists, or that it is an evil in the work or study place. But while clear violations need to be reported and perpetrators punished, it should never have become a weapon to be used against those who are merely careless or unpopular or who have merely trod on the wrong toes in the course of building their careers. It may well be up to those who started the hysteria to stop it before a "backlash" occurs that defeats whatever purposes have been achieved by those who seek to protect women—and men—from unwanted sexual advances.

Overreaction to Sexual Harassment Violates Free Speech

by Michael P. McDonald

About the author: *Michael P. McDonald is cofounder and president of the Center for Individual Rights, a Washington, D.C., public interest law firm.*

My organization, the Center for Individual Rights (CIR), represents Professor Donald Silva in a free speech lawsuit against the University of New Hampshire. The case illuminates the current national debate over sexual harassment and what has come to be known as "sexual correctness."

A Career Terminated

Professor Silva is a pastor at the Newcastle Congregational Church in Newcastle, New Hampshire. Until April 1993, he was also a creative writing teacher at the University of New Hampshire. Then, the University effectively terminated his thirty-year career because he had allegedly created a "hostile academic environment"—in short, because of sexual harassment. The evidence consisted of two offhand remarks that Professor Silva had made in class: one comparing "focus" in the writing process to sexual relations; the other, explaining the meaning of simile by means of a belly dancer's analogy of her profession to "jello on a plate, with a vibrator under the plate."

Following these two remarks, which were made in open class, and which all parties agree were neither personally abusive, gender-demeaning, nor even sexually graphic, seven female students complained that Professor Silva's speech had offended and "sexually harassed" them. At the urging of various representatives associated with the University's Sexual Harassment and Rape Prevention Program (SHARPP), the students proceeded to file formal complaints in accordance with the University's sexual harassment policy. This policy defines sexual harassment as verbal conduct or speech "of a sexual nature that has the pur-

Adapted from "Unfree Speech," by Michael P. McDonald, the original version (including footnotes) of which appeared in the Spring 1995 issue of the *Harvard Journal of Law and Public Policy*. Reprinted with permission.

pose or effect of unreasonably interfering with an individual's work performance, or of creating an offensive working environment." In response to these
complaints, University administrators promptly suspended Professor Silva and
established parallel writing courses to offer offended female students the possibility of studying with a different professor. As the situation progressed, University officials informed the professor that he would have to undergo officially
approved psychological counseling, for a period of one year and at his own expense, before petitioning for reinstatement. In October 1993, with our help,
Professor Silva filed a federal lawsuit alleging, *inter alia,* violations of his constitutional rights to free speech and academic freedom.

Regulation of Verbal Conduct

There are several interesting aspects to Professor Silva's case. Here I would
note three brief points to provide a backdrop for the discussion, followed by one
dominant theme to consider. First, realize that the University of New Hampshire's sexual harassment policy is modeled directly on rules and guidelines pro-
mulgated by the Equal Employment Opportunity Commission (EEOC) during
the early 1980s, and is similar to those now in place at many other universities
and business workplaces. The policy regulates "verbal conduct"—a clumsy cir-
cumlocution for speech. As such, the policy constitutes a speech code, regardless
of whether anybody will admit it. That being so, you might think that university
administrators would have been concerned about running afoul of the First
Amendment before promulgating it. Not so. Because the policy is ostensibly
aimed at combatting sexual harassment and came with the blessing of the
EEOC, University of New Hampshire administrators viewed it as unproblematic.
Indeed, we were told that there was not the least murmur of dissent in administrative circles when the University adopted the policy in the late 1980s.

Second, we can all agree that civility is important for creating an atmosphere
in which education can flourish. As someone once said, the university is an island of retreat for the life of the mind. It is not *The Morton Downey Show* [tele-
vision talk show known for controversial guests and shocking subject matter].
For this reason, harassment has no
place at a university. But, as Professor Silva's case illustrates, this obser-
vation is totally beside the point. His
remarks, whatever one may think of
their appropriateness, were perfectly
civil. He did not subject any students
to personal abuse. Nor did he make

> *"The purpose of these policies is not increased civility on campus but coerced sensitivity towards a constituency of pre-approved victims."*

anyone the subject of a personal attack. If anything, Professor Silva was made
the victim of a personal attack by being hounded, disciplined, and stripped of
tenure for nothing more than the fact that students disliked what he had said in
open class.

The obvious fact is that harassment policies, such as the University of New Hampshire's, are being applied not to encourage rational and civil argument on campus, but to seek a conformity of expression to the prevailing pieties of the day. The purpose of these policies is not increased civility on campus but coerced sensitivity towards a constituency of pre-approved victims—in this instance, women. That is why, for example, you rarely see the more extreme feminist instructors becoming entangled in the sexual harassment machinery for teaching, say,

> *"The zeal to extirpate hostile environment harassment from campus life . . . leads directly to the suppression of speech."*

that all consensual heterosexual sexual relations constitute rape. Or why you are not likely to see gay literary theorists running afoul of the speech codes for prattling on in graphic detail about the hidden sexual imagery in Melville's or Whitman's writings. Many reasonable students will find such teachings offensive and complain. Yet nothing happens to these professors.

Recently, at the University of Maryland, a number of feminist students, at the urging of a professor, randomly culled the names of male students from the student directory and affixed them to boards around campus under the headline: "Be careful! These men are potential rapists." The women selected the identified students solely because they were men to make the point that all men are potential rapists. In this case, University administrators did apologize; however, no action was taken against the feminist students for having created an "offensive environment" for the male students who were defamed as potential rapists. In fact, it was reported that the women received credit for their "project" as part of a course entitled "Issues in Feminist Art." Again, we see the policies being applied in a one-way direction.

Not an Isolated Case

Third, and most obviously, Professor Silva's case demonstrates how the zeal to extirpate hostile environment harassment from campus life—and I think we will see similar cases in the workplace soon—leads directly to the suppression of speech. One might argue that the University of New Hampshire's treatment of Professor Silva is a rare exception. But it is not. My organization is relatively small and not terribly well known, and yet it receives quite a few calls for help.

For example, in the CIR's first quarter of 1994 Docket Report, there is a description of another case, which we have called "Son of Silva." In this case, we are representing another tenured professor in Minnesota, Richard Osborne, who was accused of sexual harassment for opposing curriculum changes at his college. The harassment charges were based upon the fact that the course changes had been proposed by women, and that our client "had never been observed opposing similar curriculum changes put forth by men."

The charge in *Osborne v. Braxton-Brown et al., 1994* is, of course, ludicrous.

However, as in the original *Silva* case, the proper focus is not what Professor Osborne said, but rather what other professors and students on college campuses around the country will refrain from saying as a result of his being charged with "sexual harassment." The current legal rules, which define a hostile environment on the basis of a case-by-case, multi-factor analysis, are exceedingly vague. As a number of legal commentators have noted, general speech codes are remarkably similar to the Communist disclaimer affidavits required of university faculty in the 1950s. By their very nature, they deter not only genuine harassment but also harmless and desirable speech. Faced with legal uncertainty, and seeing how the Silvas and Osbornes of the world are punished, individuals will strive to avoid any speech that might be interpreted as creating a hostile environment for anyone in the class.

Moreover, it is inadequate to say that the innocent victims of the anti-harassment campaign can eventually obtain judicial relief. Mere complaints of misconduct, and their adjudication by university committees that operate with less than mathematical precision, ensure that some people are going to be found guilty even though what they said was perfectly innocent. To be sure, there is always an intricate machinery provided for the processing of sexual harassment complaints before you are allowed to go to court. But who would want to become enmeshed in such a process? The internal process established at universities to address sexual harassment issues is administered by people with a vested interest in sexual harassment programs—the equity officers who populate so many offices on college campuses and universities. And the machinery they have created itself is part of the *in terrorem* process. Witness the fact that the University of New Hampshire had Professor Silva sit through one sexual harassment hearing that lasted more than twelve hours.

Finding Help in the First Amendment

The larger theme of First Amendment concerns has played only a marginal role in sexual harassment litigation. However, this is rapidly changing. Indeed, I have high hopes that our litigation on Professor Silva's behalf will help spearhead that change. One important question concerns what the Supreme Court will do when it finally has to confront the issues of free speech and verbal sexual harassment that it avoided in cases such as *Harris v. Forklift Systems, Inc.*, 1993.

> *"For decades, civil rights and freedom of speech were thought to coexist in perfect harmony."*

For decades, civil rights and freedom of speech were thought to coexist in perfect harmony. The Supreme Court viewed a near-absolutist approach to the First Amendment as being fully consistent with an expansive civil rights jurisprudence. Its First Amendment cases, particularly those in the 1960s, reflect an abiding faith in the congruence between interests in social equality and freedom of speech. Anthony Lewis' book, *Make No Law*, for example, paints a very compelling portrait of how these two values intersect and how the justices viewed First Amendment freedoms and expansive protections for civil rights as going hand-in-hand.

But this confidence in the harmony of civil libertarian and egalitarian aspirations is fast becoming a thing of the past. Many legal scholars now argue that speech can be an instrument of oppression, and that the members of powerless and oppressed minorities should receive special protection from hateful and offensive speech. This egalitarian view of the First Amendment, once viewed as "far-out," has begun to make its mark on the law.

A History of Protected Speech

One would have thought that a general governmental prohibition of speech deemed to create an offensive environment could not possibly withstand review under any rational interpretation of modern First Amendment jurisprudence. Consider *Cohen v. California,* in which Justice John Marshall Harlan said that so long as the means of expressing one's views are peaceful, the communication in question need not meet standards of acceptability. Consider *Gertz v. Robert Welch, Inc.,* where Justice Lewis F. Powell said that no matter how offensive we find an idea, under the First Amendment, there is no such thing as a false idea. Finally, consider Justice William J. Brennan's opinion for the Court in the flag-burning case, *Texas v. Johnson,* an opinion that again condemned the idea that the State had any right to punish people for offensive utterances or symbolic speech. However, the EEOC's sexual harassment guidelines, which prohibit speech that creates an offensive environment, have seemingly been approved by the Supreme Court. How can this be? Sad to say, recently the Court has become more willing to write what one may call a civil rights exception into its First Amendment jurisprudence; that is, the Supreme Court will vigorously protect free speech and ensure the government's neutrality, except in the context of civil rights.

> *"Speech uttered that is not directed toward specific individuals should never be regulated as harassment."*

Thus, in a 1993 case, *Wisconsin v. Mitchell,* the Court unanimously upheld a Wisconsin statute that enhanced criminal penalties for a defendant who intentionally selected his victim because of his victim's race. In that case, there was no question that the state legislature had passed the penalty enhancement law in order to punish offensive beliefs; however, because the law was couched as a "civil rights" measure, it escaped searching First Amendment scrutiny by the Court.

The Supreme Court would do well to revisit this issue. A reasonable set of rules would afford comprehensive First Amendment protection for all academic speech. Speech uttered that is not directed toward specific individuals should never be regulated as harassment. And even speech targeted at particular individuals should be punished only when it results in recognizable emotional distress to the victim. It might also be useful to impose some penalty for individuals who knowingly bring false and frivolous charges of sexual harassment. If this regime were adopted, it would have the great advantage of curbing genuine harassment of the extortionate, quid pro quo kind, without intruding into the field of free speech and academic freedom.

Chapter 2

What Causes Sexual Harassment?

Chapter Preface

In the years between 1985 and 1990, the number of sexual harassment complaints filed with the Equal Employment Opportunity Commission (EEOC) went from 4,953 to 5,557. Since 1989, the number of sexual harassment charges has increased 112 percent. According to the Center for Women in Government, in 1993, 1,546 victims of sexual harassment won $25.2 million in benefits from their employers, including back pay, remedial relief, damages, promotions, and reinstatements. In response to this trend, organizations have sought the guidance of experts to help them deal with complaints before they are filed. Although the body of research on sexual harassment has grown, researchers, legal experts, and policymakers continue to disagree on what causes sexual harassment. Many authorities argue that sexual harassment is a result of differences between men and women—some claim these difference are socially learned while others believe sexual harassment is a natural phenomenon. Others propose that sexual harassment is a result of unequal power relationships not gender differences, arguing that sexual harassment is merely a form of discrimination.

Some researchers believe that society has established specific roles for men and women that are the source of sexual harassment. Men who harass women, they suggest, are simply conforming to the traditional male roles of aggression, power, and dominance while women are socialized at a very young age to believe their self-concept is dependent upon establishing and maintaining relationships. Counselors Kathy Hotelling and Barbara A. Zuber write, "Sexual harassment is not a peculiarity of human behavior, but rather a cultural pattern that establishes male-female interactions: an extension of 'normal behavior' that is taught and expected from a very early age." Other authorities argue that sexual harassment did not become a problem until women entered the workforce. These theorists believe that sexual harassment is a result of male resistance to the entry of women into a domain traditionally controlled by men. Men harass women, they argue, in order to maintain control over the workforce. According to law professor Vicki Schultz, "The fact is, most harassment isn't about satisfying sexual desires. It's about protecting work—especially the most favored lines of work—as preserves of male competence and authority." Furthermore, some policymakers suggest that tolerance of sexual harassment further reinforces the lack of acceptance of women into male-dominated fields.

Many authorities believe that identifying the cause of sexual harassment is the key to preventing it. The viewpoints in the following chapter discuss many possible causes of sexual harassment.

Male Domination of the Workplace Causes Sexual Harassment

by Vicki Schultz

About the author: *Vicki Schultz is a professor at Yale Law School who specializes in employment discrimination law, civil procedure, feminism and law, and gender and work.*

The Clarence Thomas hearings, the Tailhook incident, the Gene McKinney trial, the Clinton scandals—if these events spring to mind when you hear the words "sexual harassment," you are not alone. That such images of powerful men making sexual come-ons toward female subordinates should be the defining ones simply proves the power of the popular perception that harassment is first and foremost about sex. It's easy to see why: The media, the courts and some feminists have emphasized this to the exclusion of all else. But the real issue isn't sex, it's sexism on the job. The fact is, most harassment isn't about satisfying sexual desires. It's about protecting work—especially the most favored lines of work—as preserves of male competence and authority.

Locating the Problem

In the spring of 1998 the Supreme Court heard three cases involving sex harassment in the workplace. Along with media coverage of current events, the Court's decisions will shape our understanding of this issue into the next century, for all these controversies raise the same fundamental question: Does sex harassment require a special body of law having to do with sexual relations, or should it be treated just like any other form of workplace discrimination?

[Editor's note: In June 1998, in *Gebser v. Lago Vista Independent School District*, the Supreme Court held that federally funded schools and universities are not liable for a teacher's sexual harassment of a student unless officials actually know about the conduct and refuse to intervene. Also in June 1998, in *Burling-*

Reprinted from Vicki Schultz, "Sex Is the Least of It," *The Nation*, May 25, 1998, by permission of *The Nation* magazine.

ton Industries v. Ellerth and *Faragher v. City of Boca Raton*, the Supreme Court held that employers should be vicariously liable for the "hostile environments" created by their supervisors. However, employers can defend themselves by showing that they exercised reasonable care to promptly prevent or correct any sexually harassing behavior and by showing that the offended employee unreasonably failed to take advantage of any preventative or corrective opportunities provided by the employer.]

If the Court decides that harassment is primarily a problem of sexual relations, it will be following the same misguided path some courts have taken since they first accepted that such behavior falls under the prohibitions of Title VII of the Civil Rights Act, the major federal statute forbidding sex discrimination in employment. Early decisions outlawed what is known as quid pro quo harassment—typically, a situation where a supervisor penalizes a subordinate who refuses to grant sexual favors. It was crucial for the courts to acknowledge that sexual advances and other interactions *can* be used in the service of discrimination. Yet their reasoning spelled trouble. The courts said harassment was sex bias because the advances were rooted in a sexual attraction that the harasser felt for a woman but would not have felt for another man. By locating the problem in the sexual character of the advances rather than in the workplace dynamics of which they were a part—for instance, the paternalistic prerogative of a male boss to punish an employee on the job for daring to step out of her "place" as a woman—the decisions threatened to equate sex harassment with sexual pursuits. From there it was a short step to the proposition that sex in the workplace, or at least sexual interactions between men and women in unequal jobs, is inherently suspect.

> *"By driving women away or branding them inferior, men can insure the sex segregation of the work force."*

Harassment Is Not Always Sexual

Yet the problem we should be addressing isn't sex, it's the sexist failure to take women seriously as workers. Sex harassment is a means for men to claim work as masculine turf. By driving women away or branding them inferior, men can insure the sex segregation of the work force. We know that women who work in jobs traditionally held by men are more likely than other women to experience hostility and harassment at work. Much of the harassment they experience isn't "sexual" in content or design. Even where sexually explicit harassment occurs, it is typically part of a broader pattern of conduct intended to reinforce gender difference and to claim work as a domain of masculine mastery. As one experienced electrician put it in Molly Martin's *Hard-Hatted Women*, "[We] . . . face another pervasive and sinister kind of harassment which is gender-based, but may have nothing to do with sex. It is harassment aimed at us simply because we are women in a 'man's' job, and its function is to discourage us from staying in our trades."

This harassment can take a variety of forms, most of which involve undermining a woman on the job. In one case, male electricians stopped working rather than submit to the authority of a female subforeman. In another, Philadelphia policemen welcomed their new female colleagues by stealing their case files and lacing their uniforms with lime that burned their skin. Even more commonly, men withhold the training and assignments women need to learn to do the job well, or relegate them to menial duties that signal they are incompetent to perform the simplest tasks. Work sabotage is all too common.

> *"Sexual overtures may intimidate a woman or label her incompetent in settings where female sexuality is considered incompatible with professionalism."*

Nor is this a purely blue-collar phenomenon. About one-third of female physicians recently surveyed said they had experienced sexual harassment, but almost half said they'd been subjected to harassment that had no sexual or physical component but was related simply to their being female in a traditionally male field. In one 1988 court case, a group of male surgical residents went so far as to falsify a patient's medical records to make it appear as though their female colleague had made an error.

Men do, of course, resort to sexualized forms of harassment. Sexual overtures may intimidate a woman or label her incompetent in settings where female sexuality is considered incompatible with professionalism. In one 1993 Supreme Court case, a company president suggested that a female manager must have had sex with a client to land an important account. Whether or not the harassment assumes a sexual form, however, what unites all these actions is that they create occupational environments that define womanhood as the opposite of what it takes to be a good worker.

The Popular View Maintains Gender Discrimination

From this starting point, it becomes clear that the popular view of harassment is both too narrow and too broad. Too narrow, because the focus on rooting out unwanted sexual activity has allowed us to feel good about protecting women from sexual abuse while leading us to overlook equally pernicious forms of gender-based mistreatment. Too broad, because the emphasis on sexual conduct has encouraged some companies to ban all forms of sexual interaction, even when these do not threaten women's equality on the job.

How has the law become too narrow? The picture of harassment-as-sex that developed out of the quid pro quo cases has overwhelmed the conception of the hostile work environment, leading most courts to exonerate seriously sexist misconduct if it does not resemble a sexual come-on. In *Turley v. Union Car-*

bide Corp., a court dismissed the harassment claim of a woman whose foreman "pick[ed] on [her] all the time" and treated her worse than the men. Citing Catharine MacKinnon's definition of sexual harassment as "the unwanted imposition of sexual requirements in the context of a relationship of unequal power," the court concluded that the case did not involve actionable harassment because "the foreman did not demand sexual relations, he did not touch her or make sexual jokes."

By the same reasoning, in *Reynolds v. Atlantic City Convention Center*, the court ruled against a female electrical subforeman, Reynolds, whose men refused to work for her, made obscene gestures and stood around laughing while she unloaded heavy boxes. Not long before, the union's business agent had proclaimed, "[Now] is not the time, the place or the year, [nor] will it ever be the year for a woman foreman." When the Miss America pageant came to town, an exhibitor asked that Reynolds be removed from the floor—apparently, the incongruity between the beauty contestants and the tradeswoman was too much to take—and Reynolds's boss replaced and eventually fired her. Yet the court concluded that none of this amounted to a hostile work environment: The obscene gestures that the court considered "sexual" were too trivial, and the rest of the conduct wasn't sufficiently sexual to characterize as gender-based.

These are not isolated occurrences. I recently surveyed hundreds of Title VII hostile work environment cases and found that the courts' disregard of nonsexual forms of harassment is an overwhelming trend. This definitely works against women in male-dominated job settings, but it has also hurt women in traditionally female jobs, who share the experience of harassment that denigrates their competence or intelligence as workers. They are often subjected to sexist forms of authority, humiliation and abuse—objectified not only as sexual commodities but as creatures too stupid or worthless to deserve respect, fit only to be controlled by others ("stupid women who have kids," "too fat to clean rooms," "dumb females who [can't] read or write").

> *"Some men have taunted and tormented, battered and beaten other men in the name of purging the brotherhood of wimps and fags–not suitable to stand alongside them as workers."*

Gender-Based Harassment Hurts Men Too

Just as our obsession with sexual misconduct obscures many debilitating forms of harassment facing women, it also leads us to overlook some pernicious harassment confronting men on the job. If the legal cases provide any indication, the most common form of harassment men experience is not, as the film *Disclosure* suggests, a proposition from a female boss. It is, instead, hostility from male co-workers seeking to denigrate or drive away men who threaten the work's masculine image. If a job is to confer manliness, it must be held by those who project the desired sense of manhood. It isn't only women who can detract from that image. In some work settings, men are threatened by the presence of any man perceived to be gay—for homosexuality is often seen as gender deviance—or any other man perceived to lack the manly competence considered suitable for those who hold the job. The case logs are filled with harassment against men who are not married, men who are not attractive to women, men who are seen as weak or slow, men who are openly supportive of women, men who wear earrings and even young men or boys. Some men have taunted and tormented, battered and beaten other men in the name of purging the brotherhood of wimps and fags—not suitable to stand alongside them as workers.

We have been slow to name this problem sex-based harassment because it doesn't fit our top-down, male-female, sexual come-on image of harassment. In *Goluszek v. Smith*, the court ruled against an electronic maintenance mechanic who was disparaged and driven out by his fellow workers. They mocked him for not having a wife, saying a man had to be married to be a machinist. They used gender-based images to assault his competence, saying that if he couldn't fix a machine they'd send in his "daddy"—the supervisor—to do it. They drove jeeps at him and threatened to knock him off his ladder, and when he filed a grievance, his supervisor wrote him up for carelessness and eventually fired him. Not only did the court dismiss Goluszek's claim, the judge simply couldn't conceive that what happened to him was sexual harassment. "The 'sexual harassment' that is actionable under Title VII 'is the exploitation of a powerful position to impose sexual demands or pressures on an unwilling but less powerful person,'" the judge wrote. Perhaps lower courts will adopt a broader view now that the Supreme Court has ruled, in the recent *Oncale v. Sundowner Offshore Services* decision, that male-on-male harassment may be actionable even when it is not sexual in design.

Meanwhile, the traditional overemphasis on sex can lead to a repressive impulse to eliminate all hints of sexual expression from the workplace, however benign. Instead of envisioning harassment law as a tool to promote women's equality as workers, the popular understanding of harassment encourages courts and companies to "protect" women's sexual sensibilities. In *Fair v. Guiding Eyes for the Blind*, a heterosexual woman who was the associate director of a nonprofit organization claimed her gay male supervisor had created an offensive environment by making gossipy conversation and political remarks involving homosexuality. It is disturbing that current law inspired such a claim, even though the court correctly ruled that the supervisor's conduct was not sexual harassment.

> *"The popular understanding of harassment encourages courts and companies to 'protect' women's sexual sensibilities."*

Other men haven't fared so well. In *Pierce v. Commonwealth Life Insurance Co.*, a manager was disciplined for participating in an exchange of sexually explicit cards with a female office administrator. One of the cards Pierce had sent read, "Sex is a misdemeanor. De more I miss, de meanor I get." After thirty years with the company, he was summarily demoted and transferred to another office, with his pay slashed and his personal belongings dumped at a roadside Hardee's. True, Pierce was a manager and he was responsible for enforcing the company's harassment policy. Still, the reasoning that led to his ouster is unsound—and dangerous. According to his superiors, he might as well have been a "murderer, rapist or child molester; that wouldn't be any worse [than what he had done]." This sort of thing gives feminism a bad name. If companies want to fire men like Pierce, let them do it without the pretense of protecting women from sexual abuse.

> *"Title VII was never meant to police sexuality. It was meant to provide people the chance to pursue their life's work on equal terms."*

Policing Sexuality Is Not the Answer

Equally alarming are reports that, in the name of preventing sexual harassment, some companies are adopting policies that prohibit a man and woman from traveling or staying at the same hotel together on business, or prevent a male supervisor from giving a performance evaluation to a female underling behind closed doors without a lawyer present. One firm has declared that its construction workers can't even look at a woman for more than five seconds. With such work rules, who will want to hire women? How will women obtain the training they need if their male bosses and colleagues can't interact with them as equals?

It's a mistake to try to outlaw sexual interaction in the workplace. The old Taylorist project of purging organizations of all sexual and other emotional dynamics was deeply flawed. Sexuality is part of the human experience, and so long as organizations still employ people rather than robots, it will continue to flourish in one form or another. And sexuality is not simply a tool of gender domination; it is also a potential source of empowerment and even pleasure for women on the job. Indeed, some research suggests that where men and women work as equals in integrated settings, sex harassment isn't a problem. Sexual talk and joking continues, but it isn't experienced as harassment. It's not impossible to imagine sexual banter as a form of playfulness, even solidarity, in a work world that is increasingly competitive and stressful.

Once we realize that the problem isn't sex but sexism, we can re-establish our concept of harassment on firmer ground. Title VII was never meant to police sexuality. It was meant to provide people the chance to pursue their life's work on equal terms—free of pressure to conform to prescribed notions of how women and men are supposed to behave in their work roles. Properly conceived, quid pro quo harassment is a form of discrimination because it involves men exercising the power to punish women, as workers, who have the temerity to say no, as women. Firing women who won't have sex on the job is no different from firing black women who refuse to perform cleaning work, or female technicians who refuse to do clerical work, that isn't part of their job descriptions.

So, too, hostile-work-environment harassment isn't about sexual relations; it's about how work relations engender inequality. The legal concept was created in the context of early race discrimination cases, when judges recognized that Jim Crow systems could be kept alive not just through company acts (such as hiring and firing) but also through company atmospheres that made African-American workers feel different and inferior. That discriminatory environments are sometimes created by "sexual" conduct is not the point. Sex should be treated just like anything else in the workplace: Where it furthers sex discrimination, it should go. Where it doesn't, it's not the business of our civil rights laws.

It's too easy to allow corporate America to get away with banning sexual interaction without forcing it to attend to the larger structures of workplace gender discrimination in which both sexual and not-so-sexual forms of harassment flourish. Let's revitalize our understanding of harassment to demand a world in which all women and even the least powerful men can work together as equals in whatever endeavors their hearts and minds desire.

Social and Biological Sex Differences Can Cause the Perception of Sexual Harassment

by Joseph S. Fulda

About the author: *Joseph S. Fulda is the author of* Eight Steps Towards Libertarianism, *a contributing editor of the* Freeman, *and associate editor of* Sexuality and Culture: An Interdisciplinary Annual.

Working out the complexities of sexual harassment is an intellectually open task, requiring an interdisciplinary approach. I offer no such grand scheme here, however; only some humble questions. But if the questions are put crisply enough and asked persistently enough, perhaps some future wise man will come forward with new inspiration.

Sexual harassment may be understood as unwanted emotional and physical attention of the type designed to lead to unwanted intimacy. While each part of this definition requires elaboration, it is the key word "unwanted" that causes the most difficulty.

Women are so often characterized as coy and men as compulsive in literature that it is hardly surprising that everyday dating experience sometimes leaves men confused and women annoyed.

Accepting Human Nature

She says "yes," then "no," then "yes" again, while he, of course, says "yes, yes, yes." To criticize the female psyche as coy, insecure, and frustrating or the male psyche as hurried, obsessive, and frustrated, however, is to miss the point. Definitions of right and wrong must accommodate human nature, not deny it. If the behavior is well within the range of normal human response and, here, normal courtship behavior, to condemn it is not only futile but morally wrong.

Reprinted from Joseph S. Fulda, "The Complexities of Sexual Harassment: A Sociobiological Perspective," *Lincoln Review*, vol. 11, no. 3 (Winter/Spring 1993), pp. 13–17, by permission of the author. *Endnotes and bibliography in the original have been omitted in this reprint.*

The problem arises, of course, because relationships involve both men and women for whom physical and emotional intimacy often have different meanings, because male and female nature are fundamentally different, particularly in the area surrounding sex, love, and intimacy. This has been documented in scientific studies—especially in the fascinating field of sociobiology—and literary accounts alike.

Now the questions:

It is natural for the male to make an emotional or physical advance, for it to be mildly resisted, repeated, mildly resisted, and repeated again, this time accepted by the female. This is true throughout the animal

> *"If the behavior is well within the range of normal human response ... to condemn it is not only futile but morally wrong."*

kingdom. Perhaps the female resists to excite the male further, perhaps to excite herself further, perhaps to be sure that the male is truly interested —or perhaps because the advance is unwanted and a mild rejection is all the female can muster. It may be accepted because desired—or because the female sees its rejection as hopeless and herself as helpless.

How is a male to discern the motivation between identical behaviors? Between resistance intended to be overcome and rejection intended to be decisive. When does repetition of an advance that is being resisted become coercive, rather than playful?

It is also natural, though perhaps less common, for the female to accept an advance and then decide that it's too intense. At what point are the male's continued advances not properly judged as coercive, because no longer clearly volitional on his part?

How long do we allow the female to change her mind? Thereafter, isn't insisting on disengagement once again a criticism of, rather than an accommodation of, human nature?

Women Seek Mates with Higher Status

Women are often hypergamous, as are the females of many species, i.e. they seek mates with higher status than themselves. This can be explained by Genesis 3:16 and evolutionary theory alike. Regardless, to criticize this trait is to complain about, rather than adjust to, human nature.

Thus when thrust into a college or work environment, relationships between professors and their graduate students or managers and their employees are to be expected. Now at what point does the male drive to use his temporal status to impress the female and thus to receive emotional and physical rewards from her displace the female urge towards hypergamousness? At what point—even if no professional action has been taken for personal reasons—is the relationship tainted by an air of intimidation—subliminal, subtle, psychological coercion—merely because of the male's higher position in the power structure?

If so, is this any more unfair—in so far as the concept of fairness is coherent in a discussion of nature—than the female's initial selection of the male for that very reason?

These are all very difficult questions, questions for a future Solomon to answer. Perhaps these difficulties arise, in part, because the traditional sources of wisdom provide us with no inspiration here. In Biblical times, male-female unions were marital, quasi-marital, or chaste and the conceptual categories were clear, crisp, and distinct. Thus, we cannot look to the Bible for an understanding of relationships involving varying degrees of emotional and physical intimacy. Nor can we turn to Greco-Roman literature or the writings of the Renaissance.

"Relationships" are products of modernity, mostly unknown in earlier times or, if not unknown, a quiet deviation from the norm. As a result, any inspiration to be had must be found within ourselves. Thus far, this is a challenge that remains open. In the meantime, males and females will continue to answer these questions in accordance with their respective natures, leading to unfortunate misunderstandings.

Nevertheless, and although I have already conceded that I am far from knowing how to answer these questions in such a way as to avoid all the pain and frustration that such misunderstandings cause, I do know that the feminists are at war with human nature—male and female—when they insist that every "no" is "NO!", every turning away an indication of displeasure, every playful push a decisive rejection, and every failure by males to heed these rules acts of sexual harassment rising in some cases to the level of date rape. Life and human sexuality are far more complex and ambiguous—in a word, nuanced—than the clarity and certainty of feminist ideological doctrine.

The Masculine Gender Role Causes Sexual Harassment

by Anne Levy and Michele Paludi

About the authors: *Anne Levy is an associate professor of law, public policy, and business at Michigan State University. Michele Paludi is an expert in academic and workplace sexual harassment, editor of* Ivory Power: Sexual Harassment on Campus, *and coauthor of* Workplace Sexual Harassment, *from which the following viewpoint is taken.*

In some new theorizing about why men sexually harass women, Michele Paludi has focused not on men's attitudes toward women but instead on men's attitudes toward other men, competition, and power. Many of the men with whom Paludi has discussed sexual harassment often act out of extreme competitiveness and concern with ego, or out of fear of losing their positions of power. They don't want to appear weak or less masculine in the eyes of other men, so they will engage in rating women's bodies, pinching women, making implied or overt threats, or spying on women. Women are the game to impress other men. When men are being encouraged to be obsessively competitive and concerned with dominance, it is likely that they will eventually use violent means to achieve dominance. Men are also likely to be abusive verbally and intimidating in their body language. Deindividuation is quite common among male office workers who, during their lunch break, rate women co-workers numerically as they walk by in the cafeteria. These men discontinue self-evaluation and adopt group norms and attitudes. Under these circumstances, group members behave more aggressively than they would as individuals.

Aggression and Sexual Harassment

The element of aggression that is so deeply embedded in the masculine gender role is present in sexual harassment. For many men, aggression is one of the major ways of proving their masculinity, especially among those men who feel some sense of powerlessness in their lives. The theme of male-as-dominant or male-as-aggressor is so central to many men's self-concept that it literally carries over into their interpersonal communications, especially with women co-workers. Sexualizing a professional relationship may be the one way that such a man can still prove his masculinity when he can find few other ways to prove himself in control, or to be the dominant person in a relationship. Thus, sexual harassment is not so much a deviant act as an overconforming act of the masculine gender role in this culture.

> *"Sexual harassment is not so much a deviant act as an overconforming act of the masculine gender role in this culture."*

Harassers are found in all types of occupations, at all organizational levels, among business and professional individuals, as well as among college professors. It may be difficult for us to confront the reality that sexual harassment is perpetrated by individuals who are familiar to us and who have family lives similar to our own. Men who sexually harass have not been distinguishable from their colleagues who don't harass with respect to age, marital status, faculty rank, occupation, or academic discipline. Men who harass have a tendency to do this repeatedly to many women, and men who harass hold attitudes toward women that are traditional, not egalitarian.

For example, John Pryor noted that sexual harassment bears a conceptual similarity to rape. He developed a series of hypothetical scenarios that provided opportunities for sexual harassment if the man so chose. Men participating in this study were instructed to imagine themselves in the roles of the men in the scenarios and to consider what they would do in each situation. They were further instructed to imagine that, whatever their chosen course of action, no negative consequences would result from their choices. Men's scores on the survey, measuring their likelihood to engage in sexual harassment, were related to gender-role stereotyping and negatively related to feminist attitudes and that component of empathy having to do with the ability to take the standpoint of the other.

Characteristics of Men Who Harass

Thus, this research suggests that the man who is likely to initiate severe sexually harassing behavior appears to be one who emphasizes male social and sexual dominance, and who demonstrates insensitivity to other individuals' perspectives. Furthermore, men are less likely than women to define sexual harassment as including jokes, teasing remarks of a sexual nature, and unwanted suggestive looks or gestures. Men are also significantly more likely than women to agree with the following statements, taken from Paludi's "attitudes toward victim blame and victim responsibility" survey:

Women often claim sexual harassment to protect their reputations.

Many women claim sexual harassment if they have consented to sexual relations but have changed their minds afterwards.

Sexually experienced women are not really damaged by sexual harassment.

It would do some women good to be sexually harassed.

Women put themselves in situations in which they are likely to be sexually harassed because they have an unconscious wish to be harassed.

In most cases when a woman is sexually harassed, she deserved it.

We need to think of sexual harassment as being not the act of a disturbed man, but rather an act of an overconforming man. In other words, sexual harassment, similar to rape, incest, and battering, may be understood as an extreme acting out of qualities that are regarded as supermasculine in this culture: aggression, power, dominance, and force. Thus, men who harass are not pathological but rather exhibit behaviors characteristic of the masculine gender role in American culture.

Can and Do Women Harass Men?

We can summarize the research in this area as follows:

1. Women are highly unlikely to date or initiate sexual relationships with their co-workers or supervisors.

2. A small number of men in the workplace believe they have been sexually harassed by women. The behaviors many of these men label as sexual harassment, however, do not fit the legal definition of either *quid pro quo* or hostile environment sexual harassment.

3. Men are more likely than women to interpret a particular behavior as sexual. For example, in research by Barbara Gutek, men were likely to label a business lunch as a "date" if it is with a woman manager.

4. The great majority of men report that they are flattered by women's advances, whereas women report feeling annoyed, insulted, and threatened.

5. It is rare for a woman to hold the organizational and sociocultural power that would allow her to reward a man for sexual cooperation or punish him for withholding it, even if gender-role prescriptions did not ensure that she was extremely unlikely to demand sexual favors in the first place.

> *"Sexual harassment . . . may be understood as an extreme acting out of qualities that are regarded as supermasculine in this culture: aggression, power, dominance, and force."*

Thus, although it is theoretically possible for women to harass men, in practice it is a rare event. This is due to both the women's relative lack of formal power and the socialization that stigmatizes the sexually assertive woman. Many of men's experiences with sexual harassment are with other men. Consequently, men may be reluctant to disclose this information due to homophobic concerns.

Chapter 2

Sexual Harassment Theories

Sandra Tangri and her colleagues have labeled three theoretical models that incorporate this gender/power/aggression analysis. The *natural/biological model* interprets sexual harassment as a consequence of sexual interactions between people, either attributing a stronger sex drive to men than to women (i.e., men "need" to engage in aggressive sexual behavior) or describing sexual harassment as part of the "game" between sexual equals. This model does not account for the extreme stress reactions suffered by victims of sexual harassment.

The *sociocultural model* posits sexual harassment as only one manifestation of the much larger patriarchal system in which men are the dominant group. Therefore, harassment is an example of men asserting their personal power based on sex. According to this model, sex would be a better predictor of both recipient and initiator status than would organizational position. Thus, women should be much more likely to be victims of sexual harassment, especially when they are in male-populated occupations. This model gives a much more accurate account of sexual harassment because the overwhelming majority of victims are women and the overwhelming majority of harassers are men.

The *organizational model* asserts that sexual harassment results from opportunities presented by relations of power and authority that derive from the hierarchical structure of organizations. Thus, sexual harassment is an issue of organizational power. Because workplaces are defined by vertical stratification and asymmetrical relations between supervisors and subordinates, individuals can use the power of their position to extort sexual gratification from their subordinates.

Related to this are the research findings that suggest that individuals who harass typically do not label their behavior as sexual harassment despite the fact they report they frequently engage in behaviors that fit the legal definition of sexual harassment. Such individuals deny the inherent power differential between themselves and their employees, as well as the psychological power conferred by this differential that is as salient as the power derived from evaluation.

The behavior that legally constitutes harassment is just that, despite what the supervisor's or co-worker's intentions may be. The impact on the individual—her or his reaction to the behavior—is the critical variable.

Sex Role Stereotypes Cause Sexual Harassment

by Kathy Hotelling and Barbara A. Zuber

About the authors: *Kathy Hotelling is director at the Counseling and Student Development Center at Northern Illinois University. Barbara A. Zuber is a psychologist at the Counseling and Student Development Center at Northern Illinois University.*

Editor's Note: Scholarly references within the text and the reference list at the end of the chapter in the original version have been omitted from the following reprinted version.

Feminist paradigms of inquiry have provided scholars with the opportunity to address scientific questions and societal issues from viewpoints that formulate new questions to be answered, reconstruct prevailing theories, and develop new theories from which the world and human behavior can be viewed. Feminist thought has contended that traditional paradigms of understanding have not only been slow to address issues that face women in society, but also that they have not understood these problems adequately. . . .

Traditional Methods of Analysis

T.S. Kuhn described a paradigm shift as the alteration of viewpoints that occurs when new data or phenomena cannot be accommodated by traditional perspectives. Paradigm shifts were described not merely as extensions of the old, but rather as representing changes that shake fundamental beliefs and ways of looking at the world. New paradigms present new assumptions, new values, and new methods in generating and testing theories. The development of feminist paradigms was necessary because of the plethora of ways in which sex bias has been evidenced in scientific thought and research (in theoretical models, the formulation of questions, the choice of subjects, experimenter effects, observer effects, and bias in interpretations) and, therefore, how it has affected the understanding of both women and men and their experiences and behavior.

Traditional psychological philosophy has viewed behavior exclusively as a manifestation of individual dynamics and pathology. When considering sexual harassment and other forms of victimization, one assumption has been that perpetrators are psychologically disturbed; that is, they are the "exception" rather than the "rule." This was operationalized in early legal opinion in which sexual harassment was viewed as a personal phenomenon characterized as "egregious, infrequent behavior engaged in by powerful individuals who should know better than to use their power to extort sexual concessions"; in order to be found guilty of sexual harassment under this belief system, an individual had to be especially flagrant in his violations of the law (e.g.. termination of an employee for refusal to submit to sexual advances). A variation of the perspective that perpetrators are pathological is that men have a high sex drive and cannot control themselves. Another assumption has been that victims precipitate the perpetrator's behavior; this assumption has been evident in both general comments about sexual harassment and in courtroom questioning about a woman's dress or behavior, presumably flirtatious or provocative. A third assumption has been that victims enjoy being victimized, also demonstrated in the courtroom by questions regarding victims' sexual fantasies, previous relationships, et cetera.

> *"The development of feminist paradigms was necessary because of the plethora of ways in which sex bias has been evidenced in scientific thought and research."*

Traditional Assumptions Lack Research Support

Not straying from traditional paradigms has meant that these assumptions have been given credibility and perpetuated as fact regardless of the lack of support from research. Prevalence statistics belie the assumption that sexual harassment is rare or unique; estimates indicate that 40% or more of women workers have been sexually harassed, while 20–30% of women students have been victimized in the same way. The first major survey of sexual harassment, as well as subsequent studies and personal accounts of harassment, have indicated that women are unwilling participants in sexual harassment. In regard to the assumption that victims enjoy harassment, studies as early as 1980 found that an extremely low percentage of women were even flattered by sexual attention in the workplace. The far-reaching effects of sexual harassment on its victims, including physical problems (insomnia, headaches, digestive problems, neck and headaches, etc.), emotional problems including injury to self-esteem and confidence; and behavioral changes such as avoidance of perpetrators have been devastating beyond the immediate situation. In the long run, sexual harassment in academic settings can "reduce the quality of education, diminish academic achievement, and ultimately may lower earning power." In the work arena, sexual harassment can lead women to experience attitude changes such as loss of self-confidence and negativity toward work that can result in poor performance, loss of positions through resignations or firings, and lower wages (due to lack of raises or lack of longevity in positions).

According to feminist scholars, traditional psychological paradigms of inquiry and attendant assumptions fail to examine the social context of behavior and to acknowledge the effects of sex role socialization. Specifically in regard to sexual harassment, the saliency of gender vis-à-vis sexual harassment and the imbalance of power between men and women (which is compounded by the power relationship between employer and employee and professor and student) have not been recognized or studied through traditional paradigms. Traditional paradigms do not recognize that sexual harassment discriminates against women by limiting their ability to establish equality, thus resulting in harm to victims of sexual harassment. K. Kitchener has called the principle of "do no harm" the most fundamental ethical obligation in professions committed to helping others and benefiting society through practice and research. This ethical principle requires one to consider both the intentional and unintentional harm and the direct and indirect harm that is inflicted on others through theories and corresponding actions, such as treatment of victims of sexual harassment. A. Brownell has suggested that the harmful effects of traditional paradigms provide a compelling reason to implement feminist paradigms. . . .

The Power of Sex Roles

All conceptualizations of sexual harassment by feminist scholars have included the saliency of gender. Sexual harassment is not a peculiarity of human behavior, but rather a manifestation of the cultural patterns of male-female interactions: an extension of "normal behavior" that is taught and expected from an early age. B.A. Gutek and B. Morasch termed the carryover of expectations based on gender into the workplace as "sex role spillover." According to Gutek, this phenomenon occurs regardless of the direction of the gender skew in the workplace: The gender role of the predominant group influences the workplace expectations for that job and the treatment of women within the work group. In a workplace of primarily women, then, the jobs themselves often have assumed the characteristics of female sex roles; those that hold these jobs are expected to be nurturing, supportive, and helpful. When men are dominant, the jobs are characterized as ones requiring assertiveness, rationality, and competitiveness. These expectations are in force regardless of job requirements or skills. Also, when there are more men than women in the workplace, Gutek asserted that women are treated first as women and secondarily as workers. That is, gender is "the classifying variable

> *"Traditional paradigms do not recognize that sexual harassment discriminates against women by limiting their ability to establish equality."*

in men's perceptions of women," B.L. Glass writes.

Since gender itself represents a hierarchy with men on the top and women underneath, the sexual harassment of women occurs not only when women are on the bottom of the formal hierarchical ladder, but also when they are in lateral positions or even on top of the hierarchy. According to C. MacKinnon, men have had the experience of needing to act in certain ways or fear repercussions, which is what occurs in sexual harassment when the harasser is in a more powerful position than the victim; because of this personal experience of men, they can understand hierarchical sexual harassment. But since the inherent hierarchy between the sexes is often overlooked, lateral and reverse hierarchical sexual harassment are often not understood by men; this leads in part to its perpetuation. . . .

The potential for miscommunication that is fostered as a result of culturally induced sex role behavior has been explicated by B.L. Glass. A degree of stereotypical sexual interaction between men and women can be considered "normal" in our society. Traditionally, men have been expected to be the aggressors in all realms, especially the sexual. Women, on the other hand, are taught to be asexual since sexual interest on their part is equated with promiscuity. Passivity and silence are also part of the female role. So, women's nonresponsiveness or "no" could be interpreted as the women being good at their role and not have anything to do with their interest level. In addition, women's friendliness, another culturally induced trait, can be misperceived by men as indicative of interest in sex. The dysfunctional quality of this socialization of men and women is further exemplified by the fact that an advance may become harassment only after the man doesn't respond to evidence from the woman that she is not interested. The "boys will be boys" motto indicates both women's resignation about the existence of unwanted sexual advances and the inescapable nature of sex role socialization.

It is also gender roles that perpetuate sexual harassment once it occurs because women have been taught to avoid conflict and to doubt their perceptions, which means that they often do not report such behavior. Additionally, the importance to the self-concept of women of establishing and maintaining relationships is learned by females at a very young age and remains predominant throughout their lives. In the workplace this is exemplified by women's dependence on relationships for mobility, which reinforces passivity, again leading to the underreporting of sexual harassment.

In summary, gender identity is more powerful than work identity or social identity. No matter what the job requirements, the academic requirements, or the social situation, women are seen as women first and are treated on the basis of sex role stereotypes.

Achieving Equality Is Difficult

As a feminist theorist and attorney, Catharine MacKinnon has written extensively about the social, political, and economic underpinnings of the problem of sexual harassment and has extended the effect of the saliency of gender described above in her writings. She has pointed out that the feminist concept of the personal as political is not a metaphor, but rather refers to the experience of sexual objectification: "The substantive principle governing the authentic politics of women's personal lives is pervasive powerlessness to men, expressed and reconstituted daily as sexuality." It is because of this viewpoint regarding women's lives that MacKinnon argues that gender and sexuality are inseparable and that the home and the marketplace become the same; at work, women's role is sexualized as it is in the family.

As early as 1980, sexual harassment was viewed as more endemic than epidemic because of women's economic vulnerability. MacKinnon characterized work as potentially allowing women to gain independence, to extend abilities demonstrated in the home, and to survive economically. Because money is an exchangeable commodity, women can gain control by working outside of the home even if they are doing the same tasks as they do in the home. But, according to MacKinnon, sexual harassment in the workplace furthers social inequality because it undermines women's ability to achieve work equality; women are again dependent on men financially. When one group has been allocated fewer advantages and less power and wealth than another group, a social context is created to support this disproportionate distribution. James C. Renick and MacKinnon agree that this is the environment within which sexual harassment flourishes.

> *"Since the inherent hierarchy between the sexes is often overlooked, lateral and reverse hierarchical sexual harassment are often not understood by men."*

In the academic world, the lack of clarity about the nature of formal relationships, such as the student/professor relationship, has allowed professors to determine the importance of gender and, therefore, the degree to which sexuality has entered into interactions with students and can be used selectively to obligate students to behaviors required or encouraged by professors. D.H. Lach and P.A. Gwartney-Gibbs asserted that to whatever extent sexuality is present in a given interaction, it could be expected that women would receive more uninvited attention of a sexual nature than men.

In summary, from a feminist perspective, sexual harassment both emanates from and reinforces the traditional sex roles of men and women.

The Abuse of Power

Power, a multifaceted construct, has been defined by T. Huston as "the ability to achieve ends through influence." As pointed out earlier, power most commonly has been understood as emanating from authority or position. According to S.S. Tangri, M.R. Burt, and L.B. Johnson, organizations may provide an opportunity structure that makes sexual harassment possible because people use their power and position to influence behavior. Individuals who occupy a high-status role or position are believed to have the right to make demands of those in lower-status positions; harassing behaviors may be viewed by some high-status individuals as simple extensions of that right and that lower-status individuals are expected to comply with these demands. This reality, coupled with the fact that a gender differential has existed and currently exists in who holds organizational power (as evidenced by the 1994 Bureau of Labor statistics indicating that men hold 88.1% of upper-management positions) results in the harassment of female subordinates by male supervisors. But, as already indicated, gender also determines power: Males are more powerful in American society than women, and harassment also occurs among coworkers.

The power of the male perpetrator over the female victim and the element of coercion in sexual harassment have led many scholars to examine the similarities between sexual harassment and other forms of sexual victimization, such as domestic violence and rape. T. McCormack compared academic women to battered wives in that they both are embarrassed and worried about retaliation if they were to talk openly about the violations. MacKinnon stated that "economic power is to sexual harassment as physical force is to rape." Rape is now accepted not as a crime of sex, but rather of violence; in the same vein, MacKinnon argued that sexual harassment is the abuse of "hierarchical economic (or institutional) authority, not sexuality." Both of these crimes, sexual harassment and rape, according to MacKinnon, reinforce women's lack of power as a gender. Just because sexual harassment is representative of "normal" relationships between the sexes, and because these relationships have as their base unequal social power, does not mean that the existence of such behavior is justified; in essence, such behavior only grows out of these societal realities and, therefore, results in systematic disadvantagement based on group status. Because of this, MacKinnon has not tolerated the "differences" doctrine as a defense of sexual harassment. This doctrine allows courts to determine whether there are adequate reasons supporting the treatment of one category of persons differently from another. Except for the Japanese detention during World War II, the courts have not found compelling reasons to support the differences doctrine in regard to race, but when differences in treatment have been argued on the basis of sex, this differential treatment often has been justified. Thus, power equality is assumed, when in reality women have been subordinate in our society at the same time as

> *"No matter what the job requirements, the academic requirements, or the social situation, women are seen as women first and are treated on the basis of sex role stereotypes."*

they are distinct. Therefore, MacKinnon has argued that if sexuality were set within analyses of gender, equality (e.g., women as distinct and "fully human") would be guaranteed.

In summary, both sexual harassment itself and the potential or threat of sexual harassment create discrimination and deny women the opportunity for full participation in society as workers, as students, and as individuals. Sexual harassment is a complex phenomenon that is a social, and only derivatively a personal, problem. . . .

Preventing Sexual Harassment

Prevention from the feminist perspective is necessarily broader than prevention from a traditional perspective whereby sexual harassment training programs have focused on education regarding what behaviors constitute sexual harassment and dealing with harassment once it occurs. Awareness of what constitutes sexual harassment may not be enough to change a problem situation. Furthermore, grievance procedures and discipline are reactive measures and do not address the underlying dynamics of sexual harassment. S.L. Shullman has argued that if harassment is conceptualized as a result of cultural roles and organizational hierarchy, then prevention and training should focus on sociocultural and organizational interventions. This contention also has been supported by L.F. Fitzgerald, who argued that sexual harassment prevention must be conceptualized as ecological and proactive rather than individual and reactive. . . .

"Organizations may provide an opportunity structure that makes sexual harassment possible because people use their power and position to influence behavior."

From a feminist perspective, the occurrence of sexual harassment is fostered by cultural factors that intertwine power, gender, and sexuality as described above. By changing the cultural factors (sex role socialization, media portrayals of the objectification and victimization of women, the sex-segregated nature of the work force, and the acceptance of interpersonal violence) that essentially promote and condone sexual harassment, true prevention can be achieved. . . .

Early socialization teaches males to be aggressive and dominant and women to be submissive and passive, which contributes to the development of women's secondary social and cultural status and sexually coercive attitudes and behaviors. Because the socialization process begins early in life, alternative parenting strategies are essential in decreasing women's subordinate status and ultimately in developing equality between men and women. N.J. Chodorow recommended that parents replace traditional messages wherein boys are encouraged to be achievement oriented and self-reliant, while girls are socialized to be nurturing and obedient by teaching children that both sexes are of value; for example, fathers and mothers can model behavior representative of such messages by sharing child care and household responsibilities. This may decrease the stereotypes of "women's work" and "men's work" and give children less restrictive conceptions of masculinity and femininity than they currently hold, as well as symbolizing respect for the opposite gender as a group.

The educational system is another powerful gender socialization agent because formal curriculum and other activities convey values that shape students' perceptions of themselves and the world. Researchers have found that girls are shortchanged in their educational experiences by the type of attention they receive from teachers and as a consequence of segregation. In the classroom, teachers tend to give more time and more esteem-building encouragement to boys than girls. For example, boys are provided remediation and challenge to achieve the best possible academic performance, praise for the intellectual quality of work, and attention when answers are called out. Teachers, however, provided less assistance with problem solving to girls than boys, praised the neatness of girls' work, and completed complex tasks for girls as opposed to giving more detailed instructions for independent completion, as they did with the boys. Furthermore, teachers often used various subtle forms of sex segregation, such as seating girls and boys on opposite sides of the room and by organizing tasks by gender. As C.M. Renzetti and D.J. Curran pointed out, these practices have far-reaching implications for the lives of children:

> First, sex segregation in and of itself prevents boys and girls from working together cooperatively, thus denying children of both sexes valuable opportunities to learn about and sample one another's interests and activities. Second, it makes working in same-sex groups more comfortable than working in mixed-sex groups—a feeling that children may carry into adulthood and which may become problematic when they enter the labor force. And finally, sex segregation reinforces gender stereotypes, especially if it involves differential work assignments.

While these educational practices continue into middle school and high school, it is imperative that the issues outlined here be addressed as early as possible to improve gender relations. Specifically, teacher training to recognize gender inequity in the classroom and to remedy these inequities, through such measures as the elimination of gender segregation in work and play groups and the structuring of activities to encourage cooperation between the sexes, is necessary to achieve the type of change that is advocated to proactively address the workplace problems that females experience later in life.

Changing the Workplace

Until such societal changes occur, organizations must continue to establish policies, procedures, and climates that reinforce the prohibition against sexual harassment. The thoughtful crafting of sexual harassment policies and procedures by clearly defining sexual harassment (including examples of blatant and subtle forms of harassment, as well as recognition of harassment by peers), procedures for filing complaints, investigation procedures, consequences of harassment, and victim rights is necessary. As demonstrated in the research reviewed here, men and women have different perceptions of the appropriateness of behavior within the workplace; therefore, because women are the victims, the perspectives of women should be reflected in harassment policies and procedures. To encourage the reporting of harassment, policies and procedures must protect the confidentiality of both the victim and the alleged harasser and clearly condemn retaliatory action against complainants. Many institutions of higher education already have in place sexual harassment policies but fail to directly address amorous relationships between faculty and student. Since the power differential between faculty and student cannot be eliminated and because such relationships can never be truly consensual relationships, institutions need to develop clear policies and procedures that educate faculty about and discourage them from establishing such relationships with students.

> *"Alternative parenting strategies are essential in decreasing women's subordinate status and ultimately in developing equality between men and women."*

Institutional and organizational policies and procedures are not sufficient and must take place in the broader context of what F.L. Hoffmann calls "institution-wide efforts to create an educational and workplace environment that does not disadvantage women." This involves creating an environment that is affirming and valuing of women through a commitment from managers and administrators that a sexualized work environment will not be tolerated, through the promotion of nonsexist behavior and affirmative action policies, through an examination of the issue of comparable worth and the remedying of salary inequities, through the promotion of women into faculty and management positions, and through education about the dynamics of sexual harassment.

Enforcement of Policies and Law

Policies and procedures are necessary, but not sufficient, for addressing sexual harassment. Institutions and organizations must protect the rights of students and employees, instead of protecting perpetrators, by following through with remedies and disciplinary actions for proven charges of sexual harassment. It is imperative that disciplinary or other actions do not focus on the victim (e.g., encouraging a student to leave a class or transferring a worker to another department to avoid the situation) but on the harasser and his inappropriate behavior. Disciplinary actions must be more than a "slap on the wrist" or a letter in a personnel file and be a factor in receiving tenure, salary increases, and promotions.

The use of the reasonable person legal standard, which is male-biased and fails to take into account the discrepancy between the views of men and women about appropriate sexual conduct, must be replaced by the standard of reasonable woman as a means for determining a hostile work environment. Using this standard when investigating internal or legal charges of sexual harassment will guarantee victims of harassment greater protection than is often afforded them and takes into account their perception of the offensive behavior.

Utilizing feminist paradigms to examine the problem of sexual harassment clearly has provided scholars and researchers with alternative theories, new questions to be answered, and suggestions for prevention. This perspective has promoted a broader view of the underlying dynamics and the remedies for the longstanding problem of the sexual harassment of women by men than traditional perspectives. A feminist perspective challenges us to restructure gender roles in society to address the underlying causes of sexual harassment in our institutions of higher learning and workplaces and will enhance environments and relationships for both men and women.

Tolerance of Sexual Harassment Perpetuates Sexual Harassment in the Military

by Leora N. Rosen and Lee Martin

About the authors: *Leora N. Rosen is a research social scientist in the Department of Military Psychiatry, Division of Neuropsychiatry, at the Walter Reed Army Institute of Research. Lee Martin is a doctoral student in sociology at the University of Maryland.*

In recent years, a considerable literature has developed linking sexually assaultive behavior among men to negative attitudes toward women, acceptance of violence, and tolerant attitudes toward rape and sexual harassment. These patterns of association have been examined among incarcerated sex offenders, nonoffending men in the community, and college students who have admitted to engaging in sexually coercive, assaultive, or harassing behaviors.

Most of these studies have examined attitudes and personality characteristics as predictors of behavior or measures of tendency toward a behavior. The outcome variables have generally comprised some form of sexual violence against women, whereas the predictor variables have often included attitudes that are tolerant of rape or sexual harassment. However, attitudes that foster tolerance of sexual violence have a significance beyond predicting actual sexual violence in that they contribute to a milieu in which others may more easily perpetrate sexual violence without fearing negative consequences. Tolerance of sexual harassment may be an important enabling factor for perpetrators of sexual harassment, particularly in a group environment such as the military where harassing behavior would be severely curtailed without a supportive infrastructure.

Excerpted from Leora N. Rosen and Lee Martin, "Predictors of Tolerance of Sexual Harassment Among Male U.S. Army Soldiers," *Violence Against Women*, vol. 4, no. 4, (August 1998), p. 491. Copyright ©1998 by Sage Publications, Inc. Reprinted by permission of Sage Publications, Inc. *References and notes in the original have been omitted in this reprint.*

Attitudes Toward Sexual Harassment

The Tailhook incident, which focused national attention on the problem of sexual harassment in the military, provides an example of how such an atmosphere operates. The incident began when dozens of drunken Navy aviators sexually assaulted several women at the Las Vegas Hilton during the 1991 convention of the Tailhook Society, which was attended by top-level Navy officials. Among the revelations that ultimately reached the public was the laissez-faire attitude on the part of Navy personnel to the initial investigation, which found that there was no wrongdoing. Only after a second investigation by the Department of Defense, and after a great deal of media attention, was there a finding that assaults had actually taken place. Although there were ultimately no successful prosecutions, several top Navy personnel resigned. Tolerance of sexual harassment may be an important factor in perpetuating sexual harassment and other forms of sexual violence in the military and elsewhere.

Sexual harassment in the military is by no means limited to social events. The gravity of the problem was brought to the public's attention once again in 1996, when several female trainees at Aberdeen Proving Ground in Maryland alleged that they were raped by male drill instructors. The Army leadership made a conscious effort to avoid the mistakes of the Navy's Tailhook investigation and took immediate and decisive action. Within a short time, two drill instructors and a company commander were charged with crimes ranging from rape to obstruction of justice. In addition, the Army responded to the crisis by setting up a hot line to receive reports of sexual harassment and sexual misconduct from elsewhere in the Army. The hot line logged thousands of calls within a matter of weeks. Several hundred of these were considered serious enough to merit further criminal investigation. The Army also established a task force to review the efficacy of current policies and training on sexual harassment and to examine the role of Army culture in fostering conditions that make sexual harassment more likely to occur. The task force will make recommendations to the Secretary of the Army on how to improve the environment for soldiers with a view to the total elimination of sexual harassment.

> *"Tolerance of sexual harassment may be an important factor in perpetuating sexual harassment and other forms of sexual violence in the military and elsewhere."*

Prior to the Aberdeen scandal, several studies had documented a high prevalence of sexual harassment in the military. Whereas these studies examined sexual harassment in relation to organizational characteristics and demographic characteristics of victims, they did not attempt to relate the problem to attitudes toward women among male service members. . . .

In a survey of male and female soldiers in mixed gender Army units, we examined the prevalence, organizational predictors, and psychological consequences of perceived sexual harassment and unwanted sexual experiences in the workplace. The survey instrument also included a scale measuring tolerance of sexual harassment, that is, the extent to which soldiers take sexual harassment seriously. In the present study, we examined predictors of tolerance of sexual harassment among male U.S. Army soldiers, focusing on three indices of hostility toward women as the independent variables. . . .

Negative Attitudes Toward Women

The results of this study are consistent with those found elsewhere in the literature, indicating that among men, holding negative attitudes toward women is associated with tolerance of various forms of sexual aggression including sexual harassment. All three measures of negative attitudes toward women were significantly associated with tolerance of sexual harassment in this study. Hostility toward women and acceptance of women may directly denote negative attitudes toward women. Negative masculinity has a more indirect, but no less important association, and it is relevant to the argument that hypermasculinity may be a critical personality feature associated with sexual coercion. B. Burkhart, M.E. Fromuth, D.L. Mosher, and R.D. Anderson have argued that the socialization of the hypermasculine man results in an overvaluing of toughness, violence, and lack of empathic response, as well as the development of a personality with proclivities toward coercive sexual conduct and a need to risk danger for excitement. Sexual aggression validates and affirms this notion of masculinity because of its association with power, domination, and toughness. N.M. Malamuth and colleagues noted that certain subcultures and societies that regard qualities such as toughness, dominance, aggressiveness, and competitiveness as masculine may breed individuals hostile to women and to characteristics associated with femininity. Consequently, they are likely to be more sexually aggressive toward women. Negative masculinity may also be associated with nonsexual aggression toward women. L.K. Hamberger and J. Hastings found that recidivism following treatment for spouse battering was predicted by higher narcissism, which is a characteristic correlating highly with negative masculinity.

Opponents of gender integration in the military have equated the degradation of women with a "warrior culture," which is believed to be necessary for the maintenance of a ready and effective fighting force. Sexual harassment may therefore provide a validation of masculinity for certain men in the military, consistent with J.W. Messerschmidt's theory regarding the relationship between masculinity and criminal behavior. Messerschmidt has described the varieties of ways in which abusive acts toward women and other violent or criminal behavior contribute to the social construction of different types of masculine identities. W.S. DeKeseredy and K. Kelly have shown that peer support for abusive behavior toward women and attachment to abusive peers are predictors of sexually abusive behavior among male Canadian college students. Hostility toward women and negative masculinity may thus be particularly significant with regard to sexual harassment in the military, where they can become part of a shared masculine or warrior culture in male peer groups that may support violence against women.

The relationship of ethnicity to tolerance of sexual harassment is also of interest. White male and female soldiers were the most tolerant of sexual harassment, and African American male and female soldiers the least tolerant, perhaps because as members of a minority group, they empathized with another group that was vulnerable to discrimination. In this regard, it is worth noting that African American female soldiers in this study also reported less unwanted sexual attention than females in other ethnic groups, perhaps because of less tolerance of sexual harassment among African American males.

It is of particular interest that male soldiers' lack of acceptance of women as fellow soldiers, which was correlated with the other study variables, was among the significant predictors of tolerance of sexual harassment. Thus, general hostility toward women and lack of acceptance of women into military units are both independent predictors of tolerance of sexual harassment. These findings also highlight the need to deal with attitudes toward women and concepts of masculinity as part of any program to reduce sexual harassment.

Chapter 3

How Can Sexual Harassment Be Reduced?

Chapter Preface

According to the Equal Employment Opportunity Commission (EEOC), from 1991 until 1995, formal charges of sexual harassment rose 50 percent. A 1996 survey revealed that almost 90 percent of the Fortune 500 companies surveyed received sexual harassment complaints, and more than one-third have faced lawsuits. Because of the cost in time, money, and personnel, organizations continue to seek ways to reduce sexual harassment. As a result, a new industry has emerged that is devoted to helping organizations do just that: consultants offer harassment prevention workshops, law firms specialize in sexual harassment litigation, and insurance companies offer employment practices liability coverage. While some professionals endorse regulation in the form of formal policies and laws, critics insist that broader social changes are necessary to reduce sexual harassment.

Those who claim that regulation will reduce sexual harassment argue that because organizations have failed to reduce sexual harassment on their own, legal intervention has become necessary. Columnist Denis Horgan writes, "As much as you could hope that, on their own, individuals would have the sense not to do these things or that companies would institute the strongest rules against them, we know, instead, that only in turning to the government and its law is there any real prospect of relief." Other advocates of regulation argue that widespread confusion over what constitutes sexual harassment has forced organizations to adopt formal policies. Most of these authorities agree, however, that a clearly stated policy, consistently and promptly enforced, with a distinct complaint procedure is the most effective way to reduce the risk of sexual harassment.

Those who oppose regulation as a way to reduce sexual harassment do so for different reasons. Some authorities oppose legal intervention because the cost of litigation outweighs the cost of sexual harassment. "Sexual harassment lawsuits can be job crushers, and if the damages are big enough they can destroy a company. The way the current sexual harassment law is constructed, the company and totally innocent employees pay a bigger price than the actual harasser," writes restauranteur and writer Sarah J. McCarthy. Others argue that stringent rules are ultimately more harmful to women than sexual harassment itself because strict policies imply that women are fragile and oversensitive. Still others think that regulation of any kind is insufficient to reduce sexual harassment because it does nothing to eliminate its causes, arguing that elimination of gender inequality in the workplace and society at large is the only way to reduce sexual harassment.

The viewpoints in the following chapter explore some of the methods experts recommend to reduce sexual harassment as well as remedies they believe are ineffective.

Legal Responses Are Necessary to Reduce Sexual Harassment

by Denis Horgan

About the author: *Denis Horgan writes editorial comments on current events for the* Hartford Courant *in Hartford, Connecticut.*

Should you and I ever have the idea that the actual fault with sexual harassment in the workplace is that it could lead to a major legal problem for the owners of the workplace, then maybe we don't know what we're talking about.

What's wrong with sexual harassment is that it's wrong—not that it's costly, difficult to administer or distantly subject to manipulation. It's wrong because it's wrong.

Courts Establish Guidelines

The Supreme Court has crisply refined the boundaries of employer liability in matters of sexual harassment in the workplace, overwhelmingly men harassing women. The court has now established more precisely than ever before the legal problems of the owners of the workplace when harassment happens.

Clarifying a knotty variety of lower court rulings, the justices set out guidelines at which an employer's liability is triggered and when it is avoided. A company with a good and genuine policy can avoid the hook for its employees' activities; one without one is at fiscal peril.

Good.

What is so enduringly amazing is the steel truth that it is exactly so necessary for the courts to become involved in the question in the first place and the second place and in every place. Yet heaven help us all if the courts and government were not there in all of those places.

Charitably, those who most bemoan such engagement are those who so often think there is no problem at all or that it will solve itself—or, less charitably, that they will be able to get away with it. As it is, the fact that the Supreme Court is compelled to make such legal judgments is as much an indictment of overall attitude as it is of the specific matter under complaint.

How do these things keep happening?

You could hope that there would be no need whatever for reminders from the courts about the need for clear rules about how men treat women. You could hope that it would be unnecessary. You could hope that it would be the natural inclination of company leaders on their own to ensure that men do not sexually harass women, that one employee treats another equally and with dignity. It is not exactly new and difficult territory to explore. Bad things should not be done, should not be excused, should not be tolerated.

Yet there is obviously such a need because hoping is not enough.

It is an obvious need because the offense persists in such grim abundance. Likely, each and every one of us knows of an instance or more where a woman—someone's family member, friend, relative or acquaintance—has suffered sexual harassment in the workplace, where some oaf has intimidated, annoyed, propositioned, assaulted or diminished a woman employee. It is not rare, even now.

Awareness Is Not Enough

Mightn't we think that we'd know better by this time? Apparently not.

Here we are three dozen years from the Civil Rights Act of 1964, three-quarters of a century from women's wrenching the vote from its male-only perch, 150 years from the first Women's Rights Convention, yet the courts are still required to stand in between ham-handed males and the women of the modern workplace.

Here we are about to turn the corner on a new millennium, a marker of the anniversary of the birth of a man and a redeeming vision that commands love and mutual respect. It is a golden rule. Yet in place after place,

> *"The courts are still required to stand in between ham-handed males and the women of the modern workplace."*

women are subjected to affronts so personal and so vile as to outrage our very spirit.

Were the hurt something like someone risking getting hit by meteors or bit by penguins, you could think that the courts and government are, indeed, intrusive. Instead, the evidence shows beyond doubt that the demeaning reality goes on day after day and in every fashion offends our sense of fairness and the law.

Laws Offer Protection

As much as you could hope that, on their own, individuals would have the sense not to do these things or that companies would institute the strongest rules against them, we know, instead, that only in turning to the government and its law is there any real prospect of relief.

In the matter of sexual harassment, as in a thousand others, we find important justification for an aggressive social energy—government—separating the innocent from the power and abuse of the strong. Wishful thinking and denial aside, it is needed because there is little else to protect us—all of us—from what is simply wrong.

Well-Crafted Policies Can Reduce Sexual Harassment

by Ellen Leander

About the author: *Ellen Leander currently writes on corporate issues for* Emerging Markets Investor *and has contributed articles to* Treasury and Risk Management, CFO, *and* Global Finance.

Sex is Alan Lieban's newest obsession. No kidding.

As the risk manager at Litton Industries, the $3.6 billion defense and aerospace company, Lieban finds himself spending more and more time contemplating the topic even though only a few sexual harassment complaints still manage to cross his desk each year. Most of the ones that make it to his "in" box are already in litigation, in spite of Litton's sexual harassment policy as well as its training programs. The majority of those cases settle for amounts far below the $2 million deductible that Litton's employment practices liability, or EPL, insurance has, he notes. But just a few of these smaller cases can add up to big dollars each year, so he is seriously considering changing to a policy with a $500,000 deductible.

The Bottom Line

All across the United States, risk managers, treasurers and chief financial officers (CFOs) are beginning to look at the impact that sexual harassment lawsuits, and related suits like racial and sexual discrimination, are having on their bottom lines. The number, size and prominence of these suits being brought are unprecedented. For starters, U.S. President Bill Clinton is himself fighting off sexual harassment charges from a former Arkansas state employee, Paula Jones. At $3.5 billion W.R. Grace, a chief executive officer (CEO) was ousted because of sexual harassment involving at least five female employees over a period of several years. Female employees in April 1996 sued Astra USA, a division of a Swedish pharmaceutical manufacturer, for sexual harassment. Rampant sexual misbehavior at a midwestern Mitsubishi Motors plant was national news in 1996. Even mid-sized companies like J&J Snack Foods, a $200 million pack-

Abridged from Ellen Leander, "Unprotected Sex," *Treasury and Risk Management*, July 1997. Reprinted with permission of CFO Publishing Corp.

aged goods manufacturer, have made headlines. The company was hit with a $4.2 million judgment in a same-sex sexual harassment case in April 1997. Says J&J Snack CFO and senior vice president Dennis Moore: "Juries are out of control."

Monetary damages are forcing corporations to reckon with the problem. At Astra, the harassers were top executives who were soon fired. Still, settlements in the case have ranged from a few thousand dollars up to $100,000 per employee, and litigation is ongoing. A woman was awarded $7.1 million by a California jury in compensation for the sexual harassment she suffered while an assistant at the law firm of Baker & McKenzie. Philip Morris had to cough up $2 million to Mary Wilson, a former supervisor who was harassed by her male employees. And a Missouri jury granted a woman $50 million in a verdict against Wal-Mart. "I can't think of a week that has gone by that there hasn't been an award written about in the *Wall Street Journal*," says John Kuhn, vice president and the worldwide employment practices liability insurance product manager at $24 billion (in assets) Chubb & Sons.

> *"The first line of defense against a lawsuit is a good sexual harassment policy, but that doesn't mean three paragraphs on company letterhead."*

Managing sexual harassment risk is going to require some big changes, say risk managers who, like Lieban, have already embarked on the journey.

Woodland Hills, California–based Litton already does many things right when it comes to handling sexual harassment issues. The company has a tough written policy, does frequent training and uses arbitration. And yet to reduce its deductible from $2 million to $500,000, Litton must completely reengineer the way it deals with this type of risk internally. Right now, human resources handles all sexual harassment policies and complaints with almost complete autonomy, says Lieban. But Litton's insurer will not lower the deductible unless it receives much more say in how the company runs its sexual harassment program.

That means that Lieban must assume the role of liaison between the insurance company and Litton's human resources department.

The concept is a revolutionary one—he must learn a good deal about human resources activities, help create policy, keep the insurer in the loop and manage the risk itself. Says Lieban: "This to me is the responsible approach."

The High Cost of Litigation

Who can really blame the insurers for wanting more say, especially since huge, class action suits are popping up, many with backing from the Equal Employment Opportunity Commission (EEOC)? One of the first class action EEOC victories was a $1.1 million judgment in August 1995 against Del Laboratories in Farmingdale, New York, in favor of 15 women. The Mitsubishi case, a class action lawsuit filed in April 1996 on behalf of 289 women, alleges wide-spread misconduct in the company's facility. [This suit was settled by voluntary agreement in June 1998.] . . . In May 1996, the EEOC backed a class action suit against Merrill Lynch and Smith Barney brought by a group of women who claim both harassment and discrimination. [The suit was settled in November 1997.] The cases are part of an EEOC strategy to put its limited resources into lawsuits that will have a broader impact. But on the flip side, the agency is also promoting greater use of mediation in smaller cases, and is putting together a study on best practices in antidiscrimination policies.

Indeed, risk managers who are following the growth of sexual harassment litigation say that for a corporation, a financial hit wrought by such a lawsuit has taken on the dimensions of more traditionally catastrophic, "act of God" events such as fire, tornado, flood or earthquake. In the spring of 1992, *Treasury & Risk Management* predicted that corporate America would spend $1 billion by 1997 on sexual harassment settlements and award damages. While it is difficult to confirm that number—settlements are private—the reality looks close.

EEOC resolutions from 1992 through 1996 totaled more than $112 million—and that's just the tip of the iceberg, or less than 5%. According to Rachael McKinney, underwriting manager at Swett & Crawford, a wholesale brokerage firm based in Los Angeles, 95% of such cases settle out of court for sums likely to be

> *"One way that these policies reduce risk . . . is to prove in court that a company is firmly committed to the ideal of eliminating sexual harassment in the workplace."*

higher than the average court award of $150,000. Lawyers' fees can tack on another $250,000 to $500,000 to a litigation bill. "This is the big exposure of the 1990s, and it's bigger than environmental liabilities," says McKinney, referring to a top legal issue that frightened corporate America in the 1980s.

But sexual harassment lawsuits have not multiplied so rapidly because there is more harassment going on out there. One in three women in the U.S. has suffered on-the-job sexual harassment in one form or another, various polls report, but generally levels have remained steady or declined slightly over the past two decades.

The conventional wisdom says that lawsuits are multiplying like rabbits in springtime because those who are being harassed are now more willing to speak up about it, a phenomenon widely attributed to the Clarence Thomas–Anita Hill hearings in 1991. In those hearings, Hill, a former Thomas subordinate, said she was harassed by her boss repeatedly, and that such behavior should call into question his ability to sit as a Supreme Court justice. Although Thomas was confirmed anyway, the event created what experts now call "the sexual harassment revolution."

But another, more important reason why the lawyers are growing rich and the court dockets are more crowded is that corporations, which are usually the defendants in these cases, have not kept up with the changes that society has undergone since the Thomas-Hill hearings. Many don't have a well-crafted sexual harassment policy, most don't have employment practices liability insurance, and most take a long hard look at corporate policy only after they are hit with a huge, expensive lawsuit. In fact, an Aon [Risk Services Cos. Inc.] survey of 250 risk managers from companies with revenues of more than $500 million indicates that more than six out of 10 respondents don't have EPL insurance coverage yet.

> *"Policies should make clear what people can and cannot do. In addition, a policy should provide an internal vehicle for resolution of complaints."*

What so many risk managers and treasurers fail to realize is that companies can build a buffer against sexual harassment suits. "In terms of corporations' concerns of being socked with multi-million dollar lawsuits, there are so many things that have to happen before a case becomes a lawsuit," says EEOC Chairman Gilbert Casellas.

The first line of defense against a lawsuit is a good sexual harassment policy, but that doesn't mean three paragraphs on company letterhead. "You have to think of this as a due diligence issue," says Lynne Sullivan, senior consultant at Towers Perrin in Toronto, Canada.

The language that these policies contain is a hot topic in human resources and legal circles. But treasurers and risk managers should take a hand in crafting their company's policy, too, because a well-written and implemented policy could substantially reduce the costs associated with sexual harassment risk. Says Lieban: "When you look at the number of jury verdicts that have come down the pipeline, the cases with high punitive damages are usually the ones where the defendants have not instituted sexual harassment policies like this." (Litton's policy must be signed by each new employee.)

Policies Demonstrate Commitment

One way that these policies reduce risk, of course, is to prove in court that a company is firmly committed to the ideal of eliminating sexual harassment in the workplace. Not having a policy of some sort in place makes a company much more likely to be found guilty of having a "hostile environment" for female workers, according to EEOC guidelines.

Such a climate, which is now the most common type of harassment, can involve anything from nude photos in work spaces to outright verbal and physical abuse. The other type of legally recognized harassment is old-fashioned "quid pro quo," or the demand for sex in exchange for job security or promotion.

"You are managing the bottom line costs by demonstrating in court that you have policies and procedures in place, and that the culture has been modified because of them," says Lieban. "You want the harasser to look like the exception."

A third risk is so-called "same sex" harassment that may or may not have homosexual overtones. For example, J&J Snack Foods' case involved teasing and "horseplay," says CFO Moore. While J&J's case was fought at the state level in California, a similar federal case is now in front of the Supreme Court.

Providing for Resolution

A big step in preventing lawsuits, policies should make clear what people can and cannot do. In addition, a policy should provide an internal vehicle for resolution of complaints. Many companies use counseling or arbitration to resolve sexual harassment cases, or even just a series of discussions between a corporate referee and the parties involved.

For example, the Computer Corporation of America, a Framingham, Massachusetts–based software sales and services company, places a lot of emphasis on internal counseling to reduce litigation costs. Says Russell Lavoie, vice president of finance and administration at the $50 million company: "Internally, when issues come up, we deal with them swiftly, quickly, and at the lowest level possible."

So far, the strategy has worked. The company, which has 150 employees worldwide, has not yet been hit with a lawsuit. And at Mitsubishi, the company hired former Labor Secretary Lynn Martin to draft a new sexual harassment policy for the company. The policy establishes a dual structure to investigate, resolve and oversee disciplinary decisions in sexual harassment and other discrimination cases under 4,000 scenarios.

Such programs reduce costs, says Heather Smith, director of marketing and sales at Coregis, a Chicago-based insurance company. A strictly internal resolution, she says, costs an average of $5,000. The tab doubles to $10,000 when an attorney is brought in for arbitration, and then skyrockets to $100,000 or more for an actual trial. To implement such a policy, most companies are turning to two types of outside help—labor practice lawyers and organizations that offer employee training programs. Labor practice lawyers, also known as EPL attorneys, can help the risk manager and human resources department draft a sexual harassment policy, and can offer guidelines on how to implement it. They can also help a company cope with sexual harassment allegations before they reach the courts by providing counsel and arbitration, and give advice on the legality of different types of sanctions.

Training programs are another important way employers can reduce sexual harassment claims. "At the training sessions, the male side begins to see some recognition of issues that they never really thought about before," says James MacKinnon, vice president at the PACE Group, a diversity training company based in Farmington Hills, Mich. Another beneficial byproduct: Such sessions also demonstrate management's commitment to a harassment-free workplace.

Combating Sexism Will Reduce Sexual Harassment Among Schoolchildren

by Leora Tanenbaum

About the author: *Leora Tanenbaum writes on gender issues for magazines including* Ms., Mirabella, *and* In These Times.

A junior high school girl in Petaluma, Calif., known as Jane Doe was the target of an ugly and persistent rumor. In the fall of 1990, when she was in the seventh grade, classmates spread the word that Doe had a hot dog in her pants. Throughout the year Doe was repeatedly called a "hot dog bitch" and a "slut." And the rumor did not dissipate over the summer. When Doe returned to school the following year, the comments kept coming. One day a classmate stood up in the middle of English class and blatantly said, "This question is for Jane. Did you have sex with a hot dog?" The entire class laughed. Doe ran out in tears.

Unwanted Sexual Rumors

Doe's experience is far from rare. In fact, 42 percent of girls have had sexual rumors spread about them, according to a 1993 nationwide poll conducted for the American Association of University Women. In another survey, conducted by Nan Stein of Wellesley College in conjunction with the National Organization for Women (NOW) Legal Defense and Education Fund and distributed through *Seventeen* magazine, 89 percent of the teenage respondents said they had been the targets of unwanted sexual comments, gestures or looks. (Eighty-three percent said they had been touched, grabbed or pinched.) In two-thirds of the cases, other people were present.

The school "slut" typically endures cruel and sneering comments—"slut" is often interchangeable with "whore" and "bitch"—as she walks down the hallway, rides the school bus and gathers books from her locker. She is publicly humiliated in the classroom and cafeteria, targeted in boys' bathroom graffiti and

Reprinted from Leora Tanenbaum, "'Sluts' and Suits," *In These Times*, May 13, 1996, by permission of *In These Times*.

late-night prank phone calls. Teachers, generally speaking, do not intervene; they consider this behavior normal for teenagers.

Consider "Marcy," a Catholic girl from Queens then in the ninth grade, who was hanging out at a friend's house one evening when she drank so much she blacked out. A classmate raped her and then spread the news that they had had sex. Marcy, now a college sophomore, comments matter-of-factly that within hours she acquired a reputation as a "slut." "They'd call out 'slut' to me in the halls," she recalls. "There was graffiti." Everybody in the school knew about her, in all the grades. Marcy's reputation as a "slut" is so legendary that the new crop of incoming students at her old high school hears all about her each year.

I know what it feels like: I myself had been the subject of painful, mocking gossip in the spring of ninth grade. A friend felt betrayed after I dated a guy she'd had her eye on. In revenge, she spread the rumor that I was a "slut." It was my first lesson in the sexual double standard: Boys who bragged about their sexual status were routinely glorified, while I was belittled to an extraordinary degree. My sexuality (real or imagined) was, in effect, policed.

So what's a high school "slut" to do? Unfortunately, the solutions currently advocated by educators, many of whom consider "slut"-bashing a form of sexual harassment, are ineffective or impractical.

The NOW Legal Defense and Education Fund counsels schools to develop and enforce sexual harassment policies, so that a strong message is conveyed that verbal harassment will not be tolerated, that students know how to make a complaint and that punishments are speedy but fair. A student who is harassed by another student is advised to confront the harasser, if she feels safe and comfortable doing so. She is encouraged to write a letter to the harasser that describes the behavior, explains that it bothers her and says that she wants it to stop. This is said to be empowering and therapeutic for the student who is harassed.

But it can be incredibly difficult for anyone, let alone a child or adolescent, to confront her harasser personally. A group of 15 girls from Santa Clara High School in Santa Clara, Calif., recently banded together to complain to their school officials about boys who circulated sexual rumors, grabbed them and spit on them—and got the offenders suspended. But very often the one who is harassed is on her own, without any kind of support. In any event, in far too many cases school administrators are uninterested in developing or enforcing policies be-

> *"The solutions currently advocated by educators, many of whom consider 'slut'-bashing a form of sexual harassment, are ineffective or impractical."*

cause they don't consider sexual harassment (verbal or physical) a serious problem. Even when girls tell a teacher or administrator about incidents of harassment, nothing happens in 45 percent of the cases, according to the *Seventeen* study.

Recognizing these realities, and facing school officials who are not as quick to punish harassers as the Santa Clara officials were, a handful of "sluts" have chosen the legal route. In 1992, the United States Supreme Court unanimously ruled that students can collect monetary damages from schools for sexual harassment. The ruling in that case, *Franklin vs. Gwinnett County (Ga.) Public Schools*, applied to a student who alleged that a teacher made unwelcome sexual advances toward her during her sophomore year in high school, but it paved the way for student-to-student sexual harassment charges as well.

Students Can Sue Schools

As a form of sexual harassment, the taunting of "sluts" violates Title IX of the 1972 amendments to the Education Act, which guarantees equal access to education. Those who say they've been harassed don't have to file a complaint with the government; they can take their claims directly to court. Students who believe school officials have failed to prevent sexual harassment can file lawsuits against school districts within 180 days from the date of the last incident.

Since the Franklin ruling, several girls have already sued their school districts and settled out of court—such as a Midwestern girl whose name appeared on a list of the "25 most fuckable girls" that classmates circulated around her school. Her settlement, in 1993, was a mere $40,000. Today the stakes are much higher: Jane Doe is suing the Petaluma School District for $1 million.

> *"It is nearly impossible to fight the 'slut' label on the grounds of sexual harassment without strengthening the boundary between 'good' girls and 'bad' ones."*

Doe appears to have a strong case. She complained about the rumor repeatedly to the Kenilworth Junior High guidance counselor, Richard Homrighouse—at one point as often as five times a month. But Homrighouse did not lift a finger to help her. His attitude, she reports, was that students had free-speech rights to call her what they wanted and that, in any event, the name-calling was bound to stop sooner or later. It didn't, Doe became increasingly depressed, and as a result she transferred to another school. But her reputation was so well known that she was taunted even there. Finally, her parents moved her to a private school.

The monetary amount they are seeking is meant to include Doe's private school tuition and the costs of medical and psychological treatment. The federal district court dismissed Doe's Title IX damages claim because Doe failed to allege that the school engaged in intentional discrimination. But Doe's attorney has amended the complaint and a trial is currently pending.

Another pending case is that of Eve Bruneau, 14, who has filed a suit against the South Kortright Central School District in Delaware County, N.Y., because her teacher and school officials refused to intervene when boys would snap girls' bras, grab their breasts and call them names like "dog-faced bitch." Bruneau's teacher told her that people would call her names all her life, and that she would have to learn to deal with it. Like Doe, Bruneau dreaded going to her school so much that she was forced to transfer to another one.

Bruneau seeks to demonstrate that her school was guilty of intentional discrimination. "If we show malice," says Bruneau's attorney, Rick Rossein of the City University of New York Law School, "the school will be liable for both compensatory and punitive damages." And if the school is liable,

> *"Teenage girls have just as much a right to be sexual as boys do. Lawyers and others involved in sexual harassment claims need to remember that sexuality is not the same as sexism.*

officials will think twice before looking the other way at student-to-student harassment in the future. [A Federal jury rejected the claim in November 1996.]

These lawsuits, then, are important and necessary: They send a strong message to schools that they are obligated to try to halt cruel behavior and develop and enforce sexual harassment policies. The lawsuits also make it clear that verbal harassment can be just as damaging as physical attacks.

Lawsuits Focus on Sexuality, Not Sexism

But essential as they are, such suits also have some serious shortcomings. For one thing, the charge of sexual harassment implies that the problem is strictly gendered—that boys alone are responsible for harassing girls as "sluts." Yet nothing could be further from the truth. It is girls, not boys, who tend to be the most vicious name-callers and rumor-mongers. When the "slut" reputation is shoehorned into a legalistic framework, guilty girls get off the hook.

An even deeper problem is that lawsuits may actually promote, rather than inhibit, the targeting of girls as "sluts"—for litigation tends to reinforce the mindset that leads to girls being labeled "sluts" in the first place. Given the way suits are structured, with clear-cut victims and aggressors, it is nearly impossible to fight the "slut" label on the grounds of sexual harassment without strengthening the boundary between "good" girls and "bad" ones.

My own story is instructive. I never considered suing—I didn't even realize I could—but my reaction was typical of those who sue: I escaped into the persona of a celibate "good" girl. I feverishly sought to be known as a smart girl, not a sexual one. True, my bookish identity served me well—I succeeded academically both in high school and college—but it also made me miserable and inhibited. Looking back, I realize that my defense was a tacit endorsement of the system that says sexual girls are to be avoided while sexual boys are to be congratulated with a hearty slap on the back.

When a girl is waging a legal battle against being identified as sexually active, she shouldn't have to defend herself by claiming to be "good." Yet that is what inevitably occurs. The girl harassed as a "slut" can't be an innocent victim, the logic goes, unless she is sexually innocent.

It's precisely this mindset that led Katy Lyle—who sued her Duluth, Minn., high school because she was the object of graphic sexual graffiti and rumors—to present herself as a virginal "good" girl when she appeared on the *Donahue* show. Phil Donahue even hushed an audience member who inquired about Lyle's sexuality. ("If you weren't dating these guys," the audience member asked, "how did this all come about?") The complaints of a "slut" would never be taken seriously, the show seemed to suggest, if she were sexually active. Similarly, in an ABC "after-school special," a character who is based on Lyle was portrayed as totally asexual, her figure hidden beneath a baggy madras shirt. The program, which is used in schools across the country as a training tool, portrayed boys (with the exception of Lyle's brother) as oversexed perverts.

Only Good Girls Are Protected

Schools themselves are also perpetuating the idea that "good" girls are abstinent. Millis High School in Millis, Mass., went so far as to ban hand-holding, hugging and any other physical contact between students on school grounds. The school adopted the rule in response to a lawsuit brought against a football player who had raped or sexually assaulted 11 students. In its zeal to protect female students, administrators seem to have confused sexual harassment with female sexuality. If girls are "good," if they remain asexual, the policy implies, then they won't be harassed.

Small wonder that some former "sluts" themselves pick on others as "sluts." One college student, "Catherine," who settled her high school case out of court, tells me, "There's this 'slut' in the music department who we all pick on, and I'm guilty of it too. She has casual sex with different guys. I don't know why we don't gossip about the guys."

Is there any hard evidence against the music department "slut"? Come to think of it, she admits, there isn't. "We say things like, 'We saw her with so-and-so.' But nobody knows for sure if anything has happened. We just assume. But if the gossip starts to get graphic, then I get uncomfortable, and I let my discomfort be known. It's gotten me into trouble a few times, because people think I'm really bitchy." It seems that everyone, the school "slut" included, can always find someone less "good" than herself to police.

The lawsuits currently under way are important, but on their own they won't significantly alter the atmosphere that leads to vicious, sexist name-calling. For real progress to occur, teachers and school administrators need to be trained about sexual harassment, but they also need to be taught that teenage girls have just as much a right to be sexual as boys do. Lawyers and others involved in sexual harassment claims need to remember that sexuality is not the same as sexism. Otherwise, one girl in Petaluma may win a million dollars, but at the cost of denying girls' sexuality everywhere.

Sexual Equality in the Workplace Would Reduce Sexual Harassment

by James P. Sterba

About the author: *James P. Sterba is a professor of philosophy at the University of Notre Dame in Indiana.*

Contemporary feminists almost by definition seek to put an end to male domination and to secure women's liberation. To achieve these goals, many feminists support the political ideal of a gender-free or androgynous society. According to these feminists, all assignments of rights and duties are ultimately to accord with the ideal of a gender-free or androgynous society. Since a conception of justice is usually thought to provide the ultimate grounds for the assignment of rights and duties, I shall refer to this ideal of a gender-free or androgynous society as "feminist justice."

The Ideal Society

But how is this ideal to be interpreted? A gender-free or genderless society is a society where basic rights and duties are not assigned on the basis of a person's biological sex. Being male or female is not the grounds for determining what basic rights and duties a person has in a gender-free or genderless society. But this is to characterize the feminist ideal only negatively. It tells us what we need to get rid of not what we need to put in its place. A more positive characterization is provided by the ideal of androgyny. Putting the ideal of feminist justice more positively in terms of the ideal of androgyny also helps to bring out why men should be attracted to feminist justice.

In a well-known article, Joyce Trebilcot distinguishes two forms of androgyny. The first form postulates the same ideal for everyone. According to this form of androgyny, the ideal person "combines characteristics usually attributed to men with characteristics usually attributed to women." Thus, we should expect both

Reprinted by permission of the author from James P. Sterba, "Feminist Justice and Sexual Harassment in the Workplace," a paper submitted to the First World Congress of Business Economics and Ethics, 1996, Tokyo, Japan. *Endnotes in the original have been omitted in this reprint.*

nurturance and mastery, openness and objectivity, compassion and competitiveness from each and every person who has the capacities for these traits.

Equality in Diversity

By contrast, the second form of androgyny does not advocate the same ideal for everyone but rather a variety of options from "pure" femininity to "pure" masculinity. As Trebilcot points out, this form of androgyny shares with the first view that biological sex should not be the basis for determining the appropriateness of gender characterization. It differs in that it holds that "all alternatives with respect to gender should be equally available to and equally approved for everyone, regardless of sex."

It would be a mistake, however, to sharply distinguish between these two forms of androgyny. Properly understood, they are simply two different facets of a single ideal. For, as Mary Ann Warren has argued, the second form of androgyny is appropriate *only* "with respect to feminine and masculine traits which are largely matters of personal style and preference and which have little direct moral significance." However, when we consider so-called feminine and masculine *virtues*, it is the first form of androgyny that is required because, then, other things being equal, the same virtues are appropriate for everyone.

"A gender-free or genderless society is a society where basic rights and duties are not assigned on the basis of a person's biological sex."

We can even formulate the ideal of androgyny more abstractly so that it is no longer specified in terms of so-called feminine and masculine traits. We can specify the ideal as requiring no more than that the traits that are truly desirable in society be equally available to both women and men, or in the case of virtues, equally expected of both women and men.

Applying the Ideal to Sexual Harassment

One locus of change required by the ideal of a gender-free or androgynous society is rooted in the distribution of economic power in society, and it frequently takes the form of overt violence against women. It is the problem of sexual harassment. In what follows, I will focus on the problem as it arises in the United States. Actually, sexual harassment was not recognized as an offense by U.S. trial courts until the late 1970s, and it was only affirmed by the U.S. Supreme Court as an offense in the 1980s. The term "sexual harassment" itself was not even coined until the 1970s. So the moral problem of sexual harassment is one that many people have only recently come to recognize. The 1991 Senate Judiciary Committee hearings on Anita Hill's charge that Clarence Thomas had sexually harassed her obviously heightened people's awareness of this problem [at the time a nominee, Thomas is now a Supreme Court Justice].

According to various studies done over the last few years, sexual harassment is a widespread problem. In research done by psychologists, 50% of women in the workplace questioned said they had been sexually harassed. According to the U.S. Merit Systems Protection Board, within the federal government, 56% of 8,500 female workers surveyed claimed to have experienced sexual harassment. According to the *National Law Journal*, 64% of women in "pink-collar" jobs [support positions primarily held by women] reported being sexually harassed and 60% of 3000 women lawyers at 250

> *"We must guard against imposing special burdens on women in the workplace, when there are no comparable burdens imposed on men."*

top law firms said that they had been harassed at some point in their careers. In a recent survey by *Working Women* magazine, 60% of high-ranking corporate women said they have been harassed; 33% more knew of others who had been.

According to Ellen Bravo and Ellen Cassedy, humiliation is the term most commonly used by those who see themselves as sexually harassed to describe their experience. They see themselves as demeaned and devalued, and treated as sexual playthings. Many find themselves in a double-bind. If they fight, they could lose their jobs or alienate their boss or coworkers. If they don't fight, they could lose their self-respect. Many experience stress-related ailments: depression, sleep or eating disorders, headaches and fatigue, and take more days off from work as a result. The economic consequences for employers are also significant. A 1988 survey of 160 large manufacturing and service companies came up with the startling result: A typical Fortune 500 company with 23,750 employees loses $6.7 million a year because of sexual harassment. And this loss doesn't even include lawsuits. What it does include are financial losses due to absenteeism, lower productivity, and employee turnover. Another 1988 study showed that sexual harassment cost the federal government $267 million between 1985 and 1987. It cost $37 million to replace federal workers who left their jobs, $26 million in medical leave due to stress from sexual harassment and $204 million in lost productivity.

Defining Sexual Harassment

Given the seriousness of the problem, it is important to get clear about what constitutes, or should constitute, sexual harassment. In 1980, the Equal Employment Opportunity Commission (EEOC) issued guidelines finding harassment on the basis of sex to be a violation of Title VII of the Civil Rights Act of 1964, defining sexual harassment as "unwelcome sexual advances, requests for sexual favors, and other verbal or physical conduct of a sexual nature" when such behavior occurred in any of three circumstances:

1) where submission to such conduct is made either explicitly or implicitly a term or condition of an individual's employment,

2) where submission to or rejection of such conduct by an individual is used as the basis for employment decisions affecting the individual, or

3) where such conduct has the purpose or effect of unreasonably interfering with an individual's work performance or creating an intimidating, hostile, or offensive working environment.

In 1986, the U.S. Supreme Court in *Meritor Savings Bank v. Vinson* agreed with the EEOC, ruling that there could be two types of sexual harassment: harassment that conditions concrete employment benefits on granting sexual favors (often called the quid pro quo type) and harassment that creates a hostile or offensive work environment without affecting economic benefits (the hostile environment type).

Nevertheless, the Supreme Court made it difficult for a plaintiff to establish that either of these types of sexual harassment had occurred. For example, a polite verbal "no" does not suffice to show that sexual advances are unwelcome; a woman's entire conduct both in and outside the workplace is subject to appraisal to determine whether or not she welcomed the advances. For example, in the Vinson case there was "voluminous testimony regarding Vinson's dress and personal fantasies," and in the Senate Judiciary Committee hearings, Anita Hill was not able to prevent intensive examination of her private life, although Clarence Thomas was able to declare key areas of his private life as off-limits, such as his practice of viewing and discussing pornographic films.

Court Standards Promote Inequality

The Supreme Court also made it difficult to classify work environments as hostile to women unless the harassment is sufficiently severe or pervasive. Applying the Supreme Court's standard, a lower court in *Christoforou v. Ryder Truck Rental*, judged a supervisor's actions of fondling a plaintiff's rear end and breasts, propositioning her, and trying to force a kiss at a Christmas party to be "too sporadic and innocuous" to support a finding of a hostile work environment. Similarly, in *Rabidue v. Osceola Refining Co.*, a workplace where pictures of nude and scantily clad women abounded, including one, which hung on a wall for eight years, of a woman with a golf ball on her breasts and a man with his golf club, standing over her and yelling "fore," and where a co-worker, never

> *"A requirement that a man or woman run a gauntlet of sexual abuse in return for the privilege of being allowed to work and make a living can be as demeaning and disconcerting as the harshest of racial epithets."*

disciplined despite repeated complaints, routinely referred to women as "whores," "cunts," "pussy" and "tits" was judged by a lower court not to be sufficiently hostile an environment to constitute sexual harassment. Notice, by contrast, that the Senate Armed Services Committee, in its recent hearings, and now in fact the whole U.S. Congress regards an environment in which known homosexuals are simply doing their duty in the military to be too hostile an environment to ask particularly male heterosexuals to serve in.

Yet why should we accept the Supreme Court's characterization of sexual harassment, especially given its unwelcomeness and pervasiveness requirements?

> *"Equal opportunity is a moral requirement, and moral requirements are those that are reasonable for everyone to accept."*

As the Supreme Court interprets sexual harassment, a person's behavior must be unwelcome in a fairly strong sense before it constitutes sexual harassment. But why should a woman have to prove that an offer "If you don't sleep with me you will be fired" is unwelcome before it constitutes sexual harassment? Isn't such an offer objectively unwelcome? Isn't it just the kind of offer that those in positions of power should not be making to their subordinates—offers that purport to make their continuing employment conditional upon providing sexual favors? Surely, unless we are dealing with some form of legalized prostitution, such offers are objectively unwelcome.

Given, then, that such offers are objectively unwelcome, why is there any need to show that they are also subjectively unwelcome before regarding them as violations of Title VII of the Civil Rights Act? The requirement of subjective unwelcomeness is simply a gratuitous obstacle, which makes the plaintiff's case far more difficult to prove than it should be.

Special Burdens Are Imposed on Women

In addition, if the plaintiff is fired after refusing such an offer, the Supreme Court requires the plaintiff to prove that the firing occurred because the offer was refused, which is very difficult to do, unless one is a perfect employee. Wouldn't it be fairer, then, to require the employer to prove that the plaintiff would have been fired even if she had said "yes" to the offer? Of course, employers could avoid this burden of proof simply by not making any such offers in the first place. But when they do make objectively unwelcome offers, why shouldn't the burden of proof be on them to show that any subsequent firing was clearly unrelated to the plaintiff's refusal of such an offer? Fairness is particularly relevant in this context because we are committed to equal opportunity in the workplace, which requires employing women and men on equal terms. Accordingly, we must guard against imposing special burdens on women in the workplace, when there are no comparable burdens imposed on men. Feminist justice with its ideal of a gender-free or androgynous society will be satisfied with nothing less.

The demand for equal opportunity in the workplace also appears to conflict with the Supreme Court's pervasiveness requirement for establishing a hostile environment. Citing a lower court, the Supreme Court in *Vinson* contends that to be actionable, sexual harassment "must be sufficiently severe or pervasive 'to alter the conditions of the [victim's] employment and create an abusive working environment.'" But as this standard has been interpreted by lower courts, the pervasiveness of certain forms of harassment in the workplace has become grounds for tolerating them. In *Rabidue,* the majority argued, "[I]t cannot seriously be disputed that in some work environments, humor and language are rough hewn and vulgar. Sexual jokes, sexual conversations and girlie magazines abound. Title VII was not meant to—or can—change this. Title VII is the federal court mainstay in the struggle for equal employment opportunity for the female workers of America. But it is quite different to claim that Title VII was designed to bring about a magical transformation in the social mores of American workers."

> *"The offensiveness of sexually harassing speech becomes unacceptable from the standpoint of feminist justice when it undermines the equal opportunity of women in the workplace.*

The Supreme Court itself seems to sound a similar theme by emphasizing the application of Title VII to only extreme cases of sexual harassment as found in *Vinson.*

However, as the EEOC interprets Title VII, the law has a broader scope. Title VII affords employees the right to work in an environment free from discriminatory intimidation, ridicule and insult. According to the EEOC, sexual harassment violates Title VII where conduct creates an intimidating, hostile, or offensive environment or where it unreasonably interferes with work performance.

Definitions Do Not Support Equality

But how are we to determine what unreasonably interferes with work performance? In *Rabidue,* the majority look to prevailing standards in the workplace to determine what is reasonable or unreasonable. Yet Justice Keith, in dissent, questions this endorsement of the status quo, arguing that just as a Jewish employee can rightfully demand a change in her working environment if her employer maintains an anti-Semitic workforce and tolerates a workplace in which "kike" jokes, displays of nazi literature and anti-Jewish conversation "may abound," surely women can rightfully demand a change in the sexist practices that prevail in their working environments. In *Henson v. Dundee,* the majority also drew an analogy between sexual harassment and racial harassment:

> Sexual harassment which creates a hostile or offensive environment for members of one sex is every bit the arbitrary barrier to sexual equality at the workplace that racial harassment is to racial equality. Surely, a requirement that a man or woman run a gauntlet of sexual abuse in return for the privilege of being allowed to work and make a living can be as demeaning and disconcerting as the harshest of racial epithets.

And this passage is also quoted approvingly by the Supreme Court in *Vinson*.

Moved by such arguments, the majority in *Ellison v. Brady* propose that rather than look to prevailing standards to determine what is reasonable, we should look to the standard of a reasonable victim, or given that most victims of sexual harassment are women—the standard of a reasonable woman. They contend that this standard may be different from the standard of a "reasonable man." For example, what male superiors may think is "harmless social interaction" may be experienced by female subordinates as offensive and threatening.

Nevertheless, if we are concerned to establish the equal opportunity in the workplace that feminist justice with its ideal of a gender-free or androgynous society demands, there should be no question about what standard of reasonableness to use here. It is not that of a reasonable woman nor that of a reasonable man for that matter, but the standard of what is reasonable for everyone to accept. For equal opportunity is a moral requirement, and moral requirements are those that are reasonable for everyone to accept. This assumes that apparent conflicts over what is reasonable to accept, e.g., conflicts between the standard of a reasonable woman and the standard of a reasonable man, are conflicts that can and should be resolved by showing one of these perspectives is more reasonable than the other, or by showing that some still other perspective is even more reasonable. However, at least in the context of sexual harassment, this standard of what is reasonable for everyone to accept will accord closely with the standard of a reasonable woman, given that once women's perspectives are adequately taken into account, the contrasting perspective of a reasonable man will be seen as not so reasonable after all.

The Conflict with Free Speech

It is also important to recognize here that achieving equal opportunity in the workplace as required by the ideal of a gender-free or androgynous society will conflict, to some degree, with freedom of speech. Consider the recent case of *Robinson v. Jacksonville Shipyards*, in which a United States District Court upheld claims of sexual harassment on hostile work environment grounds, and issued extensive remedial orders. Plaintiff Lois Robinson was one of a very small number of female skilled craftworkers employed at the Shipyards, actually one of 6 out of 852 craftworkers. Her allegations of sexual harassment centered around "the presence in the workplace of pictures of women in various stages of undress and in sexually suggestive or submissive poses, as well as remarks by male employees and supervisors which demean women." Although there was some evidence of several incidents in which the sexually suggestive pictures and comments were directed explicitly at Robinson, most were not.

In analyzing this case, Nadine Strossen, past president of the American Civil Liberties Union (ACLU), argues that even sexually offensive speech should be protected unless it is explicitly directed at a particular individual or a particular group of individuals. Accordingly, Strossen endorses the ACLU's amicus brief in *Robinson v. Jacksonville Shipyards* case which regarded the court's ban on the public display of sexually suggestive material without regard to whether the expressive activity was explicitly directed at any employee as too broad. However, in light of the fact that Jacksonville Shipyards had itself banned all public displays of expressive activity except sexual materials, the amicus brief went on to favor the imposition of a workplace rule that would right the balance and permit the posting of other materials as well—materials critical of such sexual expression, as well as other political and religious or social messages which are currently banned. Such a rule would implement a "more speech" approach to counter offensive speech.

But would such a rule work? Would it work to protect the basic interests of women, especially their right to equal opportunity in the workplace? It is not clear that it would work in male-dominated workplaces like Jacksonville Shipyards, where women are a tiny minority of the workforce, and so they are apt to have their voices drowned out in the free market of expression that this rule would permit.

Inequality Is Offensive

Nor does Strossen's distinction between offensive speech explicitly directed at a particular person or group and offensive speech that is not so directed seem all that useful, given that most sexual harassment is directed at women not because they are Jane Doe or Lois Robinson, but because they are women. So why should we distinguish between sexual harassment that is explicitly directed at some particular woman because she is a woman, and sexual harassment that is only directed at some particular woman because it is explicitly directed at all women? Of course, sexually harassing speech can be more or less offensive, and maybe its offensiveness does correlate, to some degree, with the manner in which that harassment is directed at women. Nevertheless, what is crucial here is that the offensiveness of sexually harassing speech becomes unacceptable from the standpoint of feminist justice when it undermines the equal opportunity of women in the workplace—that is, when it imposes special burdens on women in the workplace where there are no comparable burdens on men. It is at that point that feminist justice requires that we impose whatever limitations on sexually harassing speech are needed to secure equal opportunity in the workplace.

I have argued in this viewpoint that the achievement of feminist justice requires changes that implement new programs against sexual harassment in the workplace in order to achieve that equal opportunity which feminist justice promises to everyone. These changes, and more, are required by feminist justice's ideal of a gender-free and androgynous society. Of course, these requirements were arrived at by examining the problem of sexual harassment as it exists in the U.S., but there is good reason to think that these requirements hold in other societies as well.

A Policy of Zero Tolerance Will Reduce Sexual Harassment in the Army

by Dennis J. Reimer

About the author: *Dennis J. Reimer has been chief of staff for the U.S. Army since June 20, 1995.*

Editor's note: The following viewpoint was excerpted from senate testimony delivered in response to allegations of rape and sexual harassment of enlisted women by male officers at the U.S. Army's Aberdeen Proving Grounds in November 1996.

It is a privilege for me to appear before you to report on any issue concerning the Army, even on one as troublesome as sexual harassment. I will provide you an assessment of how we have responded, and I assure you that the Army's senior leadership, led by the Secretary of the Army, is committed to eliminating sexual harassment and sexual misconduct across the Total Army. We have been as forthright as possible, and we are taking the steps necessary to rid the Army of a plight that detracts from morale and readiness, and most importantly, erodes basic human dignity.

Sexual Harassment Is Contrary to Army Values

We will deal with this issue head-on, not only because public scrutiny compels us, but also because the very idea that any soldier is forced to endure an act of sexual harassment is absolutely contrary to the basic principles that define the United States Army as a values-based institution. Duty, honor, courage, loyalty, integrity, respect and selfless service are the core values that define the essence of every soldier's character. However, the responsibility goes much deeper than that. Those of us serving in the Army today are caretakers with a solemn obligation to preserve this organization that has served our nation and

Reprinted from "On the Issue of Sexual Harassment and Misconduct in the United States Army," Dennis J. Reimer's statement before the Senate Armed Services Committee, February 4, 1997.

guarded its freedom for over two-hundred-twenty-one years. I don't want anyone to misunderstand that ultimately this issue must be and will be resolved by those of us wearing the uniform. We spent too much time helping make this Army what it is today to back away from what's required to make it even stronger.

To accomplish this vital task, we must openly and completely eliminate the circumstances that allow sexual harassment to take place. Sexual harassment, in any form, is repugnant to the Army's traditions and America's values. We have committed ourselves to providing an environment that is free of sexual harassment and free of the conditions that would spawn sexual misconduct. We will reaffirm our commitment to those principles by how we deal with the allegations that have been made.

> *"Sexual harassment, in any form, is repugnant to the Army's traditions and America's values."*

We have approached this situation with a crystal clear message—zero tolerance. Zero tolerance means that every Army leader will take immediate corrective action to address inappropriate conduct whenever and wherever it occurs. This might be as simple as ordering an offensive calendar off the wall, on-the-spot counseling of a group of soldiers for offensive comments, or as serious as preferring charges under the Uniform Code of Military Justice. As Secretary of Defense William S. Cohen recently said in an interview, "That zero means zero." The reason for zero tolerance is obvious in the military where a premium is put on teamwork, and when that element is missing or lacking, it can often lead to failure of the mission, or even injury or death. The Secretary continued, ". . . It is not acceptable . . . because a great deal depends on building moral [morale] and cohesion in units, and these are people who are going to be out putting their lives on the line, and we can't have that kind [of] conduct."

We will fix any menacing environment that intimidates soldiers and prevents them from coming forward, and we will ensure that those who do report instances of sexual harassment are not ostracized for their actions. We will take care to ensure that those accused and subsequently cleared are not further penalized. Any sexual harassment infraction will be dealt with swiftly and in a rational and measured way. Our approach is to instill values and develop a culture of respect for others regardless of race or gender.

Soldiers Must Trust Their Leaders

Our concern is not only with losing the trust and confidence of the American people but also with allowing circumstances to continue that erode the very foundation of the Army. As a values-based institution, soldiers must have absolute trust and confidence in their leaders. Soldiers must trust that their leaders are selfless, objective, knowledgeable, and dedicated to doing what is best for them, their unit, and the Army. They must be confident that their leaders' decisions always support these same core values. In short, they must have confidence in the chain of command, and that confidence must be earned.

Trust and confidence are intangibles, but I guarantee you that without them no organization, especially a military one, will be able to function and work as it should. Military leaders potentially have to make life and death decisions that affect their soldiers through the orders they issue. At the critical time when orders need to be followed without question, doubt and lack of confidence in the chain of command will cause casualties. Confidence and trust engender discipline, which saves lives. The circumstances that foster trust and confidence must prevail. Leader-subordinate relationships defined by these tenets are absolute and essential to mission accomplishment. It is no exaggeration to say that this is what makes the actions of those who use their leadership positions to sexually harass soldiers in their charge so repugnant.

We have a legitimate responsibility to fix any circumstances and climate that permits sexual harassment to occur. We are well aware that the Army's reputation has been tarnished by the allegations of sexual misconduct. We will conduct thorough and complete investigations of the allegations; if allegations are true, we will discipline individuals involved; and we will conduct an in-depth examination of any institutional climate that abetted these acts. To do anything less would further erode the institution we are so ardently striving to preserve, and which we are so proud of.

Sending the Zero-Tolerance Message

We have begun several initiatives, and I would like to discuss them with you. Some of these programs were in place before the recent allegations surfaced, others are in direct response.

As the Army's Chief of Staff for the past nineteen months, I have preached values to soldiers at every opportunity, but particularly by speaking to all of the battalion and brigade pre-command courses at Fort Leavenworth, Kansas. This course is attended by every lieutenant colonel and colonel commander selected to lead soldiers, including program managers and specialists like physicians. I have continually highlighted the importance of caring for our soldiers and the commander's solemn responsibility to create an environment in their units that sends the zero-tolerance message to their soldiers. This message is repeated at the Sergeants' Major Academy where the future leaders of the Army's Non-commissioned Officer Corps are trained.

> *"The circumstances that foster trust and confidence must prevail. Leader-subordinate relationships defined by these tenets are absolute and essential to mission accomplishment."*

Additionally we are conducting training on sexual harassment at all levels of institutional schooling to include initial entry; officer, warrant officer, and non-commissioned officer basic and advance courses; first sergeant and command sergeants major courses; Command and General Staff College, and Pre-command courses. Our recent experience is causing us to go back and review this instruction as well as add an additional course at the Army War College where we had not taught it before.

I also tasked the Deputy Chief of Staff for Personnel to develop a "Chain Teaching" packet on sexual harassment, and I was personally involved in its preparation. In fact, the packet contains a videotape with a segment where the Sergeant Major of the Army and I personally introduce the subject. The major point we stress is that sexual harassment, in any form, will not be tolerated in the Army. Along with the tape, commanders receive slides with a prepared text. The training program explains what sexual harassment is, how individuals should handle a sexual harassment incident, and the fact that sexual harassment, in any form, will not be tolerated in the Army.

Commanders Set the Example

The packet, which includes a segment that tells leaders how to conduct the training, and outlines their specific responsibilities, was distributed to the field on January 27, 1997. I have directed that all soldiers receive the training directly from their brigade or battalion commanders—no lower. This is a chain-of-command issue, and that's why I'm charging commanders with the responsibility to deliver the message and set the climate in their units. Units are required to conduct the training and will report back up through the chain-of-command when the training is complete. We recognize, however, that this issue is far more complex than this, and plan to follow up with a more detailed sustainment program patterned after the successful "Consideration of Others" program implemented at West Point.

The Sergeant Major of the Army and I also have embarked on a program to visit Army installations where our drill sergeants train our young soldiers. As a former basic training company commander, I know that life in our training centers is stressful, particularly for those great drill sergeants. The purpose of our visits is two-fold: first, to let them know that I have the greatest respect and admiration for all they do and that we know that 99+ percent are the Army's best. Second, we need to reaffirm to them and ensure they know they have our full support in their vital mission. We cannot let the alleged misconduct of a few detract from the absolutely superb job being done by the finest trainers in the world. There has been no fanfare associated with these visits, but by word-of-mouth the story is getting out.

Earning Respect

We need to instill in our soldiers a basic belief that soldiers take care of each other regardless of race or gender. We must ensure that respect for the chain-of-command is absolute and that that respect has been duly earned. We ask soldiers to sacrifice many things, but we must never ask them to sacrifice their dignity. Soldiers must know they are respected, and commanders at all levels need to recognize the weight of their responsibility to care for their soldiers.

I firmly believe that we will come out of this a much stronger institution. The key to how well we do lies in two things. First, the chain-of-command must execute and set the example—to do what's right legally and morally. Secondly, we have to reemphasize the importance of values. One of those values is respect—respect for the chain-of-command and for each other. We need to not only talk about it a lot, but also most importantly, we must exemplify it.

I often say that "soldiers are our credentials," because they truly are. They ask for so little and they do so much for our Army and for the Nation. As General Creighton W. Abrams once said, "The Army is not made up of people—the Army is people." Our soldiers—the Nation's credentials—deserve every ounce of respect and admiration that we can give them. They are entitled to duty and living conditions free of harassment and prejudices of any kind. I am committed to this, the Army's leadership is committed to this, and we will intensively focus our efforts and resources on delivering a quality environment for America's sons and daughters so they can be all that they can be.

Lawsuits Are Not the Solution to Sexual Harassment

by Sarah J. McCarthy

About the author: *Sarah J. McCarthy is a restauranteur and writes on sexual harassment issues for* Forbes, Regulation, *and* Restaurant Business.

Mitsubishi Motors, facing what is threatening to become the biggest sexual harassment case in history, gave 3,000 of its employees a day off with pay to demonstrate against a lawsuit filed by 29 fellow employees with the Equal Employment Opportunity Commission (EEOC). [Mitsubishi voluntarily settled with the EEOC in June 1998 for $34 million.]

One of the protesters, Kathleen McLouth, 42, a parts-deliverer at the Mitsubishi Motors plant near Chicago, exhibited more common sense than the collective wisdom of the National Organization for Women, Congress, and the U.S. Supreme Court when she said, "Sexual harassment has got to exist—you can't have 4,000 people and not have it exist."

The Cure Is Worse than the Disease

This does not mean, of course, that McLouth wants sexual harassment to exist, or that she approves of it, but that she knows it will recur as inevitably as crabgrass or stinkweed. When weeds or pests appear on the scene, most of us have learned the big lesson of Vietnam—that it's better not to destroy a village we're trying to save. When you call the Weed-B-Gone man, you don't expect him to blow up your house.

Unfortunately, when it comes to sexual harassment law, Congress and the Supreme Court have concocted a cure that's worse than the disease. A sort of sexual harassment hysteria has erupted because of a definition so broad and so vague as to cause people like Bernice Harris, 58, a cashier in the U.S. Senate cafeteria, to be accused of harassment for calling her customers "honey" and

Reprinted from Sarah J. McCarthy, "The Sexual Harassment Lemon Law," *The Freeman*, December 1996, by permission of *The Freeman*.

"sugar." Being called "baby," complained Christopher Held, an employee of Senator Mitch McConnell, was "real bothersome."

In the days before $300,000 fines could be levied for a "sweetie" in the cafeteria line, such petty slights would have been overlooked. To ignore a slight nowadays is like tossing out a winning lottery ticket.

With global sales of $38 billion, Mitsubishi employs workers who are among the best paid in the auto industry, but has only one assembly plant in the United States—the one being sued for sexual harassment. "I get fair wages. I get fair benefits. There's an opportunity for me to move up," says Jane Hieser, a 43-year-old body shop worker. "I get better backing here as a woman than I've ever gotten before."

> *"When it comes to sexual harassment law, Congress and the Supreme Court have concocted a cure that's worse than the disease."*

Hieser sounds like the women I heard testify at the trial of a bartender at the former Pittsburgh Sports Garden, a nightspot frequented by Steelers, Penguins, Pirates, and their fans. Many women said it was the best place they'd ever worked before it collapsed under the weight of a sexual harassment suit. Though the owners knew nothing about the dispute between a bartender and a waitress, the small business closed down the day the guilty verdict was announced.

Sexual harassment lawsuits can be job crushers, and if the damages are big enough they can destroy a company. The way the current sexual harassment law is constructed, the company and totally innocent employees pay a bigger price than the actual harasser.

Everyone Pays the Price

The economic threat to a company through a class-action lawsuit is often so large as to border on extortion, but the threat of economic extinction is only part of the picture. The employees of Mitsubishi are in for a rough, ugly ride where their sexual histories, family relationships, and workplace interactions are dragged into the courtroom like a huge pile of dirty laundry. Every workplace comment, joke, flirtation, and relationship will be grist for the mill. The ugly soap opera could end relationships and marriages. The media, lawyers, and sexual harassment crusaders will pick over the details of workers' lives like vultures feeding on a carcass. Some of those involved will profit mightily.

Just as in a family quarrel or a divorce, no one will ever agree on what really happened—whether the women involved were damaged, whether they did or didn't bring the harassment on themselves, or whether they were just trying to win some easy money. Their character and the reputations of witnesses on both sides will be impugned. Careers will be derailed.

In the end the Mitsubishi plant may be prosperous enough to survive this lawsuit. But given the near impossibility of monitoring the sexual speech of over 4,000 workers who may be dating, flirting, breaking up, or fighting, it's likely they may decide against opening additional assembly plants in the United States. The necessity of extensive monitoring by employers who are trying to protect themselves from sexual harassment lawsuits should raise concerns about the chilling effects on free speech and freedom of association. The silencing of workplace clowns, elimination of social gatherings, and implementation of no-dating policies are the usual outcomes of sexual harassment lawsuits.

If the case goes to trial, it's a near certainty that the plant's culture will be destroyed. Employee will be pitted against employee, man against woman, friend against friend, and everyone will blame someone else while the real culprits—the National Organization for Women, the trial lawyers' lobby, and the Congress of the United States, who were the architects of this incendiary law—will remain self-righteously above the fray.

Sensible Alternatives

There are, of course, many more sensible ways to curb sexual harassment, or any other kind of harassment, in the workplace. Counseling and mediation, backed up by escalating fines and firings if the problem remains unresolved, could actually induce more women to report earlier. At present many hold back complaints because the fallout is so draconian. Alternative, common-sense solutions, however, lack the glories and moral victories sought by sexual harassment crusaders and their big-government allies. There would be no lottery-size wins and banner headlines for the crusaders and their lawyers. Resolving a problem through the sensible-shoes approach is not as thrilling as hobbling a multinational corporation.

> *"The media, lawyers, and sexual harassment crusaders will pick over the details of workers' lives like vultures feeding on a carcass."*

After the crusaders have marched off to the next glorious battle, Kathleen McLouth and Jane Hieser may be left like soot-covered soldiers on a deserted battlefield without a workplace and without jobs. Defective cars that roll off the Mitsubishi Motors assembly plant are subject to recall under the lemon law. It's time to repair the sexual harassment lemon law.

Banning Erotic Words and Pictures Will Not Reduce Sexual Harassment

by Feminists for Free Expression

About the author: *Feminists for Free Expression is an organization devoted to defending freedom of speech and opposing censorship of sexually explicit material.*

Feminists for Free Expression (FFE) is deeply concerned about sexual harassment in schools and workplaces, and believes that gender-based harassment—like all serious social problems—requires thoughtful, fundamental solutions. We are alarmed by the facile proposals popular today among some policy makers and activists who claim that banning a list of "bad" words and images will improve the condition of women. It will not. Such quick fix solutions ignore the substantive causes of sexual harassment and establish restrictions on words and images that will harm women's interests. Without this country's tolerance for a broad range of words and images, women could never have founded a feminist movement—considered dangerous and sinful by many Americans—25 years ago. Without that tolerance, the goals of women will be harmed today.

> Sanitizing workplace speech in defense of women workers enshrines archaic stereotypes of women as delicate, asexual creatures who require special protection from mere words and images.

> —From FFE's brief to the United States Supreme Court in *Harris v. Forklift Systems, Inc.*

When Harassment Becomes Censorship

Current law defines sexual harassment as a form of discrimination, and generally protects against harassment on the basis of race and religion, as it should. The law recognizes two forms of sexual harassment: (1) "quid pro quo" harassment, which typically involves a supervisor's demand for sexual favors, and (2) "hostile work environment" harassment, which holds that offensive words and pictures can hinder women's ability to work or study.

FFE emphatically supports laws prohibiting quid pro quo harassment and hostile work environments, except when hostile work environment policies are misused to censor controversial opinions voiced in schools or work-places or expressed in books, magazines, etc.

As a remedy to sexual harassment, some activists and policy makers propose to ban all erotic words and pictures, without regard to the damage such broad restrictions would do to women's expression—including expression about sexual issues. In the last 25 years, women have won the right to talk about sex, reproduction, contraception and pleasure. Overbroad restrictions on sexual material would return women to the confining "propriety" from which they worked so hard to escape.

> *"Overbroad restrictions on sexual material would return women to the confining 'propriety' from which they worked so hard to escape."*

In our briefs to the Supreme Court in the recent *Harris v. Forklift Systems* case, and in other courts, FFE has advocated that a work or school environment becomes hostile when an employee suffers physical abuse such as unwanted touching and quid pro quo pressures. Words alone may constitute a hostile work environment when an employee suffers a pattern of targeted and/or intentional verbal abuse. Controversial, offensive opinions, books or posters—even sexist ones—should not constitute sexual harassment unless they are directed to harass individual workers or additional evidence shows discriminatory intent to harass women or minority workers.

Censorship Hurts Women

Should the law prohibit all words and pictures that someone in a workplace or school finds offensive, much speech—certainly, much interesting speech—would soon be illegal. Women's speech might well be thought offensive because it runs counter to a worker's religious beliefs. Feminist material on reproductive choice would be particularly vulnerable. Should the state force a woman to remove a pro-choice poster or magazine article from her office because another worker finds it objectionable? History teaches us that once in place, censorship schemes are used to stifle feminist advocacy of social change. Birth control pioneer Margaret Sanger was jailed under censorship laws; today in Canada, feminist books (ironically, including two by Andrea Dworkin, who has long advocated restrictions on erotic speech) have been prosecuted by the courts and seized by customs under the shadow of a new, ostensibly "feminist" obscenity law.

Those who focus on sexual speech, presuming it to be inherently offensive to women, miss the point. Gender-based harassment should be illegal whether or not it relies on sexual language or imagery. A woman is likely to be more intimidated by comments that she is "slow" or "dumb" than by sexual jokes. Moreover, women themselves make and enjoy sexual banter. Overbroad restrictions on sexual material infantilizes women and shores up destructive Victorian stereotypes that women are (or should be) so pure that any expression about sexuality offends and demoralizes them. This is not a feminist position.

Finally, a focus on sexual material diverts attention from the underlying causes of harassment. Gender-based harassment (whether it uses sexual or non-sexual language) is typically a power play by men who feel threatened by women's progress toward equality or even by their presence. It is the deeply-rooted social causes of such hostility that policy makers need to address.

Abusive demands for sexual favors and targeted verbal harassment should be addressed at all levels—legal, educational and in personnel offices. Research shows that sexual harassment is most likely where women are few in number. Where women make up a good portion of the work force (including at high-level positions), sexual harassment decreases. The most potent remedy to sexual harassment is to increase the number of women

> *"Should the law prohibit all words and pictures that someone in a workplace or school finds offensive, much speech–certainly, much interesting speech–would soon be illegal."*

in the work-place—a real advance for women rather than the window dressing that image-banning provides.

It is precisely because FFE is concerned about the causes of gender-based harassment and wants to see real solutions that we oppose misguided, ineffectual campaigns against supposedly "bad" words and images. They are meaningless substitutes for measures that will benefit women in school and on the job.

> The urge to censor "offensive" expression in pursuit of lofty goals is ever a strong force in our society, and one which has of late made itself increasingly felt in American culture. It is, however, an urge the First Amendment requires that we staunchly resist, in favor of the fundamental values of tolerance, pluralism, and the free exchange of ideas.

—From FFE's brief to the Unites States Supreme Court in *Harris v. Forklift Systems, Inc.*

Chapter 4

Are Legal Definitions of Sexual Harassment Useful?

Legal Definitions of Sexual Harassment: An Overview

by Gloria Jacobs and Angela Bonavoglia

About the authors: *Gloria Jacobs is the editor of* Ms. *magazine. Angela Bonavoglia is contributing editor to* Ms. *magazine and the author of* The Choices We Made: 25 Women and Men Speak Out About Abortion.

Ruby S. was working late one night when the supervisor of her department at a large banking firm came up behind her and started massaging her back. She hadn't been working for the company long; didn't know the guy very well; and didn't particularly like him: "He was a little too slick for my taste." She turned to him and said, "Thanks for the back rub, but I have to go; I'm meeting someone in a few minutes." He laughed, let go of her shoulder, and asked, "Who's the lucky guy?" As he helped her on with her coat, he brushed his hand over her hair, tucking a strand behind her ear. She grabbed her things and got out of there, even though she still had a lot of work to do on an important project that was due the following week. "He gave me the creeps," she says, "but I never felt like I could be more firm about telling him to leave me alone, because it had taken a long time to find that job, and I really liked it except for him. I didn't want to risk losing it." After about six months, she switched to another department with another supervisor. Her ex-boss stayed right where he was.

What exactly was going on in Ruby's office? Was it sexual harassment? Was it illegal? Was it someone trying to be friendly who just wasn't Ruby's type? And who gets to decide? Ruby? Her boss? Her company? A judge?

A Need for Clarity

If you asked ten different people those questions, you'd probably get ten different answers. The truth is that just as the United States has become mired in media overkill on the topic of sexual harassment—was it or wasn't it? Did he or didn't he?—many people of perfectly good intentions have absolutely no idea what such harassment really is. Short of the most egregious cases, we still don't "get it."

The lack of clarity at all levels has left corporate counsels shaking in their boots, haunted by visions of financial ruin (sales of employment practices insurance, which covers sexual harassment settlements, have more than doubled since 1997, from $100 million to over $200 million, according to *U.S. News & World Report*). Government employees and workers in companies and universities all across the country, private and public, large and small, are completely confused—many are convinced that the new rules forbid everything from flirting to joking to falling in love with your cubicle mate.

> *"Sexual harassment law . . . is constantly evolving as each new case comes before the courts and establishes new precedents."*

Confusion may be inevitable when it comes to personal relations: so much of it is based on nuance, anyway. But it's also true that sexual harassment law, perhaps more than most, *is* constantly evolving as each new case comes before the courts and establishes new precedents. Thus, what today would be a perfectly obvious (and winnable) case of harassment—a woman loses her job because she won't sleep with her boss—was far from obvious to judges in the early 1970s.

The Evolution of a Definition

Discrimination based on race, color, religion, national origin, or sex was outlawed in 1964 by Title VII of the Civil Rights Act. But over the next decade more than one sexual harassment case was lost when judges ruled that being punished for refusing to have sex with your boss had nothing to do with discrimination per se—these were "personal" relationships—and therefore did not fall under Title VII. Eventually several cases were successfully argued—by lawyers who claimed that because of the sexual stereotyping of women, an unwanted sexual advance by a person with supervisory power did amount to discrimination. In 1980, the Equal Employment Opportunity Commission (EEOC), which enforces federal antidiscrimination laws (some states have their own laws, in addition), issued specific guidelines on sexual harassment. Title VII covered nonsexual harassment as well, the kind used to keep women from competing with men for jobs—such as tampering with their work or equipment, threatening them, or deliberately jeopardizing their safety. But the EEOC emphasized sexual relations—the guidelines focused only on harassment between members of the opposite sex, and so have the courts over the years. It was not until March 4, 1998, that the Supreme Court declared same-sex harassment (whether against gays or straights) illegal.

The EEOC's guidelines identified two types of harassment: quid pro quo and hostile environment. As more and more cases were won using these categories, legal precedents were established, and expectations of what was acceptable behavior began ponderously but steadily shifting, like tectonic plates lumbering under the earth. As with many of the changes feminism has brought about, the idea that men—and some women—would have to question male prerogatives has elicited hostility and hosannas, as well as bewilderment and confusion. This discomfort, along with fear of litigation, has frequently led employers to overreact: if they don't know for sure where the line is, they'll draw it far enough back so hardly anyone can claim they didn't know they were stepping over it. Often companies end up with policies that don't make distinctions between office romances (given all the hours we spend at work, where else are we going to find a date or a mate?) and harassment.

Quid pro quo is Latin for "this for that"—it involves a boss demanding sexual favors in exchange for things like a job, a promotion, a raise, or benefits. Sexual favoritism is an offshoot of quid pro quo: it postulates that if a boss has sex with an employee and gives her promotions, better hours, and other benefits in return, the other women on the job can argue that they're being penalized for not sleeping with the boss.

It took 12 years for quid pro quo to be recognized by the courts. In 1976 in *Williams v. Saxbe*, a district court in Washington, D.C., finally ruled that sexual harassment is a form of unlawful sex discrimination. A year later, a higher court, the D.C. court of appeals, one of the most influential courts in the country, concurred. In *Barnes v. Costle*, the court ruled that having a job be "conditioned upon submission to sexual relations" was illegal. In response to *Barnes* and several big settlements that followed it, many employers took drastic steps, banning all romantic involvement between supervisors and their subordinates. The same thing happened in universities that created policies forbidding teachers from having a sexual relationship with students.

> *"Sexual harassment is deliberate, repeated, unwelcome, not asked for, and not returned."*

No-Dating Policies

Not surprisingly, there's a lot of disagreement about the effect of such sweeping policies. Some people believe they are essential, others say they rob us of the ability to make personal decisions. In 1997, the president and chief operating officer of Staples, the office supply giant, resigned after it was revealed that he had had a consensual affair with his secretary. Staples' policy was that anyone in a close reporting relationship with another employee is prohibited from sexual relations with that person. That resignation received a great deal of media attention and set off a lot of second-guessing—the man was considered a top-notch leader, and if the woman consented, and he didn't show her any favoritism at work, who was harmed?

What is surprising in all the debate about no-dating's pros and cons is that, despite backlash rantings in the media against puritanical feminists, few feminists involved in workplace issues actually support policies like Staples'. "A no-dating policy is a quick-fix solution," insists Ellen Bravo, codirector of 9to5, a working women's advocacy group, "and a foolish policy." Carol Sanger, who teaches sexual harassment law at Columbia University in New York City, says these policies simply set women up as victims. "What women don't need is for the law to say, 'Guess what, you thought you were consenting to have sex, but we say you couldn't possibly have, because you're in an inferior power position, you're only a secretary.' Women's sexuality has been repressed too long. Let them consent." On the other hand, warns Sanger, if the initiator of an unwanted sexual advance is the person with more power, they must be willing to pay the price, if necessary: "If you fuck around with your young employees or your students, and they decide they're injured, then the risk should be on your head."

Defining a Hostile Environment

The Supreme Court first addressed the issue of sexual harassment in a 1986 ruling that set precedent by recognizing "hostile environment" harassment. In *Meritor Savings Bank v. Vinson*, the Court ruled that harassment could occur even if the victim hadn't lost any job benefits. In this case, the plaintiff had slept with her boss, but the justices said that he had sexualized the workplace to such an extent that it amounted to a hostile environment—which, according to the EEOC guidelines, consists of "unwelcome sexual advances, requests for sexual favors, and other verbal or physical conduct of a sexual nature" when it affects employment, interferes with work performance, or creates "an intimidating, hostile, or offensive working environment."

Since *Meritor*, the largest number of legal cases brought to the courts involve hostile environment. It is also the murkiest area of the law. What type of sexual conduct are we talking about exactly? When does harmless workplace behavior morph into a potentially hostile environment? When a guy e-mailing "The 50 Worst Things About Women" to several of his buddies hits the "all" key by mistake? When a man asks a female coworker for a date by e-mail, then voice mail, then sends a fax, then goes back to e-mail again, even though she has said no each time? When a male manager insists on checking a problem with a female coworker's computer and leans over her shoulder and whispers compliments in her ear? When the guys in the mail room begin the day with the latest raunchy joke, within

> *"At the core of sexual harassment law lies a concept that the 'victim' gets to decide if she has been victimized."*

obvious earshot of an older woman worker? When a male professor uses *Hustler* to teach female anatomy despite students' concerns? When a female administrator whose office brims with posters and cartoons that rag on men is assigned a male office mate?

With the exception of the e-mail of the "50 Worst Things" (assuming it was a one-time mistake, and recognizing the risk of using company e-mail for personal communiqués), all of the other examples may amount to sexual harassment. "Sexual harassment is deliberate, repeated, unwelcome, not asked for, and not returned," says Susan Webb, the author of *Shades of Gray*, a guide on sexual harassment in the workplace. Her Seattle-based consulting firm that advises corporations on preventing harassment was one of the first to enter the field.

Companies React with Strict Policies

Firms like Webb's are multiplying because most companies feel they're on shaky ground when it comes to figuring out what a hostile environment is. "Sexual harassment is not black and white," says Webb. "You've got to take the whole thing in the context in which it occurred." It's not surprising that some of the examples given above could leave people scratching their heads. And many companies have established guidelines that go beyond the EEOC or their state laws. So you could lose your job for having violated company rules, but not have committed an illegal act. Companies are creating these policies because

> *"This attempt to give some flexibility to the law and prevent frivolous lawsuits has led to endless legal debates about just what is 'reasonable' in a multicultural society, anyway."*

they are legally liable if they knew or should have known that harassment existed and failed to act. So far, the courts have said that the company is somewhat less liable for a hostile environment than for quid pro quo harassment, but most employers are trying to avoid as much risk as possible. With the sheer potential for liability—there are 137.6 million people working in the U.S.—and the damage that can be done to a carefully honed corporate image by one sensational suit, many employers have gone off the deep end in their efforts to control personal behavior.

Often, they've turned to what are known as "zero tolerance" policies. These say, in effect, one wrong move and you're out the door. But how to interpret that wrong move? Employers develop exhaustive lists of all the behaviors that won't be tolerated, which they generally post and distribute. Some behaviors on the lists are understandable: no unwelcome physical contact; and some are unrealistic: absolutely no touching. "One of my favorite examples of the stupidity of these lists," says Freada Klein, a longtime consultant on corporate policy, "is when some corporation did the typical thing after a lawsuit. They overreacted and put in a policy that said no touching ever. One of the first complaints came from someone who had observed a manager embracing his secretary—well, she had just found out her mother had died and he came out and consoled her."

When it comes to the people who truly use these behaviors to harass, the lists don't do much good, insists Klein. "Do you really think that someone who would engage in that kind of behavior, if they had a laminated card in their pocket with dos and don'ts, would decide not to act that way?" This rigid approach is "bizarre, insulting, infantilizing, and ineffective." She adds: "For every other workplace issue, we're talking about driving decision-making down. On this one, we say, 'You can't think for yourself, you're not a grown-up, you will only do as you're told.'"

Some Schools Overreact

Schools are another place where a "dos and don'ts" approach to harassment can melt down into the ludicrous. In 1996, two little boys, ages 6 and 7, were accused of sexual harassment for stealing kisses (and, in one case, the button of a dress) from female classmates. Each was briefly suspended from his school. The impetus was fear of liability by the schools involved: families have been successfully suing school districts for sexual harassment involving kids. And plenty of awful cases abound. A study by the American Association of University Women (AAUW) has shown that harassment of teenage girls in middle and high schools is pervasive and has devastating effects.

Based on its own studies, as well as reports like the AAUW's, and complaints received by the agency, in 1997 the U.S. Department of Education issued guidelines for stopping student-to-student harassment, as well as harassment between students and teachers, that hold schools responsible for their implementation. Unfortunately, despite the fact that the guidelines made distinctions according to age, cases like the ones involving the two little boys indicate, as in corporate America, a tendency to overreact, to see discipline problems involving children of different genders as harassment, and to disregard what any good educator should know: moral standards develop with age. "A 12-year-old's understanding of what is right and wrong on this subject can be very different from what a 7-year-old thinks," Gwendolyn Gregory, who was the deputy general counsel for the National School Boards Association at the time of the incidents, told the Washington *Post*.

The cases involving these young boys were exceptional, but they re-

> *"Others argue that men should know by now when their behavior is unacceptable, it shouldn't be up to women to teach them."*

ceived an enormous amount of derogatory press, some of it implying that sexual harassment as a concept was so off the wall, it made these kinds of cases inevitable. "By playing up the ridiculous, the exaggerations, or the aberrations, what the right wing tries to do is make it seem that that's the main thing that's going on, and it isn't," argues Ellen Bravo. "The main thing going on in the schools is not a 6-year-old being kicked out for kissing a girl on the cheek, but grabbing, groping, and sexual assault that borders on criminal behavior. By trivializing sexual harassment that way, they can dismiss it."

At the core of sexual harassment law lies a concept that the "victim" gets to decide if she has been victimized. (This strikes fear in the hearts of many—and may have contributed to employer overreaction.) If a coworker tells dirty jokes in your presence, and they don't bother you—you laugh along with everyone else—that's not harassment. If a coworker tells those same jokes as part of a pattern of hostility that makes you so uncomfortable it's hard to do your job, it's harassment. To those who have to implement the law, this can seem like a fairly subjective standard. Especially when it comes to trying to win a case in court. Recognizing that, the courts have ruled that the standard must be that of the so-called reasonable person. Because most plaintiffs in sexual harassment cases have been women, the standard is often referred to as that of a "reasonable woman."

> *"Topping off the debate on what's reasonable is the question of bigotry. Is someone's homophobia . . . reasonable because a lot of people might share it?"*

This woman is a kind of Jane Doe/Everywoman: not too sensitive, not too idiosyncratic, sort of "just right," like Goldilocks' porridge. It would seem like an impossible task to figure out what's "reasonable" under such an amorphous standard. But the point, many lawyers insist, is that women do have a certain experience of the world that the courts should take into account. "We realize there's a broad range of viewpoints among women as a group," says Carol Sanger, "but we believe many women share common concerns which men do not necessarily share. For example, because women are disproportionately victims of rape and sexual assault, women have a stronger incentive to be concerned with sexual behavior. If a man gets a note from a female coworker who's been making sexual overtures, he's not afraid she's going to come up behind him in the parking lot one night."

Speaking Up

But this attempt to give some flexibility to the law and prevent frivolous lawsuits has led to endless legal debates about just what is "reasonable" in a multicultural society, anyway. One of the biggest areas of contention involves the issue of speaking up. Because the law gives the victim the power to decline the offense, many lawyers feel strongly that, when possible and safe, women ought to let the potential harasser know that his behavior is offensive. One law professor describes an incident when she served as ombudsman for her students. "A girl comes in and tells me that a guy says to her, 'I'd love to see you naked.' I say to her, what did you do? And she says, 'Well, I giggled and ran into my room.' That wasn't good enough. All you have to do is say, 'Don't do that to me again.'" A few days later, the woman came back, furious that she was expected to confront her fellow student. The professor eventually convinced her to write a letter, if for no other reason than to document his behavior should he repeat it. In this case, says the professor: "he really didn't know it was wrong. This is a guy who lives in a completely sexualized culture and he's a complete nerd and he's trying to be cool."

Others argue that men should know by now when their behavior is unacceptable, it shouldn't be up to women to teach them, and it isn't always possible to speak to a harasser. "In principle, it makes sense," says Katherine Franke, a professor of law at New York City's Fordham University, who specializes in sexual harassment. "But as a practical matter, a lot of women don't feel in a position to say to their boss, cut that out. What the law requires is often very different from what people feel empowered to do."

Topping off the debate on what's reasonable is the question of bigotry. Is someone's homophobia, for example, reasonable because a lot of people might share it? Vicki Schultz, a professor at Yale Law School in New Haven, Connecticut, describes a case in which a gay man was sued by a female coworker for sex harassment because he talked about his sex life at work. Although the woman lost, Schultz cautions, "I can see this being a very punitive measure in the hands of socially conservative people who don't want to hear people they perceive to be sexually deviant talk about their lives at all."

Feminists Just Want a Safe Workplace

So here we are, women at the turn of the century who have transformed the workplace and the rules that govern it, by our presence. The good that has come from that transformation is now inevitably bogged down in the messy, complicated task of trying to make sure all the pieces of this particular puzzle fit together. It's a task that makes many people uncomfortable, and feminists have taken the brunt of the backlash. "The accusation lies there: you're just a frigid feminist, all you want to do is regulate sexuality," says Sanger. "But what kind of lives have people led that they don't know what awaits women?"

Ellen Bravo makes the point that "people have described in a trivializing, minimizing, and parodying way those of us who fight sex harassment, as if what we want is a repressive workplace where no one can tell a joke, no one can flirt, no one can date. This is not what we want. We want an end to unwelcome, offensive behavior of a sexual nature."

"Nearly everyone agrees that you can't just teach people a set of rules, expect them to memorize them, and that's it."

That is what we want, but nevertheless, the question remains—and it's a huge one—how can the average well-intentioned person figure out what behavior is acceptable in the workplace, especially when the damage is always in the eye of the beholder? The answer, say those who help devise the corporate rules, is deceptively simple: respect. Nearly everyone agrees that you can't just teach people a set of rules, expect them to memorize them, and that's it. It takes communication and discussion over a period of time. Not a one-day training session. Not handing people a manual and saying, "Read this." It takes a willingness to listen, respect for the concerns and fears of others, and an ability to honor differences, in order to reach some common ground. "Boilerplate policies are preposterous," says Freada Klein. "You have to respect the culture of the organization. Many of us are not in the same businesses, and even when we are, one company may be much looser than another." So the company has to set the tone and the standard.

A Matter of Respect

Several companies are starting to do just that. DuPont, for example, has created a sexual harassment training program called A Matter of Respect. It consists of several workshops, some lasting several hours, some several days. The workshops use role playing, videos, and group discussions to help all levels of employees understand harassment. According to the company, about 75 percent of its 60,000 workers have attended some part of the program. DuPont diversity consultant Bob Hamilton says the goal is to "get people to build relationships so that they can talk freely, and so that if someone does something that bothers them, they can feel comfortable knowing they have the support of management and the organization to say something."

> *"It takes a willingness to listen, respect for the concerns and fears of others, and an ability to honor differences, in order to reach some common ground."*

DuPont is one of the leaders in the attempt to create policies that rely on judgment and communication rather than specific rules. Even those who are most in favor of such policies say the effort is not easy. It demands that people do some second-guessing of themselves. One female executive says she now controls her impulse to touch her staff. "All of a sudden I realized I can't go out there and stand behind one of my employees and put my hand on his shoulder. That may be offensive to him and may be misinterpreted by him. So I've had to change my behavior."

Other executives say it's possible to get to a point where the decision-making about what's acceptable is more couched in the moment and the context. Burke Stinson, a spokesman for AT&T, which has an antiharassment program based on individual judgment, says women and men are definitely more comfortable about where to draw the line now. "If colleagues from different offices run into each other, there will be a hug, a 'God-it's-good-to-see-you' exchange that is nonsexual, nonthreatening, nongroping, based on one human being to another. Five or six years ago, I would say each party would have thought three times about it, and then just shaken hands."

People are more relaxed, Stinson believes, because they know the company will support them if there is a problem. "Employees who grew up in the work environment of the seventies and eighties feel that corporate America's hallways are not as threatening, are more secure, that there is recourse if there is some nasty business with words, deeds, or actions, a policy to fall back on. We're beginning to see a new sense of confidence."

Let's hope he's right. And that, along with that sense of confidence, there is a willingness to continue to struggle to figure out what's right, rather than resorting to inflexibility and archaic notions of women's "protected" status.

Legal Definitions of Sexual Harassment Are Useful

by Barry Spodak

About the author: *Barry Spodak is cofounder of a management and training firm that specializes in the prevention of sexual harassment in the workplace.*

Robert Samuelson's [Samuelson is a syndicated columnist who writes on social and economic policy issues] critique of sexual harassment law reminded me of a recent conversation I had with a lawyer from a large media company. The lawyer had just finished telling me about a series of thorny sexual harassment problems that he had handled for his company, when with a wan smile he said, "I just don't ever meet alone with female employees anymore."

This man was echoing what I had been hearing with increasing frequency from corporate executives from across the country. I pointed out that by isolating himself from women in his office, he was violating the very antidiscrimination law that he was trying to protect himself from.

Definitions Are Clear

It's easy to see why some people have come to believe that sexual harassment law exists in a land where "Catch-22" meets the law of unintended consequences. If you listen to the analyses of some very intelligent observers, you would come to the conclusion that sexual harassment is an offense for which there is no definition. This is just untrue.

The Supreme Court, in a unanimous decision, offered a clear definition of Title VII sexual harassment law a number of years ago. The problem is that the definition requires that judges and juries make a number of subjective judgments that rely on the social and psychological context in which the behaviors occurred. This is hardly a novel concept in the law. Charges of murder, assault, rape and obstruction of justice are just a few of the criminal areas where context plays a crucial role in determining guilt. Yet nobody says that these crimes are undefined.

People have erroneously come to believe that any behavior of a sexual nature

Reprinted from Barry Spodak, "Defining Harassment," *The Washington Post*, August 29, 1998, by permission of the author.

that someone at work finds offensive can make a person guilty of sexual harassment. Indeed, there have been a number of ludicrous lawsuits and verdicts that would seem to back up this conclusion. While most judges and juries have reacted reasonably to complaints, the sensational or unreasonable findings have garnered the most attention. In addition, some well-meaning companies have overreacted with policies that are counterproductive. For example, the term "zero tolerance" has crept into policies about sexual harassment, but what zero tolerance means rarely is defined. It's little wonder, then, that some people fear being fired for something as innocuous as flirting.

The Law Encourages Mutual Respect

There is another way. A calm and reasoned analysis of the current state of the law has led America's most progressive companies to a more thoughtful and nuanced approach. It is an approach that views sexual harassment law not as a confining social prison but rather as the outer perimeter of an organizational culture that allows people to go about their work in an atmosphere of mutual respect and courtesy. Their policies stress the importance of effective communication between supervisors and workers and offer individuals many options when reporting unprofessional or offensive behavior. They also emphasize that discipline, when appropriate, will be commensurate with the offense. These are measures that not only prevent sexual harassment but offer the best defense against unjust litigation.

> *"While most judges and juries have reacted reasonably to complaints, the sensational or unreasonable findings have garnered the most attention."*

Does the need for self-restraint in the workplace seem anachronistic in the midst of a popular culture that revels in the individual's right to do or say whatever he or she pleases? Perhaps it does, but many Americans spend more of their waking hours at work than anywhere else. Is it too much to ask that co-workers remain respectful of each other's social boundaries?

It is a bit ironic that the Supreme Court, which has been pilloried over the years for contributing to a cultural degradation of our society, should now be criticized for trying to set a standard for discrimination law that encourages common decency in the workplace.

Legal Definitions of Sexual Harassment Do Not Restrict Free Speech

by George Rutherglen

About the author: *George Rutherglen is a professor of law at the University of Virginia, in Charlottesville.*

If we take the comments of Maggie Gallagher [a syndicated columnist and author] and Michael McDonald [president of the Center for Individual Rights, a public interest law firm] seriously, we now find ourselves in the midst of a great liberal witch hunt where the law of sexual harassment is used to enforce political correctness. I have no doubt that the law of sexual harassment could be misunderstood to serve this purpose, but in this respect, I think, it is more sinned against than sinning. Upon closer inspection, the actual law scarcely resembles the caricature that has been offered by its detractors—or occasionally, for that matter, by its supporters. The law of sexual harassment instead is surprisingly moderate, and for reasons that should have wide appeal, even if they do not satisfy those who would drastically restrict or expand its scope.

The framers of the law of sexual harassment are not the feminist, leftist liberals of conservative myth. The author of existing law is not Catharine MacKinnon, although she must be recognized as the single individual most responsible for raising the issue of sexual harassment. And neither is it the Equal Employment Opportunity Commission (EEOC), although this agency formulated the single most influential guideline on sexual harassment. Instead, the unlikely leaders of this supposed liberal witch hunt are Chief Justice William Rehnquist and Justice Sandra Day O'Connor, who, respectively, wrote the opinions in *Meritor Savings Bank v. Vinson* and *Harris v. Forklift Systems, Inc.* The standard established in these cases requires a plaintiff who alleges a hostile environment to prove that sexual advances and comments are "sufficiently severe or pervasive 'to alter the conditions of [the victim's] employment and create an

Adapted, with permission, from "Sexual Harassment: Ideology or Law?" by George Rutherglen, the original version (including footnotes) of which appeared in the Spring 1995 issue of the *Harvard Journal of Law and Public Policy*.

abusive working environment.'" Correctly understood and applied, this standard raises few questions under the First Amendment. To the extent that it raises any problems at all, they are problems of implementation, mainly in evaluating conflicting evidence of sexual harassment. . . .

Not All Speech Is Protected

Mr. McDonald and others have relied upon a variant of an old argument to find that a hostile sexual environment is constitutionally protected by the First Amendment. The argument is this: Forms of expression that are not obscene and that do not aid independently illegal conduct constitute protected speech under the First Amendment. Because such forms of expression—in particular, various forms of soft-core pornography and other non-obscene speech—can create a hostile sexual environment, any liability imposed on employers for engaging in or allowing such forms of expression violates the First Amendment. For all its appealing simplicity, this argument is simply invalid. It does not follow from the fact that speech is entitled to some protection under the First Amendment that it is entitled to complete protection, or, to be precise, to as much protection as political speech in a public forum.

This fallacy becomes plain in exactly the kind of case discussed by Mr. McDonald: discipline of a professor in a state university for remarks made in class. I happen to teach at a state-supported law school. Suppose that I became bored with my course in Civil Procedure and decided to devote several weeks to telling dirty jokes instead of teaching pleading and discovery. Suppose further that each of these dirty jokes had some redeeming social value, so that none were legally obscene. Nevertheless, it is clear that I could be disciplined for this lapse of professional judgment. Now suppose that instead of telling dirty jokes, I simply seized on every possible opportunity to make demeaning remarks about women, expressing the view that women had no place in the legal profession. Again, my remarks would be constitutionally protected, arguably as political speech, but in a course on Civil Procedure, they would count simply as poor teaching.

> *"Speech that receives constitutional protection may still be regulated and restricted, so long as it is not entirely prohibited."*

Nor does this argument fare any better when it is framed in terms of academic freedom rather than protected speech. The constitutional protection for academic freedom must necessarily be qualified, not absolute. Suppose that I made my remarks about the appropriate role of women in a course on employment discrimination law. Such remarks are plainly relevant to the course, but if they had the predictable effect of antagonizing all the female students in the class, these effects could be taken into account in evaluating my teaching. The point, which I will not belabor further, is that otherwise constitutionally protected speech is routinely evaluated in the academic setting without raising any claim of absolute protection under the First Amendment. Anyone who has any further doubts should merely consider the evaluations used in considering a teacher for tenure.

Speech Can Be Regulated

What holds true inside the ivory tower, at least in this one situation, also holds true outside it. Speech that receives constitutional protection may still be regulated and restricted, so long as it is not entirely prohibited. For example, certain forms of speech, such as commercial speech, receive only qualified protection. Additionally, all constitutional scholars recognize that some forms of speech, notably political speech, receive greater protection. Even if they do not agree with this principle, they recognize it as an accurate statement of existing law. As Justice Stevens wrote in a case allowing regulation of pornographic movies that were not legally obscene, "few of us would march our sons and daughters off to war to preserve the citizen's right to see 'Specified Sexual Activities' exhibited in the theaters of our choice."

> *"The law against sexual harassment is not a license for judges to censor appropriate speech and manners in the workplace."*

Similarly, few of us should be concerned about the regulation of sexually harassing speech within the workplace. The supervisor's statement in *Harris,* that the plaintiff was "a dumb ass woman," does not require absolute constitutional protection. Equally undeserving of such protection is the pervasive display of soft-core pornography. The crucial question in these cases, and in the case in which Mr. McDonald is currently representing a college professor accused of sexual harassment, is not the constitutional question whether the speech was immune from regulation. Undoubtedly it was not. The crucial question is whether the speech was so "severe or pervasive" as to constitute sexual harassment. An isolated remark in casual conversation or a single pin-up inside a locker door not does satisfy this definition of a sexually hostile environment, a definition that the Court formulated wholly apart from free speech concerns. The law against sexual harassment seldom raises any substantial questions under the First Amendment because it applies only to speech already found to constitute "severe or pervasive" harassment.

Employers Are Free to Express Their Views

This practical conclusion from existing legal doctrine is obvious enough, but curiously it has been overlooked in the debates over sexual harassment. Its neglect is all the more puzzling because this conclusion reveals important structural similarities between the law of sexual harassment and the law of free speech. In both areas of law, judges evaluate individual decisions about appropriate gender roles only when necessary to secure equal opportunity for members of both sexes. Under the First Amendment, an employer is free to espouse and publicize his views about the proper role of women in society, even if the women who work for him find his views offensive. Likewise, the law of sexual harassment leaves an employer free to express those views, but he cannot use them as an excuse to deny women an equal opportunity to work in his business. Contrary to what its critics fear—and some of its supporters hope—the law of sexual harassment does not take a position on the inherent desirability of different gender roles, only on their exclusivity. Gender roles cannot be used to deny women and men equal opportunities for employment. Otherwise, like the First Amendment, the law of sexual harassment leaves the question of appropriate gender roles to be resolved by the individuals themselves.

Nor does this result follow only from liberal principles of sexual equality. It also follows from general libertarian principles of limiting governmental interference with sexual conduct. All of us should be concerned about judicial activism in making nice distinctions between proper and improper sexual advances. The "young in one another's arms" is not a subject for old men—or any judge of any age.

In a diverse society like ours, in which several different gender roles are possible for anyone, and all are objectionable to someone, only the most extreme forms of expression should be excluded from the workplace. "Extreme," in this context, should have a quite specific meaning: likely to deny women equal opportunities for employment. The law against sexual harassment is not a license for judges to censor appropriate speech and manners in the workplace. Limited by the First Amendment's protection of political speech, this form of judicial regulation guarantees only equal opportunity, not proper etiquette. An employer who made general statements about his social philosophy, such as his belief that a woman's place is in the home, would not be held liable for harassment on that ground. I know of no case that has imposed liability for such a careful statement of political views. On the contrary, the standard of "severe or pervasive" harassment has been a significant barrier to finding liability based on a hostile environment.

Harassing Speech Is Admissible Evidence

Some critics of the law of sexual harassment would go further than simply barring liability for protected speech. They would also deny the use of protected speech as evidence of discrimination. This position, however, is obviously untenable. Unlike the Fifth Amendment, the First Amendment creates no evidentiary privilege, and even if it did, any privilege would have to be heavily qualified to allow protected statements to be used as evidence of state of mind. It is difficult to imagine how a prohibition against intentional discrimination could be sensibly administered if the best evidence of intentional discrimination could never be considered by the trier of fact. Whatever doubts that might have arisen on this score were recently laid to rest in *Wisconsin v. Mitchell,* which held that criminal punishment could be enhanced by proof that the defendant selected his victim on the basis of race.

The use of protected expression as evidence also dispenses with the argument that rules against sexual harassment have an impermissible chilling effect on speech. If employers effectively prohibit statements demeaning women—a supposition that the widespread perception of continued harassment casts into doubt—they do so for reasons in addition to their potential exposure to liability for sexual harassment. They do so because these statements, such as the supervisor's reference to "a dumb ass woman" in *Harris,* can be used against them to prove other forms of sex discrimination. Wholly apart from legal liability, employers also have good reason to avoid the disruptive effect of harassing speech, not to mention a genuine desire, among some employers at least, to attract and retain female employees. The law against sexual harassment does not chill protected speech any more than do other forms of permissible workplace regulation.

> *"The law against sexual harassment does not chill protected speech any more than do other forms of permissible workplace regulation."*

Harassment Is Not Political Speech

Because these arguments for broader protection of harassing speech do not work, critics of the law against sexual harassment must move in the opposite direction: toward arguments for narrower protection under the First Amendment based on viewpoint discrimination. Like the broader arguments for immunity of harassing speech, however, these arguments do not have much force in the only circumstances in which they can be applied: when the preliminary requirement of "severe or pervasive" harassment has been met. These arguments presuppose that speech that demeans women needs to be protected so that it can compete on fair and equal terms with speech that carries a contrary message. In fact, however, if harassment is "severe or pervasive," it already has an overwhelming advantage. Harassing speech, therefore, cannot be treated simply as a strident and more effective form of political speech. If it were, then any form of censorship based on viewpoint would be unconstitutional. But if it is recognized for what it is—a form of nonpolitical speech—then it is subject to a wide range of regulation based on viewpoint. Advertising for cigarettes, for instance, can be restricted while advertising against cigarette smoking is not. And in terms of an earlier example, harassing speech is different from an employer's speech that simply states his own views about appropriate gender roles.

The difference has to do both with the reason for regulating harassing speech and the way in which harassing speech distinguishes itself from political speech. The reason for regulation is to protect women from a hostile environment that discourages them from seeking employment or remaining employed.

This goal is not the same as protecting women from political views that they find offensive. Harassing statements, whether sexually oriented or simply insulting, are not necessary to carry on a political debate over gender roles. On the contrary, such statements are addressed to an unwilling and captive audience that must face the choice of tolerating the speech or searching for a job elsewhere. For these reasons, harassing speech inside the workplace does not deserve the same degree of protection that either political speech in the same forum or harassing speech in a different forum deserves. People will use harassing speech as often—and in all probability far more often—to exclude women from the workplace than to carry on a political debate over feminism.

This is not to say that a bright line separates these two forms of speech. Theoretically, it may well be impossible to draw any such distinction in the abstract. But once again, the requirement of "severe or pervasive" harassment avoids most constitutional problems. Judging by the absence of cases imposing liability for purely political statements, this practical piece of legal doctrine has had the desired effect, at least in the courtroom. Most of the public controversy over sexual harassment has focused on cases, tried before inexperienced and inexpert tribunals, in which the law has been applied loosely and without adequate procedural safeguards. These cases demonstrate both the wisdom of the existing law against sexual harassment and the need to apply it correctly. In the end, Mr. McDonald's arguments in his case have less to do with the inadequacies of the law of sexual harassment than with the procedures for applying it. In some institutions, this procedural problem may be severe, but it is hardly unique to claims of sexual harassment. It can arise over any charge of serious misconduct and it can be cured only by providing the accused with a fair hearing before any finding of guilt. It cannot serve as yet another excuse for repealing the laws against sexual harassment. . . .

If we step back from overheated arguments and look at what the law against sexual harassment really is, we see that it need not be another battleground between the sexes, or between censorship and the First Amendment, or between Eros and its enemies. Despite the best efforts of its critics—and some of its supporters—the law should not be inflated into a vehicle for transforming sexual relations in our society. It is enough if it contributes to the opportunities of women in economic and public life. In just the few decades since Title VII first prohibited gender discrimination in employment, that change has been dramatic enough. There is no doubt that more and better changes could have been brought about, and in some instances, fewer and more effective changes. If legal reform is to be improved, however, it requires some attention to what the law is and what the facts are.

Schools Are Protected by Sexual Harassment Law

by Ralph R. Reiland

About the author: *Ralph R. Reiland is associate professor of economics at Robert Morris College in Pittsburgh.*

By a 5-4 vote on June 22, 1998, the Supreme Court made it much tougher to hold a school district financially responsible for an employee's sexual misconduct. "The only way to find a school liable for damages," wrote Justice Sandra Day O'Connor for the court's majority, would be to prove that a district official knew of the misconduct of a teacher, administrator, coach or principal and did little or nothing about it.

When School Officials Are Unaware

The case began in 1993 when police in Lago Vista, Texas, found social-studies teacher Frank Waldrop, 52, a former Marine colonel, naked in the woods with student Alida Gebser, 15. There was no evidence that school officials knew about the ongoing relationship, which the girl kept secret. After being nabbed by the police, Waldrop quickly was fired by the school district and later stripped of his teaching certificate. He eventually pleaded no contest to a charge of attempted sexual assault.

"We're gratified by the Supreme Court's decision," said Anne Bryant, executive director of the National School Boards Association. "It is important not to divert financial resources from the public schools when the school district itself engaged in no wrongdoing."

The court's four dissenters—its most liberal members: Justices John Paul Stevens, David Souter, Ruth Bader Ginsburg and Stephen Breyer—criticized the ruling as a rather dramatic departure from settled law, a break with the "should-have-known standard." Under that legal paradigm, the school district should have known about Waldrop and Gebser.

On top of opening deeper pockets to the plaintiff's lawyers, the should-have-known standard would have had the effect of shifting the bulk of the price for Waldrop's wrongdoing to the school district's taxpayers, students and other employees.

That price, given both the highly subjective definition of harassment and today's draconian penalties, represents a major-league threat to the financial stability of school districts, or any other enterprise. We're now at the point, for instance, where schools are overflowing with students who claim to have been victims of sexual harassment. "High-school kids" says Cathy Young, vice president of the Women's Freedom Network, "are herded into seminars where they are taught that sexual attention is demeaning to women, any annoying sexual overture is a crime and skepticism toward a sexual-harassment charge is the worst kind of insensitivity."

School districts themselves, in short, are manufacturing a student body of neo-Victorian plaintiffs who are conditioned to become indignant at racy classroom metaphors. Some 85 percent of girls and 76 percent of boys claimed to have been harassed at school, according to Hostile Hallways, a 1993 report issued by the American Association of University Women. Of those students, one in four girls and one in 10 boys reported being harassed by an adult employee of the school.

Private Companies Are Not Protected

For business owners, the Supreme Court's departure from the standard that allowed the emptying of pockets of organizations that were unaware of any wrongdoing is a welcome change. The next question is whether the Supreme Court will expand this tougher legal test to the private sector.

As it now stands, a clear double standard exists. Private companies, held to the should-have-known standard, continue to be regularly targeted for huge penalties because of the behavior of their employees, even when the behavior violates company policy and is hidden from the company. Worse, the alleged liability of private businesses has been expanded to include the actions of anyone who just happens to drop by.

In the case of Sunrise Sunoco in a high-crime section of Pittsburgh, the gas station's owner, Frank Salvati, received a letter from an attorney maintaining that a murder in Salvati's lot was caused by "your failure in not having proper security when the station was known to be located in a crime-ridden neighborhood with known street violence and drug dealing taking place." Added a paralegal in the attorney's office, "Someone going into a gas station doesn't expect to be shot."

"It is important not to divert financial resources from the public schools when the school district itself engaged in no wrongdoing."

Pittsburgh's Zone One police station happened to be right across the street from Sunrise Sunoco. To supplement this public-sector attempt at proper security, what should Salvati have done to avoid a charge of inadequate security? A fortress gas station with metal detectors and plastic cars? A drawbridge, perhaps, and a moat? Pumps inside, with every car occupant searched before a fill up? Instead of getting hit by lawsuits every time a crime happens to occur on or near their property, men such as Salvati should be given medals for creating jobs in urban America's highest-risk neighborhoods and for fighting off criminals who keep coming at them through the revolving jailhouse doors.

Legal Definitions of Sexual Harassment Have Stood Up in Court

by Alba Conte

About the author: *Alba Conte is a legal consultant and author of* Sexual Harassment in the Workplace: Law and Practice.

The concept of sexual harassment as sex discrimination spent a decade earning judicial acceptance before the U.S. Supreme Court announced its first relevant ruling in *Vinson v. Meritor Savings Bank* in 1986. It took another five years and a contracts professor named Anita Hill to finally catapult the issue into the public arena. [Hill testified that Supreme Court nominee Clarence Thomas had sexually harassed her. Despite the allegations, Thomas was confirmed in 1991.]

Thanks to the military and a number of other public servants, a week rarely goes by without a reminder of the pervasiveness of sexual harassment as a social problem. More women than ever before are seeking redress, and employers are on notice that this conduct will no longer be tolerated in the workplace.

Challenging Sexual Harassment Charges

Interestingly, the increase in sexual harassment litigation has generated a new body of law in the form of suits by people accused of and disciplined for sexual harassment. Some have challenged their termination or discipline directly. These claims may be subject to the provisions of the Labor Management Relations Act or other labor laws. Others have brought Title VII suits claiming that the sexual harassment charge and the subsequent adverse employment action were simply a pretext for sex, race, ethnic, religious, or age discrimination or retaliatory discharge.

Claims brought by alleged sexual harassers include wrongful termination, invasion of privacy, violation of due process and free speech rights, defamation, and intentional infliction of emotional distress. Alleged harassers have also

Reprinted from Alba Conte, "When the Tables Are Turned: Courts Consider Suits by Alleged Sexual Harassers," *Trial*, March 1996, by permission of *Trial*. Copyright by the Association of Trial Lawyers of America.

challenged denials of workers' compensation benefits.

There may be a number of reasons for the emergence of these claims. The integration of women into a discrimination-free workplace has been an arduous process. These cases seem to indicate that perhaps alleged harassers cannot yet accept the breadth of inappropriate conduct and do not grasp that the rules regarding interaction between men and women at work are different from the rules that apply to them in other social situations.

> *"Except when the discipline was clearly improper, judges have supported employers in their efforts to curb sexual harassment in the workplace."*

A 1995 report by the U.S. Merit Systems Protection Board indicates that there are still some behaviors that many people do not recognize as sexual harassment—even though the law does. The report also shows that many people believe that whether conduct constitutes sexual harassment depends on the intent of the harasser. These results support the notion that people disciplined for harassment may tend to feel wronged and may want to be vindicated.

Whatever the reason for these claims, they have generally faced a cool reception in the courts. Except when the discipline was clearly improper, judges have supported employers in their efforts to curb sexual harassment in the workplace.

Discharging Employees

When an employer discharges an employee for violating a sexual harassment policy, the relevant inquiry is whether "the decisionmakers believed at the time of the discharge that the employee was guilty of harassment, and, if so, whether this belief was the reason for the discharge." Alleged harassers with records of other disciplinary problems have had less success challenging their termination or discipline.

For example, in *Carosella v. United States Postal Service,* the court found that a supervisor was properly discharged when a preponderance of the evidence showed that he had sexually harassed six female subordinates. But in *Downes v. Federal Aviation Administration,* the court held that a manager was improperly demoted and reassigned when the alleged harassment was "trivial," did not establish a pattern, and did not alter the woman's job status.

Many states adhere to the employment-at-will doctrine. This gives the employer and the employee the right to terminate the employment relationship at any time with or without cause unless there is an agreement to the contrary. To sustain an action for wrongful termination in these states, the terminated employee must show that the employment relationship was based on a contract that specifically indicated the employment was not terminable at will.

Some courts have held that an employee may not rely on the existence of an employment handbook to create such a contract. In *Johnson v. J.C. Penney Co.,* in which an employee challenged his termination for alleged sexual harassment, the court held that the company's employment manual did not change the plaintiff's status as an employee-at-will under Texas case law. The court noted that if a manual has a disclaimer stating the manual does not constitute a contract, the disclaimer will negate any implication that the personnel procedures restrict the at-will relationship.

Courts Reject Privacy Claims

Employers have a duty to investigate allegations of sexual harassment, and their employees have a legitimate interest in knowing what activities could result in their termination. Courts have rejected most privacy claims by alleged harassers because other employees or the public at large have an overriding interest in the information.

In *Smith v. Arkansas Louisiana Gas Co.,* the court reversed a judgment against an employer for invasion of privacy. Management had distributed memos advising staff managers of the plaintiff's demotion and another employee's termination because of alleged sexual harassment. The plaintiff said the employer violated his privacy rights when it disseminated the memos both inside and outside the company.

At trial, the employer had relied on a defense of qualified privilege, which protects employers from liability for communicating to selected employees its reason for disciplinary action against another employee. This privilege arises from the need to allow unrestricted communication—

> *"The general public may have a legitimate interest in the disclosure of facts surrounding a sexual harassment investigation of a public employee."*

without threat of liability—about a matter in which the parties have an interest or duty. The trial judge had not instructed the jury about this defense, but the appeals court held that the defense applied.

The general public may have a legitimate interest in the disclosure of facts surrounding a sexual harassment investigation of a public employee. For example, the Montana Supreme Court rejected a mayor's privacy claim relating to a sexual harassment investigation. In an action against the mayor and city council of Hamilton by a public interest group under the state open meetings law, the city counterclaimed. It asked for a declaratory judgment on whether the mayor's constitutional right of privacy prevented disclosing the results of an investigation into his alleged harassment of city employees.

The court held that because the mayor, as an elected official, did not have a "reasonable expectation of privacy," he could not assert an overriding privacy interest in preventing publication of the report. Moreover, the city had already used public funds to settle with the complainant, and public funds would possibly be used to indemnify the mayor for his attorney fees. The court said the public was entitled to know the reason for this expenditure.

Due Process and Free Speech Claims

Alleged harassers have also pressed due process and First Amendment claims against their employers. In most reported opinions, these cases have been unsuccessful.

For example, in *Kennedy v. Marion Correctional Institution,* the Ohio Supreme Court rejected the plaintiff's argument that he was entitled to prehearing discovery and a formal evidentiary hearing before being disciplined. The court noted that he had been given written notice of the charges, copies of statements regarding the alleged harassment, and an opportunity to present his side of the story. These steps were sufficient to constitute due process, the court held.

Similarly, in *Black v. City of Auburn,* the court dismissed an action by a municipal police officer who was demoted for alleged sexual harassment of female officers, holding that the plaintiff did not prove that his demotion violated his due process or equal protection rights. The court found that the plaintiff was not denied procedural due process for a number of reasons, including that he was afforded ample notice of the charges, a hearing was held, and he was aware of what types of behavior might offend female officers because he had attended seminars about sexual harassment.

Even employees who have been exonerated of sexual harassment charges have had difficulty bringing constitutional claims against their employers. In *Workman v. Jordan,* a discharged captain in a sheriff's department sued after he was reinstated with back pay when it was determined in a hearing that he had not committed sexual harassment. He claimed procedural due process and First Amendment violations by the sheriff and others.

The captain claimed he was deprived of a liberty interest in his good name and his property interest in continued employment when his supervisors placed allegedly stigmatizing documents in his personnel file. The court disagreed because the documents did not contradict the finding by the hearing officer exonerating the captain of the harassment charge.

The court also rejected the captain's First Amendment claim, which alleged that the sheriff's department had retaliated against the captain for, among other things, testifying at his own post-termination hearing. To

> *"Even employees who have been exonerated of sexual harassment charges have had difficulty bringing constitutional claims against their employers."*

proceed with a First Amendment claim, the captain had to show that the testimony he gave at the hearing related to a matter of public concern.

The court held that a sexist atmosphere in the workplace is a matter of public concern but that internal personnel disputes are not. According to the court, the captain's testimony regarding the alleged sexual harassment and the department's alleged tolerance of a sexist environment did not touch on a matter of public concern but was motivated by the captain's desire to show that his behavior was not anomalous.

However, under certain exceptional circumstances, courts have allowed due process claims to proceed. One example is *Civil Service Employees Association v. Southold Union Free School District.* The court held that a "formal reprimand" was improperly placed in the personnel file of a school custodian accused of sexual harassment because the custodian had not been afforded due process protections under state civil service law. Documents like critical administrative evaluations or admonitions intended to warn or instruct an employee may be placed in personnel files without a formal hearing, the court said, but placing in the file documents that are a form of discipline intended to punish an employee for improper conduct may violate due process if no hearing is held.

> *"Communications between employees in the regular course of business cannot be subject to defamation claims."*

Defamation Claims

The key issues in a defamation claim are generally whether the allegedly defamatory information is true and whether the person spreading the information did so with actual malice. These elements make defamation claims difficult to prove, particularly in the face of evidence that the employer actually believed the harassment allegations or passed on true information to its own employees or to the public.

In *Duffy v. Leading Edge Products, Inc.,* the Fifth Circuit affirmed a lower court's rejection of a defamation claim. The court found that a man who charged that his former employer made false allegations against him failed to establish actual malice, necessary to overcome the employer's qualified privilege with respect to alleged defamatory statements. There was no evidence that the supervisor who investigated two coworkers' allegations did not believe their statements or that the alleged conduct did not constitute sexual harassment.

In *Harper v. Walters,* the court held that a former Equal Employment Opportunity Commission (EEOC) attorney did not state a claim for defamation against a television news operation. It had reported that the attorney was charged with sexually harassing 13 women while he worked at the agency and that the agency had recommended terminating him, although he ultimately was allowed to retire first.

According to the court, the reports—which were made without actual malice—were complete and accurate representations of EEOC notices of adverse employment actions specifying particular acts of harassment allegedly committed by the attorney as required for the broadcast to be privileged under District of Columbia law.

In another case, an alleged harasser unsuccessfully brought a claim for defamation and intentional interference with a business relationship against a coworker. The coworker had complained to their employer of a touching incident. The plaintiff in *Miller v. Servicemaster by Rees* alleged that the written and verbal reports filed after the incident were defamatory as a matter of law because they adversely damaged his professional reputation.

The Arizona Court of Appeals found that the man failed to make a prima facie case that the woman's report of the alleged harassment was improper. The court found there was no actual malice in the report.

Also, according to the court's ruling, "[T]here is strong public policy to protect a worker's right to report alleged sexual harassment. Workers should be free to report alleged sexual harassment without fear of liability, absent malice in fact."

In *Lambert v. Morehouse,* an action by a discharged employee against other employees who had accused him of sexual harassment, the Washington Court of Appeals held that complaints of harassment made in the context of workplace investigations were conditionally privileged under the laws of both defamation and tortious interference. The court affirmed the trial court's finding that the discharged employee—who did not deny specific facts alleged by subordinate employees but denied the conclusion that he had sexually harassed them—did not create a genuine issue as to the truth or falsity of the allegations or as to whether the subordinate employees had abused the conditional privilege.

Rattray v. City of National City was an action by a former police officer who was terminated for dishonesty regarding allegations that he had sexually harassed a female coworker. A jury returned a verdict in the officer's favor on his defamation claim.

The judge granted the city's motion for a new trial, holding that the evidence showed that the chief who terminated the officer made his statements regarding the officer's dishonesty in good faith. The Ninth Circuit affirmed the district court's ruling.

At least one court has held that statements about alleged sexual harassment—even if false and malicious—may fall within the intracorporate immunity exception in defamation law. This holds that communications between employees in the regular course of business cannot be subject to defamation claims.

In *Lovelace v. Long John Silver's,* the Missouri Court of Appeals held that female employees' oral and written statements to their employer regarding a manager's alleged sexual harassment toward them were not publications of defamatory material under Missouri law.

As the court stated, "A corporation has an interest to see that business runs efficiently. The sexual harassment of an employee by a supervisor not only affects the efficiency of the employee—and hence of the business—but also may incur the legal obligation of the employer to take steps against the practice."

In most states, in order to prove intentional infliction of emotional distress a plaintiff must show that the defendant acted outrageously and that the plaintiff suffered severe or extreme emotional distress as a result. Generally, courts have held that disciplining an employee for alleged sexual harassment is not outrageous conduct likely to result in severe emotional injury.

Ekokotu v. Pizza Hut, Inc., involved an action by a former assistant manager of a restaurant against his employer and two supervisors. The case alleged conspiracy to fabricate false charges of sexual harassment, libel, tortious interference with employment, and severe mental and physical anguish.

The Georgia Court of Appeals held that reporting the results of sexual harassment investigations against the plaintiff to his supervisors and firing him did not constitute the outrageous conduct necessary for a claim for intentional infliction of emotional distress in the absence of physical injury. Another court held that even if a termination is shown to be illegal, this is not normally enough to constitute extreme and outrageous conduct.

Workers' Compensation Claims

Several alleged harassers have attempted to obtain workers' compensation benefits for alleged injuries stemming from accusations of sexual harassment. In *Martone v. State of Rhode Island/Registry of Motor Vehicles,* the state supreme court held that an employee who alleged psychological injury from coworkers' treatment of him after he was disciplined for harassment could not receive workers' compensation. The court said he had not shown a causal relationship between his injury and his employment. The court also found that the sexual harassment was not a deviation from work that was substantially motivated by influences that originated in his job; rather, the employee was motivated by his own desire for sexual excitement and his wish to manipulate the victim.

Similarly, in *Crowley v. SAIF Corp.,* the Oregon Court of Appeals held that the state workers' compensation board properly concluded that an employee's mental disorder was not compensable under the state workers' compensation statute. The employee claimed his disorder resulted from a conference with his supervisor in which he was advised that a female employee had accused him of sexual harassment.

The court said the conference was reasonable, corrective action and rejected the contention that the disorder resulted from the false accusation, not the discipline. According to the court, "The board gave a reasoned conclusion on the basis of findings that are supported by substantial evidence. It rejected the fine distinction that claimant wishes to draw that his awareness of the allegations, not the supervisor's corrective action, produced the reaction."

> *"Courts have held that disciplining an employee for alleged sexual harassment is not outrageous conduct likely to result in severe emotional injury."*

Alleged harassers have pressed other claims not discussed here, including claims for libel, breach of contract, and negligent investigation. They have also challenged denials of unemployment and severance benefits.

Despite increased attention to sexual harassment issues in recent years, there is still some confusion in U.S. workplaces regarding what types of conduct are offensive. Some male workers fear that even the most benign compliment will be parlayed into a sexual harassment suit. Many male employees are tentative in their interactions with female coworkers, and employers are vigilant in avoiding liability. The cases discussed above indicate that many employers are carefully evaluating the implications of their employment decisions.

Although alleged harassers have been largely unsuccessful in cases against their employers or accusers, courts have recognized the need for fairness to all parties when these sensitive charges are brought. When due process is lacking, courts will not allow disciplinary actions to stand.

For example, in *Starishevsky v. Hofstra University*—a sexual harassment case involving a student rather than an employee—a university panel fired an administrator who allegedly kissed a student. The panel found the behavior inappropriate but concluded that no sexual harassment had occurred.

The New York court discussed the care an employer must take to give due process to those accused of sexual harassment. The court found the termination of the administrator arbitrary and capricious, holding that he was denied his right to a fair and reasonable hearing.

The court noted that with the recognition of the need to eliminate sexual harassment has come an awareness of how difficult the task will be. As the court stated, "The process of eliminating sexual harassment must go forward with recognition of the rights of all involved and without the creation of new wrongs. The process must be propelled by a sense of fairness and not motivated by any other less appropriate notions."

Confusion about sexual harassment seems inevitable as employers and workers try to come to grips with changing social mores. While there will always be shades of gray with respect to inappropriate workplace behavior, increasing numbers of women in positions of power and sexual harassment prevention through training and education will ultimately lower the number of suits by all parties.

Legal Definitions of Sexual Harassment Are Harmful

by Richard Dooling

About the author: *Richard Dooling is an employment-discrimination lawyer and novelist.*

Just as the O.J. Simpson trial was a public demonstration of the laws of evidence and procedure in criminal cases [Simpson was acquitted on October 2, 1995, of the June 12, 1994, murder of his ex-wife, Nicole Brown Simpson, and her friend Ron Goldman], so Paula Jones and her lawyers have provided the American public with an object lesson in the awesome scope and power of our current sexual-harassment laws. One woman's unsupported allegations are grounds for hauling even the President of the United States into a deposition where he can be forced to testify under oath about sexual encounters with former lovers, the size and shape of his penis, his shopping habits, and what books he gives as gifts. [Paula Jones' allegations of sexual harassment by Bill Clinton while he was Governor of Arkansas were dismissed on April 1, 1998.]

It was not always so. As one pundit after another has reminded us, President John F. Kennedy's escapades remained private, and the country was arguably better for it. Kennedy died in 1963, and Title VII of the Civil Rights Act was passed in 1964; before that there were no civil laws which pretended to referee the timeless scrimmage between men and women for power, money, sex, and influence—a contest which was fought by individuals in the marketplace and in the bedroom, until group rights and identity politics came into fashion.

Destructive Side Effects

Title VII began as a statute requiring employers to make decisions about the "terms and conditions of employment" without regard to race, color, religion, sex, or national origin. As any employment lawyer or line supervisor knows, the statute had precisely the opposite effect, because what the company lawyer now needs to know in order to assess hirings, firings, and promotions is the race, color, religion, sex, national origin, age, and disability of the employees involved. This is one of the many pernicious side effects itemized by Richard Epstein and other legal scholars who argue that Title VII is not only unnecessary but actively destructive.

Title VII and the other federal employment laws now protect so many minorities that they in effect confer a right to sue on a majority of employees. Still, to the extent that Title VII prohibits "discrimination" (that is, hiring or firing because of sex or race), it forbids an activity which, in theory, most people discriminated against

> *"Legal scholars . . . argue that Title VII is not only unnecessary but actively destructive."*

can easily prove and most employers can easily avoid. Give similarly situated individuals the same pay for the same work. Hire and fire on the basis of objective, quantifiable criteria. Or get sued.

When Title VII acquired tremendous potential for abuse was when the courts decided it prohibited not just discrimination, but something vague called "harassment." As Justice Scalia noted in 1993, Title VII's "inherently vague statutory language . . . lets virtually unguided juries decide whether sex-related conduct engaged in (or permitted by) an employer is egregious enough to warrant an award of damages."

Amen. Any law that can be interpreted as forbidding lewd comments and dirty pictures in the workplace in one jurisdiction, and then as permitting dropping one's pants and saying "kiss it" in another, should be, in constitutional-law lingo, void for vagueness. This is the major complaint of legal scholars like Eugene Volokh and Kingsley Browne, who have argued for years that Title VII's vagueness chills workplace speech and therefore violates the First Amendment. Employers instinctively prohibit any "sexual" speech for fear of punitive damages.

Ever since Title VII was interpreted as prohibiting "harassment," a parade of women—some arguably harassed, some merely annoyed—have come before the courts. After months, sometimes years, of costly discovery, juries are asked to determine whether she is more believable than he, whether the overture was "sexual," and whether it was "unwanted." And every year charges and suits paralyze companies all over America.

At the height of the Clinton scandal, every other pundit legitimately asked: "Is this how we want our President spending his time?" But this is precisely the question the stockholders ask when a secretary brings a global corporation to a halt by alleging that the CEO told her a dirty joke in the coffee room.

Better Remedies Are Available

What would happen if Congress passed an amendment to Title VII, which simply confined its interpretation to its original plain language, namely, prohibiting discrimination in the terms and conditions of employment? Would boorish chauvinists have at unprotected women and minorities, who would suddenly be left with no legal remedy? Hardly. Many behaviors prohibited by the "harassment" components of Title VII are already prohibited by other civil and criminal laws. Any unauthorized touching is a battery. Abusive and threatening language may rise to the level of assault. Defamation prohibits injurious statements intended to harm a person's reputation. And so on. In short, what would happen if we simply allowed the same laws that protect us from one another on the street also to protect us in the workplace?

Unlike Title VII, which holds companies liable for their supervisors' behaviors, the tort and criminal laws make individuals liable for their own behaviors. How's that for deterrence? But of course, victimized plaintiffs need the employer's deep pockets—which should prompt us to ask ourselves whether it is more important to deter individual harassing behaviors, or to compensate victims with corporate checks under some construct of vicarious liability.

If it is too early in the season of public opinion to call for a repeal of Title VII, the time is ripe at least for pruning its most unworkable and unenforceable sections. Even the feminists quickly stopped talking about vague "power differentials" when the amorphous theory was about to be applied to their guy; maybe we could also do away with the equally vague admonition that all employees have "the right to work in an environment free from discriminatory intimidation, ridicule, and insult."

But above all, the nation should be asking itself: Do we really want to live under a law that pretends to be able to adduce evidence and settle a dispute between a man and a woman who went into a room alone together and came out with different stories?

Feminist Legal Definitions of Sexual Harassment Promote Injustice

by Michael Weiss and Cathy Young

About the authors: *Michael Weiss is an adjunct professor at the University of Houston Law Center. Cathy Young is an associate policy analyst at the Cato Institute, a columnist with the* Detroit News, *and author of* Gender Wars.

Feminist legal theory has become a formidable presence in many of America's top law schools. Feminist activism has also had a major impact on many areas of the law, including rape, self-defense, domestic violence, and such new legal categories as sexual harassment. However, the ideology of legal feminism today goes far beyond the original and widely supported goal of equal treatment for both sexes. The new agenda is to redistribute power from the "dominant class" (men) to the "subordinate class" (women), and such key concepts of Western jurisprudence as judicial neutrality and individual rights are declared to be patriarchal fictions designed to protect male privilege.

The Rise of Feminist Legal Theory

Many feminist-initiated legal reforms have addressed real wrongs, such as the tendency to treat rape victims more harshly and suspiciously than victims of other crimes, and inadequate protection for victims of domestic violence. But feminist pressure has also resulted in increasingly loose and subjective definitions of harassment and rape, dangerous moves to eviscerate the presumption of innocence in sexual assault cases, and a broad concept of self-defense in cases of battered wives that sometimes amounts to a license to kill an allegedly abusive spouse.

Courts and legislatures should resist efforts to limit individual rights in the guise of protecting women as a class, and reaffirm the fundamental principle consistent with the classical liberal origins of the movement for women's rights: equality before the law regardless of gender. . . .

Excerpted from Michael Weiss and Cathy Young, "Feminist Jurisprudence: Equal Rights or Neopaternalism?" *Cato Policy Analysis*, June 19, 1996. Reprinted with permission of the Cato Institute. *Endnotes and references in the original have been omitted in this reprint.*

The liberal feminism inherited by the women's liberation movement of the 1960s was based on emancipatory theory and sought to dismantle the positive legal barriers that had denied women equal opportunity with men. The theory behind those goals was that the rights of individuals as traditionally understood in a liberal society should transcend gender differences. This brand of legal feminism was in many ways exemplified by Ruth Bader Ginsburg, now associate justice of the Supreme Court, who said in a 1988 speech, "Generalizations about the way women or men are . . . cannot guide me reliably in making decisions about particular individuals." As general counsel of the American Civil Liberties Union's Women's Rights Project in the 1970s, Ginsburg challenged laws that gave health benefits to wives of servicemen but not to husbands of servicewomen and prohibited women from engaging in certain types of business (such as running a bar) without a male co-owner. Feminists were also involved in efforts to overturn legal restrictions on contraception and abortion.

The illiberal feminist legal theory (also known as "radical feminism"), which emerged during the 1980s, urges women to renounce traditional notions of rights and justice, now viewed as perpetuating male dominance. Some of the new feminists charge that the reforms achieved by "equality feminists" have dismantled protections beneficial to women while doing nothing to eliminate their disadvantages.

Rejecting Traditional Legal Principles

For radical feminists, the key concept is "patriarchy," the male-dominated social structure. Patriarchy is perceived to be as all-encompassing and all-infecting as the Communist conspiracy of earlier days. Hence, even such liberal principles as neutrality of the law, equality, and individual autonomy must be discarded because of their "patriarchal" roots. The new feminism attempts to replace those notions with a new breed of philosophy and jurisprudence premised on "connection" between persons. Law is seen as an instrument to "change the distribution of power," which requires not equal treatment but "an asymmetrical approach that adopts the perspective of the less powerful group with the specific goal of equitable power sharing among diverse groups," Martha Chamallas writes. . . .

Catharine MacKinnon, a feminist lawyer and scholar and now a professor at the University of Michigan School of Law, spearheaded the first major court victory of radical feminist jurisprudence. In 1986, in *Meritor Savings Bank v. Vinson*, the United States Supreme Court adopted her theory that women should be able to sue an employer for sexual harassment based on a "hostile work environment." In contrast to earlier cases in which employers were found liable for sexual harassment because they pressured employees for sexual favors, in *Vinson* the Court held that the employer need do nothing to be liable and that there was no need for anyone else to have made sexual demands.

The problem of sexual imposition on women by male bosses is hardly a new one; the plight of innocent factory girls or maids being preyed upon by employers was a subject of much concern (and prurient interest) in the nineteenth century, though not a target for legal action. As women entered the workforce in great numbers in the 1970s and sought equal career opportunities, the issue of the burden imposed upon them by sexual demands became a more prominent one. The term "sexual harassment" came into use around 1975.

Abandoning Traditional Remedies

In some early cases, female plaintiffs were able to combat unwanted sexual overtures in the workplace by using the common-law remedies of tort and contract. Yet in formulating her theory MacKinnon expressly rejected the common-law approach because of what she saw as "the conceptual inadequacy of traditional legal theories to the social reality of men's sexual treatment of women." Her main objection to a tort remedy was that it would treat sexual harassment as a personal affront rather than systemic persecution of women as a gender: "By treating the incidents as if they are outrages particular to an individual woman rather than integral to her social status as a woman worker, the personal approach . . . fails to analyze the relevant dimensions of the problem." MacKinnon also felt that labeling harassment a breach of contract would subject women to male standards of behavior and limit the scope of the law to exclude most speech offenses. Instead, she wanted the courts to classify both sexual extortion and verbal insensitivity as a form of sex discrimination, already prohibited under Title VII of the 1964 Civil Rights Act.

Initial attempts to apply this theory were rejected. In *Corne v. Bausch & Lomb* (1975), in which two women claimed that sexual advances by their supervisor had driven them to quit their jobs, Judge Frey found that such behavior was not actionable under Title VII. His decision, and some other rulings of the time, noted that unlike discrimination in hiring, sexual overtures from supervisors or coworkers were personal actions, not company policy. Moreover, such overtures could be made toward a man (by a man or a woman) or toward men and women equally (by a bisexual supervisor).

However, before too long proponents of the sexual-harassment-as-discrimination theory scored their first victories. In 1976, the federal district court for the District of Columbia accepted their view in *Williams v. Saxbe*. The following year, the Court of Appeals for the D.C. Circuit became the first appellate court to find that sexual harassment was indeed sex discrimination. Finally, in 1986, the Supreme Court decided *Vinson*, adopting the most expansive part of MacKinnon's theory: that sexual harassment "sufficiently severe or pervasive" to create "an abusive work environment" is illegal even if

> *"Feminist legal theory . . . urges women to renounce traditional notions of rights and justice, now viewed as perpetuating male dominance."*

sexual demands are not linked to concrete employment benefits. The court further went along with MacKinnon's theory by finding that "'voluntariness' in the sense of consent" is not a defense to a sexual harassment charge. MacKinnon summed up, "What the decision means is that we made this law up from the beginning, and now we've won."

Some dissenting voices have continued to criticize the radical paradigm of sexual harassment as sex discrimination, arguing for a return to the common-law structures of tort and contract in handling such claims. The common-law system is more than just a method of resolving legal disputes one case at a time; it embodies basic historical principles such as neutrality, objectivity, and equality before the law. As legal philosopher Karl Llewellyn put it "Cases . . . build and become stones for further building." The evolutionary nature of the common law ensures that it is drawn in the direction of greater fidelity to those basic principles yet is sufficiently flexible to meet the demands of new social problems.

> *"'Discomfort' as the test of harassment is not only broad enough to outlaw many forms of previously legal speech but is also too subjective."*

Developing Vague Definitions

Once the tort and contract approach had been jettisoned, the problem that arose after *Vinson* was how to define harassment. The National Organization for Women defines it as

> any repeated or unwanted sexual advance, sexually explicit derogatory statements, sexually discriminatory remarks that cause the recipient discomfort or humiliation. . . .

Given this broad category, it is not surprising that many feminists claim 85 percent of all women have been sexually harassed in the work force at some point in their lives. That degree of vagueness in a statute would never pass constitutional muster. It is comparable to replacing speed limits with a law under which one could be fined for driving through a neighborhood at any speed which made some of its residents uncomfortable. "Discomfort" as the test of harassment is not only broad enough to outlaw many forms of previously legal speech but is also too subjective. According to Susan Strauss, "Whether harassment has occurred is truly in the 'eye of the beholder'—or the ear. . . . The deciding factor is the feelings a particular phrase, gesture, or behavior evokes in the individual on the receiving end."

The imposition of restrictions on such a large class of speech in the workplace angered several civil liberties groups, but that has done little to stem radical feminist influence on judicial thinking. A major step in the direction of remaking the law in the neo-feminist image occurred early in 1991 (nearly a year before the testimony of Anita Hill at the Clarence Thomas confirmation hearings brought the issue of sexual harassment to the forefront of public consciousness). In *Ellison v. Brady*, the Ninth Circuit Court of Appeals in California abandoned the traditional test for offensive conduct—the "reasonable person" standard—and substituted a "reasonable woman" test, dealing yet another blow to common-law construction.

In its ruling, the Ninth Circuit panel drew on legal feminist texts for the proposition that "men tend to view some forms of sexual harassment as 'harmless social interactions to which only overly sensitive women would object'" and that "because of the inequality and coercion with which it is so frequently associated in the minds of women, the appearance of sexuality in an unexpected context or a setting of ostensible equality can be an anguishing experience." The court stated:

> We . . . prefer to analyze harassment from the victim's perspective [which] requires . . . an analysis of the different perspectives of men and women. Conduct that many men consider unobjectionable may offend many women. See, e.g., *Lipsett v. University of Puerto Rico*, 864 F.2d 881, 898 (1st Cir. 1988). ("A male supervisor might believe, for example, that it is legitimate for him to tell a female subordinate that she has a 'great figure' or 'nice legs.' The female subordinate, however, may find such comments offensive"). . . . We adopt the perspective of a reasonable woman primarily because we believe that a sex-blind reasonable person standard tends to be male-biased and tends to systematically ignore the experiences of women.

A New Standard

The court found that behavior that would seem trivial to a man could be quite harmful to a woman because "women who are victims of mild forms of sexual harassment may understandably worry whether a harasser's conduct is merely a prelude to violent sexual assault." Thus, even "well-intentioned compliments by co-workers or supervisors" might be sufficient to bring a lawsuit based upon this new legal definition of sexual harassment if a "reasonable woman" could find them offensive, reversing an almost century-long march toward a more expansive view of free speech rights. The court also uncritically embraced the neo-feminist notion that men and women do not and perhaps cannot see the same events similarly, gutting the concept of neutrality under the law. Ironically, it was in part the earlier wave of "equality feminism" that led to the abolition of most traditional laws against indecent speech directed at women. As recently as May 1993, the South Carolina Supreme Court struck down a law making it a misdemeanor to communicate "any obscene, profane, indecent, vulgar, suggestive or

"It is difficult to imagine how any behavior with sexual overtones could escape classification as harassment—defined by the reaction of the most sensitive woman."

immoral message" to a woman or girl: "Statutes . . . that distinguish between males and females based on 'old notions' . . . that females should be afforded special protection from 'rough talk' because of their perceived 'special sensitivities' can no longer withstand equal protection scrutiny."

> *"Restrictions on such a large class of speech in the workplace angered several civil liberties groups, but that has done little to stem radical feminist influence on judicial thinking."*

In March 1991, applying the reasonable-woman standard, a federal district court in Jacksonville, Florida, found a working environment at a shipyard abusive and in violation of civil rights laws because of nude pin-ups on the walls and frequent lewd remarks. To buttress his findings, Judge Howell Melton quoted several feminist law articles. There was no evidence of obscene language or sexual demands being directed at the plaintiff, Lois Robinson—although, *after* she had complained about sexually explicit materials at work, some of the male employees retaliated by posting a "Men Only" sign in one area and by leaving abusive graffiti at Robinson's workstation. Here are the main elements of the "hostile work environment" found by the court:

> A Whilden Valve & Gauge calendar for 1985, which features *Playboy* playmate of the month pictures on each page. The female models in this calendar are fully or partially nude. In every month except February, April, and November, the model's breasts are fully exposed. The pubic areas are exposed on the women featured in August and December. Several of the pictures are suggestive of sexually submissive behavior. . . . Among the remarks Robinson recalled are: "You rate about an 8 or a 9 on a scale of 10." She recalled one occasion on which a welder told her he wished her shirt would blow over her head so he could look, another occasion on which a fitter told her he wished her shirt was tighter . . . an occasion on which a foreman candidate asked her to "come sit" on his lap, and innumerable occasions on which a coworker or supervisor called her "honey," "dear," "baby," "sugar," "sugar-booger," and "momma" instead of calling her by her name.

Although the plaintiff felt sexually harassed, other female workers said that they did not. To the judge, however, that merely provided additional evidence of victimization: "For reasons expressed in the expert testimony . . . the Court finds the description of [their] behavior to be consistent with the coping strategies employed by women who are victims of a sexually hostile work environment." In light of that, it is difficult to imagine how any behavior with sexual overtones could escape classification as harassment—defined by the reaction of the most sensitive woman, even if she is the only one who takes offense.

Increased Regulation of the Workplace

This is not to say that Lois Robinson was hypersensitive. The Jacksonville Shipyard, as described in the record, appears to have been a working environment that most women, and probably a good many men as well, would have found an unpleasant place to work. Traditionally, however, the law has posited that when a person takes a job in what is known to be a rough environment, she or he willingly assumes the risk of being offended. While such an approach arguably limits some people's choice of jobs, it avoids the intrusiveness of the government regulating the mental comfort level of a workplace.

Judge Melton ordered all pinups, sexually oriented remarks, and sexually explicit magazines banned from the workplace, even in the men's locker room. The decision was perceived by many as a green light for an expanded attack on offensive speech and images, and sparked similar suits. Several women suing Stroh Brewery Company for harassment by male coworkers (which they claimed included lewd touching, indecent exposure, and sexual demands) added to their suit a complaint that the company's use of seminude female images in its ads, particularly the "Swedish bikini team" promotional campaign, contributed to a hostile environment. (In November 1993, a judge ruled that the advertising could not be used as evidence in the harassment suit.)

Under the guise of combating sexual harassment, radical feminists have imposed a speech regime that the Supreme Court of the 1930s would not have allowed. In *Ellison*, the Ninth Circuit panel suggested

> *"Courts and legislatures have restricted the employer's authority over his workplace."*

that women's sensitivities were not only "special," but might become further refined with the passage of time. Thus, even employers who have taken steps to stamp out any workplace conduct that might not pass muster with the "reasonable woman" should not rest on their laurels:

> We realize that the reasonable woman standard will not address conduct which some women find offensive. Conduct considered harmless by many today may be considered discriminatory in the future. Fortunately, the reasonableness inquiry which we adopt today is not static. As the views of reasonable women change, so too does the Title VII standard of acceptable behavior.

There is no doubt that some of the conduct addressed by sexual harassment litigation would be egregious by most people's standards—sufficiently so to meet the tort standard applied to intentional infliction of emotional distress: a "case . . . in which the recitation of the facts to an average member of the community would arouse his resentment against the actor, and lead him to exclaim, 'Outrageous.'" (That may even be true of *Ellison*, in which the plaintiff had been subjected not merely to persistent but obsessive and delusional attentions by a coworker, and had filed a suit only after her attempts to get him transferred to a different office failed because of intervention by the union.)

However, the label of sexual harassment is being used in increasingly trivial cases. Since most of the effects of legal theories take place "in the shadow of the law," many of the most expansive applications of the new standards have occurred in nonlitigation, compliance actions. For instance:

- At the *Boston Globe* in 1993, veteran columnist David Nyhan humorously taunted another male staffer, who had declined a game of basketball after work, for being "pussy-whipped." The remark was overheard by a female staffer who complained about it. Nyhan was assailed in a memo to the staff by editor Matthew Storin and fined $1,250, to be contributed to a women's organization. After abject apologies from Nyhan, the fine was rescinded.

- A senior vice president of the New York City transit authority was demoted for making a ribald statement over a speakerphone from his hospital bed. While recuperating from triple-bypass surgery, he said on a conference call to his office mates that he felt good enough to have sex on stage with one of them. Unimpressed by his recuperative vigor, transit authority president Alan Kiepper, enforcing regulations based on new sexual-harassment rulings, demoted him. Commented Kiepper, "He can't push this aside by saying it was just a joke. A lot of demeaning things are said under the guise of being a joke. We have to become more sensitive to what we say."

Obviously, sexual-harassment laws target not only speech but noncoercive sexual behavior—another sphere where the lessening of state controls has been commonly regarded as progressive. Penalizing "unwelcome" advances even when the initiator has received no sign that they are unwelcome clearly reduces opportunities for consensual relationships. (As one young woman writer notes, "The truth is, if no one was ever allowed to risk unsolicited sexual attention, we would all be solitary creatures.") University of Southern California law professor Susan Estrich, considered a mainstream legal scholar, wants to eliminate the "welcomeness" test altogether, since it implies that women must express their objections to harassing behavior before they can sue. Estrich also says that she would have "no objection to rules which prohibited men and women from sexual relations in the workplace, at least with those who worked directly for them."

While no formal rules of that kind exist anywhere, it seems that existing sexual-harassment regulations have had the same effect for many women and men. A recent *New York Times* article about romance by electronic mail quoted a Los Angeles lawyer who had met his future wife in the late 1980s through a computer forum as saying that such a thing would have been "much more difficult" today: "With all the sexual harassment danger, it's a risky business."

In a truly free market, private employers would have a right, absent contractual agreements to the contrary, to prohibit or ignore employees' workplace behavior, including crude language or sexual overtures toward coworkers. In today's political environment, however, courts and legislatures have restricted the employer's authority over his workplace. Toward limiting

> *"Such rules seek to redress alleged generalized injuries to more than half of the population by silencing the other half."*

governmental intrusion in the workplace, political scientist Ellen Frankel Paul has called for replacing the civil rights model of sexual-harassment-as-sex-discrimination with a tort of sexual harassment. . . .

Such a tort, Paul notes, "would encourage companies to provide an effective mechanism for dealing with sexual harassment" while setting the threshold high enough to deter frivolous complaints and requiring women (and men) who are sexually harassed to object to the behavior before they can file a suit. It would also give employers reasonable assurance that an effective mechanism of processing nontrivial complaints would shield them from lawsuits.

Prohibiting Campus Speech

Not content to limit their assault on free speech to the workplace, radical feminists have been in the forefront of the effort to establish campus speech codes that prohibit "discriminatory" or "harassing" speech. A student at the University of Michigan was threatened with disciplinary action for pointing out in a computer bulletin-board exchange that a charge of date rape could be false. A memo from the dean informed him that his opinion constituted "discriminatory harassment."

In an attempt to counteract restrictions on speech on college campuses across the country, Senator Larry Craig of Idaho sponsored the Freedom of Speech on Campus Act of 1991. The bill would have prohibited universities that receive federal funding from taking "official sanction" against any student for speech protected under the First and Fourteenth Amendments that had caused offense to others.

In 1992, MacKinnon testified in Congress against the bill. First noting that to the extent that the legislation tracks the First Amendment, it is redundant, she proceeded to advocate what amounts to an evisceration of the First Amendment, defending speech codes as "policies . . . regulating discrimination that takes expressive and other forms . . . for the purpose of promoting equality in university settings." That is to say, it is appropriate to stifle words and ideas if the purpose is to "promote equality." Unlike laws covering libel or slander, which redress a particular injury intentionally directed at an individual, such rules seek to redress alleged generalized injuries to more than half of the population by silencing the other half. And, typically erasing the distinction between words and conduct, MacKinnon asserted that for a student to call another a "fucking faggot" was an "assault" that "effectively threw [the listener] off campus and out of class."

Ironically, MacKinnon uses workplace sexual-harassment rules to support the effort to police expression on campus. Completing the circle, she castigates courts that "have rendered discriminatory harassment as protected speech" for failing "to follow the clear workplace precedents which have recognized the activity the policies cover as actionable for over 15 years." She marvels that without speech codes, "KKK scrawled on the wall [is] discrimination at work but

. . . protected speech in school." The court-approved feminist concept of harassment in the workplace turns out to be a legal toehold to extend its influence to other areas such as colleges.

Silencing Ideas

As the University of Michigan example cited above illustrates, campus speech codes often affect not only racial or sexual slurs but the expression of "insensitive" ideas. In the spring of 1993 on the same campus, several students sent a letter to the Sociology Department, the Affirmative Action Office, and the university president accusing sociology professor David Goldberg of "racial and sexual harassment" in his graduate course on statistics. His crime was not insulting or mistreating anyone, but using statistical analysis to challenge some claims of race and sex discrimination—such as the assertion that blacks were disproportionately denied mortgage approval because of race, or that women earned 59 cents to a man's dollar because of discrimination. Although the university did not pursue harassment charges, Goldberg was forbidden to teach the statistics class or any other required course. His punishment was reduced after protests by senior faculty members: the 35-person class was split into two sections, one of which Goldberg was allowed to continue teaching.

The true agenda of the radical feminists (and other campus radicals) is revealed by MacKinnon's comment that the "real issue of free speech on campus [is] the silencing of the disadvantaged and those excluded by the advantaged and powerful." In this view, all debates are nothing but struggles for power.

> *"Radical feminists are aiming to impose their view of 'correct' action and speech at the earliest stages of development."*

The Freedom of Speech on Campus Act never got out of committee. Recently, several campus speech codes (including those of the universities of Michigan and Wisconsin) have been struck down by courts as too broad; other colleges, including Tufts University and the University of Pennsylvania, have "voluntarily rescinded speech codes after concluding they were ineffectual, divisive or illegal," Sarah Lubman writes. Still, according to a survey by the Freedom Forum First Amendment Center, nearly 400 public colleges and universities in the United States have speech regulations. About a third of the codes target not only threats of violence but "advocacy of offensive or outrageous viewpoints . . . or biased ideas."

Punishing Childhood Behavior

Another radical feminist proposal is that harassment policies should cover schoolchildren. In California and Minnesota, state legislatures have passed laws "to end sexual harassment by children." The California law penalizes "physical, visual or verbal actions of a sexual nature" that "have a negative impact upon an individual's academic performance or create an intimidating, hostile or offensive educational environment," and covers children from fourth through twelfth grade.

For some, even that is not enough. Sue Sattel, a gender equity specialist for the Minnesota Department of Education, complains that "California is sending a message that it's okay for little kids to sexually harass each other. . . . Title IX protects kids from kindergarten through college." On her home turf, Sattel has been more successful. The Minnesota sexual harassment law covers children all the way down to kindergarten. In the 1991–92 school year in Minneapolis alone, over 1,000 children were suspended or expelled on charges related to sexual harassment. In 1993, Cheltzie Hentz of Eden Prairie, Minnesota, became the youngest complainant ever to win a federal sexual-harassment suit—at the age of seven. She had been the target of abusive language by boys on the school bus.

Once again, the language defining prohibited behavior is extremely broad and speech is punished as conduct. What is "a verbal action of a sexual nature" that has a negative impact on academic performance? Should ten-year-old children be expelled from school for making comments about each other's developing bodies? Margaret Pena of the California Civil Liberties Union correctly complains that the laws are not only vague but confusing and unnecessary—as redundant as the Freedom of Speech on Campus Act was according to MacKinnon. School administrators already have authority to discipline students who attack other children or use obscenity, and they generally use their discretion to decide what action is warranted in each case. Feminist activists are trying to take that discretion away by raising the specter of lawsuits if the complainant feels that adequate steps were not taken. In the case of Cheltzie Hentz, school authorities had responded to letters from the girl's mother, Sue Mutziger, by suspending a few of the boys and replacing the school bus driver, after which the teasing stopped. Mutziger was not satisfied and pursued her complaints with the federal and state governments. The U.S. Department of Education ruled that the school had "failed to take timely and effective responsive action."

Not content to allow traditional parental and school supervision to set the boundaries of children's behavior, radical feminists are aiming to impose their view of "correct" action and speech at the earliest stages of development. Susan Strauss lists such "sexually harassing behaviors" as "name-calling (from 'honey' to 'bitch')," "spreading sexual rumors," "leers and stares," "sexual or 'dirty' jokes," "conversations that are too personal," "repeatedly asking someone out when he or she isn't interested," and "facial expressions (winking, kissing, etc.)." In some states, such behaviors—long considered a normal part of childhood and adolescence—can now be severely punished.

Regulating Street Harassment

What if some people still fall through the cracks of sexual-harassment regulations? Increasingly, the argument that women are entitled to a working or learning environment free of offensive or unwelcome sexual expression is expanding to claim that they are entitled to such an environment everywhere. Cynthia Grant Bowman, a professor of law at Northwestern University, has proposed more legislation to stop behavior that radical feminists dislike: "street harassment."

Writing in the *Harvard Law Review*, Bowman defines street harassment as "the harassment of women in public places by men who are strangers to them." This includes wolf whistles, leers, winks, grabs, pinches, and remarks ranging from "Hello, baby" to "You're just a piece of meat to me, bitch." Examples are taken from sources that include *Mademoiselle* magazine and a novel by Joyce Carol Oates.

> *"The risk of occasionally being offended is the price we pay for living in a free society."*

According to Bowman, street harassment is not merely vulgar or distasteful, but political. "By turning women into objects of public attention when they are in public, harassers drive home the message that women belong only in the world of the private." It can also "serve as a precursor to rape." In any event, it "takes a toll on women's self-esteem," restricts women's mobility and, even when seemingly trivial, objectifies women.

Bowman's solution, of course, is a legal remedy. She argues that laws directed at such behavior could be modeled on defamation laws or the sexual-harassment laws under Title VII, and also suggests that street harassment could be regulated as "low-value speech." Moreover, she calls for the passage of statutes specifically targeting street harassment, and litigation aimed at redefining the torts of assault, intentional infliction of emotional distress, and invasion of privacy. Her proposed model statute includes this language: "Street harassment occurs when one or more unfamiliar men accost one or more women in a public place . . . and intrude . . . upon the woman's attention in a manner that is unwelcome to the woman, with language that is explicitly or implicitly sexual."

In fact, truly egregious street harassment is covered by existing legal remedies. Sexually aggressive physical contact such as grabbing or pinching constitutes indecent assault or sexual battery. However, most of the expression that Bowman and other activists seek to curb does not fall into those categories. (An article in a women's magazine deploring the plague of street harassment featured the "harassment diaries" of 10 women. Although among them they totalled over 50 incidents in a week, none involved physical contact and only one involved obscene language. Many consisted merely of ogling or staring; typical remarks were, "Hi, baby. It's a nice day. You enjoying the weather?," "Have a nice day. God bless you," "Nice," "Sexy," and "You're beautiful.")

The statute proposed by Bowman would punish a man for starting a conversation with a female stranger with any sort of implicitly sexual language—including, perhaps, an "unwelcome" pickup line in a singles bar. Unconstitutional vagueness and overbreadth would appear to stand in the way of such legislation.

Even Bowman concedes that the "Supreme Court would be inclined to strike down any such regulation as gender-based, content-based, or underbroad."

Such action by the high court is not only likely; it is mandated by longstanding legal precedents. The risk of occasionally being offended is the price we pay for living in a free society. The Supreme Court cautions us against "the facile assumption that one can forbid particular words without also running a substantial risk of suppressing ideas in the process. Indeed, governments might soon seize upon the censorship of particular words as a convenient guise for banning the expression of unpopular views."

However, most feminist legal theorists do not even deny that their intent is to censor particular words because they serve as conduits for evil ideas—namely, that it is proper for men to treat women as objects of sexual attraction. Even if one agrees with their view that such "sexual objectification" is detrimental to women's status, that hardly warrants eviscerating First Amendment freedoms.

Vague Sexual Harassment Policies Threaten Academic Freedom

by Harvey A. Silverglate

About the author: *Harvey A. Silverglate is a graduate of Harvard Law School and specializes in criminal defense and civil liberties work in Boston.*

Repression at American universities continues apace and has reached the mighty Harvard Law School.

The faculty, in a move that received surprisingly little attention, voted overwhelmingly in April 1996 to adopt a set of "Sexual Harassment Guidelines." Weighing in at 11 single-spaced pages of substantive text, and bolstered by eight pages of enforcement procedures and a 15-page "appendix of related materials," the guidelines contain a provision that critics contend violates the rights of free speech and academic freedom. It punishes, among other things, "any . . . speech . . . of a sexual nature that is unwelcome . . . abusive . . . and has the purpose or effect of unreasonable interfering with an individual's work or academic performance or creating an intimidating, demeaning, degrading, hostile, or otherwise seriously offensive working or educational environment at Harvard Law School."

A Clause for Concern

Even though the guidelines were adopted with only one dissenting vote (not counting those professors who absented themselves from the faculty meeting), there are signs that some of the brighter lights at the institution had qualms.

For one thing, the faculty inserted a wishful clause that declares "no speech . . . shall be deemed violative of this guideline if it is reasonably designed or intended to contribute to legal or public education, academic inquiry, or reasoned debate on issues of public concern or is protected by the . . . First Amendment."

Putting aside the faculty's elevation of public discourse above private communication, one marvels that such an august group of legal scholars and teachers has adopted a speech code so ambiguous that they find it necessary to assure those under its authority that if charged with uttering words that an American (non-Harvard) citizen would be free to speak, they may argue the First Amendment in their defense. How many students, however, are likely to take the risk of being prosecuted for their "speech of a sexual nature" and rely upon the law school's good faith and good sense in accepting this defense? Indeed, can this exception for constitutionally protected speech

> *"Students with a sharp tongue (or perhaps just an independent mind) walk on egg shells at Harvard Law School these days."*

really cure the chilling impact that the guidelines will surely exert on speech at Harvard Law?

Harvard Law students (as well as many faculty members, for that matter) are not widely known as risk-takers when their careers are at stake. Furthermore, there is already a perception that the decks are stacked at the disciplinary tribunals.

Although adopted in April 1996, the guidelines did not go into effect until October. The six-month delay was occasioned by the requirement that the guidelines be vetted and approved by Harvard's Office of the General Counsel. Here we have the specter of some of the nation's leading constitutional law scholars being second-guessed by the university's staff of 13 in-house lawyers.

Students Do Not Need Protection

Why did the faculty see fit to adopt such a speech code? Was there an epidemic of gross sexual misconduct that provoked curtailment of speech? Dean Robert Clark, queried on the subject in a letter I wrote him in April 1996, said little to justify the code, but what he did say was pregnant with meaning:

"Thank you for your letter . . . about your thoughts on the Harassment Guidelines. Your sentiments have been echoed in the faculty chambers along with many others. This discussion is a sign of the times, as is the need perceived among students that we have to discuss this or be seen as uncaring of their concerns."

What Dean Clark pointedly failed to claim was that there was a *demonstrated need*, rather than merely a *perceived occasion* for curtailment of speech. He also failed to explain why the faculty had to follow up "discussion" with actual censorship, lest it be seen as "uncaring." Finally, let the record reflect that the law school did not dare to have a referendum (preferably by secret ballot) among the students to see if a majority really needed or wanted such "protection" at the expense of their free-speech rights.

Indeed, to my knowledge, no academic institution has ever dared to put restrictive speech codes to a vote to see if students really feel the need to be "protected" by a sacrifice of their liberties. As far as one can tell, these codes are simply another example of the university's unilaterally acting *in loco parentis*—a distant but direct relative of the rules of prior decades, imposed from the top, that prohibited the sexes from visiting each other's dormitory rooms.

Some administrators have sought to defend speech codes by claiming that federal Department of Education guidelines require universities to take unspecified steps to prevent and deal with "harassment" of "vulnerable classes," and that failure to do so invites lawsuits. However, it is clear that no bureaucrat has the power to force a university to curtail free speech, since the Constitution trumps a mere regulation every time. In any event, none of these academic bureaucrats have demonstrated sufficient integrity to launch a court challenge to these alleged governmental censors.

Banning Hate Speech

Of course it could have been worse, according to Dean Clark. An earlier proposed version of these guidelines proposed banning "sex-based harassment by personal vilification," which would have included speech directed to individual members of the law school community that is "intended to insult or stigmatize . . . on the basis of their gender or sexual orientation" and conveys "visceral hatred or contempt." Faced with the prospect of this near-total ban on any kind of personally discomforting gender-based speech, Dean Clark and some faculty members appear to feel that the code actually adopted is the lesser of evils. Certainly Dean Clark's letter makes that appear to be so, dubbing the "harassment by vilification" language to be a "hate speech" ban.

Yet it is hard to understand how and why the current "hostile environment" language is any less restrictive of or threatening to free speech and, for that matter, how it differs from a "hate speech" ban. Further, if experiences on other campuses are a guide, any speech ban at Harvard will be applied with the all-too-familiar double standard, where only students with politically incorrect views will be charged and convicted.

A 1992 incident at Harvard Law makes one pause over the meaning and scope of the speech ban, notwithstanding the faculty's assurance that nothing violative of the First Amendment will be penalized.

The March 1992 issue of the *Harvard Law Review*, setting aside what the editors called "traditional editorial policy," published "an unfinished draft" of an article by Mary Joe Frug, a feminist legal scholar tragically murdered the year before. The manuscript, an example of the kind of controversial politicized scholarship that traditional legal scholars do not consider scholarship at all, was parodied the following month by a group of students in what was denominated by them, in a "warning" on the cover, as admittedly "highly insensitive."

Censoring Unpopular Ideas

The publication provoked a storm of outrage from many faculty members and administrators, some calling for the disciplining of the offending students and the wrecking of their legal careers. Ultimately, the students survived, as it became clear that their attempt at parody, though perhaps in abysmally poor taste, should be protected.

However, when at least one faculty member asked the drafting committee—whether the Frug parody would be viewed as nonprotected hate speech under the guidelines, the committee failed to deal with this crucial question. Had the guidelines been in effect in 1992, it is thus not at all clear whether the law school parodists would have been punished. What *is* clear is that students with a sharp tongue (or perhaps just an independent mind) walk on egg shells at Harvard Law School these days. To quote Dean Clark (who appears to have used the phrase more with resignation than enthusiasm), this is "a sign of the times."

To make matters worse, it appears that in caving in to the authoritarians, the faculty has not ended its agony, and the administration has not guaranteed itself "no trouble on this watch."

A first-year law student wrote in the Dec. 8, 1995, issue of the *Harvard Law Record*, the official student-run newspaper, that it was "tragic and ultimately short-sighted" for the faculty to adopt a policy that "seeks to protect students from offensive behavior or dialogue on the basis of sex, yet failed to adopt a comparable policy on the basis of race." Ominously, but instructively, what the student columnist was complaining about was the showing of a film in his criminal law class, which depicted a debate between a prosecutor and defense attorney over an encounter between a black college student and a white police officer who used a racial epithet.

"I became miffed, confused, and ultimately offended as the film progressed," wrote the student. Showing the film in class without giving students "proper warning" of its offensive content constituted racial harassment, he argued in all seriousness.

Dean Clark and the faculty are about to learn that once principle is sacrificed in the name of expedience, there is no end to the demands from ever-proliferating groups of self-described victims seeking to cleanse the campus—and the classrooms—of unpleasant speech, not to mention uncomfortable ideas.

Sexual Harassment Policies Can Be Applied Unfairly

by Kirstin Downey Grimsley

About the author: *Kirstin Downey Grimsley is a staff writer for the* Washington Post.

Social worker Hank McGovern loves David Letterman and his flippant late-night talk-show style. One day at work in March 1995, he found himself trying to emulate what he thought was the host's offbeat conversational manner with a new female co-worker at the Cleveland Center counseling facility in Shelby, N.C.

"I'm gonna flirt with ya," he told the woman one afternoon. About a week later, he repeated the same thing. She told him she didn't like it. Then accounts differ. She alleges that he said it a third time; he says he told her he wouldn't say it again.

One month later McGovern, 42, was fired. According to the letter of dismissal McGovern received from his supervisors at the Cleveland Center, the triggering event was the woman's charge of sexual harassment.

"I was shocked," McGovern says. "I feel the person victimized the most was me. I was the person fired from the job. It was traumatic."

Alleged Harassers Are Often Victims

McGovern has joined a small but growing fraternity of people who claim they were punished unduly harshly or fired for minor incidents that seem to them and some experts as relatively trivial, compared with the egregious behavior that is documented in sexual harassment cases that have emerged elsewhere.

How to react to allegations of sexual harassment is one of the trickiest questions facing corporate managers today. Many consultants, lawyers and other experts in sexual harassment say that as companies grow more aware of the issues and potential legal liabilities, many managers are stumbling in their responses. Some under-react by denying, deferring or ignoring serious charges. Others overreact by firing or severely punishing employees for lesser allegations.

Reprinted from Kirstin Downey Grimsley, "The Punishment Doesn't Always Fit the Crime," *The Washington Post*, January 27, 1997, by permission; ©1997, The Washington Post.

"There's a dichotomy in our economy," says employment attorney Rita Risser, a principal in Fair Measures, a workplace training and advisory firm in Santa Cruz, Calif. "Some organizations will tolerate gross harassment—rape, stalking, attempted murder—and won't do anything, but other organizations will fire someone for doing something minor that is not illegal but is a violation of the [zero-tolerance] harassment policy."

In some cases, the overreaction appears to stem from corporate concerns about the potentially large damage claims or bad publicity that can result from ignoring sexual harassment. In other situations, supervisors are using sexual harassment claims as an easy excuse for supervisors to fire unpopular people.

Nobody knows how many employees have been hurt by this kind of corporate overreaction. Risser, who has been tracking the phenomenon, says she has seen at least a dozen examples in the past 18 months among her 50 corporate clients.

Those numbers are dwarfed by the thousands of individuals who bring complaints of sexual harassment to government agencies because they believe their employers failed to respond appropriately. These numbers are growing rapidly: There were 15,549 sexual harassment complaints made to the U.S. Equal Employment Opportunity Commission and state human rights organizations in 1995, up from 6,127 in 1990.

Overreaction Damages Careers

Yet, in a handful of cases, it's clear that corporate or organizational bureaucracies have bungled or manipulated investigations of complaints in ways that may unfairly damage people's careers. These cases of overreaction are caused partly by lawyers and human resources consultants, who sometimes counsel companies to avoid litigation by quickly firing people who are accused—with or without completing a full investigation.

"The thinking and teaching is that you are better off firing them, because the second [incident] will hit you really hard," employment attorney Mike Neill says. "They are branded for life."

The right approach, experts say, is to conduct a careful investigation and respond quickly with appropriate disciplinary action, such as an official warning, suspension or transfer. If the behavior continues, a company may have no choice but to dismiss the worker or face an eventual lawsuit.

Complicating matters is the fact that most harassers deny the allegations against them. Even people charged with repeated, serious misconduct, where there is ample evidence of wrongdoing, will refuse to acknowledge the effects of their behavior. And harassers typically contend that their accusers are overreacting.

> *"Supervisors are using sexual harassment claims as an easy excuse for supervisors to fire unpopular people."*

The best guide for corporate managers in this new area of the law is to assess whether an employee's actions would bother a "reasonable" person. That is the standard used by the courts, which have generally defined sexual harassment as conduct that is repeated, unwelcome, creates a hostile work environment and would offend a "reasonable" woman or man.

An analysis by Risser of 13 federal sexual harassment cases from 1994 to 1996 found that those won by the plaintiffs generally involved menacing actions, such as rape, stalking, attempted murder, extremely vulgar language and repeated propositions, particularly by supervisors.

When Reasonable People Disagree

But what about less-extreme behavior, where reasonable people might disagree? McGovern, the therapist who was fired after saying he wanted to flirt with a co-worker, contends that his behavior wasn't sexual harassment. "It's an insult to me, because I would not say anything to someone if I knew it was unwanted," he says.

Support for McGovern's contention that he was fired unfairly comes from the North Carolina Employment Security Commission, which reviewed the facts in the case and ruled in July 1996 that he was eligible for unemployment compensation because he hadn't been discharged from his job for "substantial fault or misconduct connected with the work."

Yet in dismissing McGovern, Cleveland Center area director D.S. Brenneman and outpatient treatment services director Chris von Stade, said he was being fired because of a "failure in personal conduct."

In the memorandum, Brenneman and von Stade said McGovern had failed to take full responsibility for the negative consequences of his "gonna flirt with ya" comments. They said it indicated a pattern of poor judgment, and that he had been argumentative about the significance of his words. They said he had attended sexual harassment training when he was hired by the agency and had been told that a sexual harassment charge could cause an employee to lose his job.

"Cleveland County government and Cleveland Center cannot afford a reputation of excusing this kind of behavior," they wrote.

Brenneman and von Stade each were contacted twice, but both declined to comment on the dismissal and referred calls to Cleveland County attorney Julian Wray. Wray says that by law, county officials are not permitted to comment publicly on personnel matters.

An example of an accused harasser who won back his job is Richard Dinsmore, a professor of European history at the University of Maine at Fort Kent. Many accused harassers take to the courts to try to avenge themselves, but he is one of a handful who have succeeded.

In early 1992, one of the women students in Dinsmore's History of Ideas class complained to school administrators that he had sexually harassed her by touching her shoulder during a viewing of a film, by helping her put on her coat and by acting overly friendly while taking her out for coffee.

An investigation was conducted by Myrna Cassel, the campus's vice president for academic affairs and student services. In addition to supporting the student's claims, she also said Dinsmore was "guilty of using inappropriate academic content" by requiring students to read a book by psychologist John Bradshaw called *Homecoming,* which Cassel said could be "dangerous to students who might not be sufficiently mature." She recommended that Dinsmore, who had been suspended, should be terminated.

He was fired from his tenured position in May 1992.

Dinsmore sued, charging that his rights to free speech and due process had been violated and that he had been defamed. He won nearly $1 million in damages and attorneys fees in a jury verdict in 1995. His case was later resolved in a mediated settlement for $500,000 and he was reinstated to his previous job. He returned to work at the college campus in the fall of 1996.

> *"Sexual harassment charges can sometimes become weapons in corporate competition."*

Dinsmore said in an interview that the charges were "preposterous," and that he had become a victim of "man-hating feminists." He said he did not blame the young woman who had made the complaint because he believed she was a pawn in an ongoing dispute he had with administrators.

Dinsmore's attorney, David G. Webbert, says Dinsmore had become a controversial figure on the campus by espousing unpopular views on gender issues. "In a university setting, sexual harassment is a weapon people can use to get people fired," Webbert says.

Vendean Vafiades, counsel for the University of Maine System, confirms that the university has settled the case and reinstated Dinsmore. But she says the university's views about Dinsmore's conduct have not changed, despite the jury's verdict.

"Professor Dinsmore's conduct caused us great concern," Vafiades says. "We feel we have an institutional obligation to protect our students."

False Accusations Become Weapons

Group dynamics appear to play an important role in these cases, experts say, as people join in denouncing those they mistrust. Particularly vulnerable are African American men, especially if the alleged victim is white, or highly paid older white men in an era of salary cutbacks, experts say.

In a relatively small number of cases, alleged victims have invented harassment stories, experts say. These rare instances of false accusations stem from psychological problems, a desire to earn money in a lawsuit, or an attempt to protect their jobs if they are performing badly and fear they may be fired, according to attorneys who specialize in handling sexual harassment cases.

One case cited by sexual harassment prevention trainer Monica Ballard involves a woman teacher who was coming to work late and leaving early; she was confronted about it by the male principal, who told her he had been tracking her schedule of missed work. The next day, the woman falsely charged he had sexually harassed her, and the school district fired him immediately to avoid negative publicity.

Sexual harassment charges can sometimes become weapons in corporate competition.

Employment attorney Risser says that at one company she advises, two competing sales managers, both men, were drinking at a bar and exchanging war stories about their staffs and their strengths and weaknesses. One of the men described a woman salesperson as "hot," referring to the blizzard of business she brought the firm.

His drinking buddy returned to the office and reported his competitor for sexual harassment. The man who had made the "hot" comment was written up for a disciplinary infraction, Risser says.

Sometimes companies treat accused harassers differently, depending on who they are, Risser says. At one high-tech Silicon Valley company she advises, a fast-track, up-and-coming engineer jokingly patted a woman subordinate on the rear one day. The woman complained, but the company wanted to do nothing, hoping to protect the rising star. Risser disagreed, saying they were required to enter it in his record.

But at the same company, Risser was brought in to provide last-chance counseling to a service manager who had been issued a final written warning about another one-time incident. This male service manager had complained to a female colleague, after she chewed him out in public, that she had "raped" him. The woman then complained his use of the term was sexual harassment.

The company agreed and sanctioned the man severely. But in her counseling session with the man, Risser says the service manager had documented 12 uses of the word "rape" at their office, by both men and women, as a verb meaning to take advantage, abuse or overwhelm another worker. He believed he had been unfairly singled out for punishment. "He said, 'This is political,'" Risser says. "And I said, 'You're right. This is what they are doing to get you on the way out. They want to get rid of you.' "

A Chilling Effect on the Workplace

Not surprisingly, such overly harsh policies can have the same chilling effect on the workplace as sexual harassment that goes ignored. It can also boomerang on women complainants because other co-workers will blame them if someone is fired for what appears to be a minor issue. Male workers also may start avoiding working with women because they fear that some small misstatement will result in their dismissal.

Glenn Ricketts, a spokesman for the Princeton, N.J.–based National Association of Scholars, who reviewed Prof. Dinsmore's case and believes it is not unique, says he thinks that women ultimately may suffer because of men's fears of false accusations or unjust punishment.

"The sad situation is a number of my male colleagues won't ever meet with a female student without the door to their office open, and without a colleague present," Ricketts says.

"When you go nuts and fire somebody for something minor, then you have a whole new set of problems," says Susan Webb, president of Seattle-based Pacific Resource Development Group, a pioneer in the field of sexual harassment prevention training and an expert witness on the topic for the past decade.

"If you under-react and punish people too lightly, it shows you don't care," she says. "If you overreact, a lot of women will be impacted too."

The Reasonable Woman Standard Hurts Women

by Kathryn Abrams

About the author: *Kathryn Abrams is a professor of law and women's studies at Cornell University in Ithaca, New York.*

Is sexual harassment understood differently by men and women? If so (as seems likely), whose understanding should set the standard for court decisions? These questions, which lawyers have argued about for almost a decade, reached the general public with the Senate testimony of Anita Hill. [Hill alleged she had been a victim of sexual harassment at the confirmation hearings of Supreme Court justice Clarence Thomas.] But the ensuing debate—between partisans of a universal common sense and those who see perceptions of sexual harassment as gender-differentiated—has thus far produced more heat than light. Although the debate has offered a fascinating window on movements within feminist theory, it has rarely yielded sufficient guidance for the judgment of actual cases.

Measuring Sexual Harassment

The central challenge of sexual harassment litigation has been to define when harassment becomes sufficiently pervasive to create a "hostile environment." The Supreme Court accepted the idea of hostile-environment sexual harassment in 1986, but its pronouncements on the question of pervasiveness have been frustratingly vague. Sexual harassment violates the law when it is "severe or pervasive [enough] to alter the conditions of plaintiff's employment and create an abusive working environment," or when it "unreasonably interferes with [plaintiff's] work performance and creat[es] a hostile, intimidating or offensive" environment. This proliferation of adjectives has raised more questions than it has answered. Is an "intimidating" or "offensive" environment different from an "abusive" one? Do certain kinds of conduct contribute more to the creation of such environments than others? Compounding these difficulties has been a question of perspective or vantage point in assessing the alleged abuse. Courts are frequently confronted with a plaintiff who argues that certain conduct

Abridged from Kathryn Abrams, "The Reasonable Woman: Sense and Sensibility in Sexual Harassment Law," *Dissent*, Winter 1995. Reprinted by permission of the author and *Dissent* magazine.

starkly interferes with her work performance, and a defendant who argues that the same conduct is trivial, episodic, jocular, or nonintrusive. How can judges find an independent ground on which to stand in assessing these allegations?

The first solution offered by the courts was to assess the claims of the plaintiff from the perspective of the "reasonable person." This approach offered several advantages. First, it had the legitimizing pedigree of a long history in the law: courts had assessed the conduct of torts defendants from the standpoint of the "reasonable man" and later the (gender-neutral) "reasonable person" to determine whether they had met the required duty of care toward plaintiffs. Second, the specification of a vantage point distinct from that of the actual plaintiff offered reassurance to employers; it protected them from liability arising from idiosyncratic claims. Finally, the resort to a vantage point ostensibly accessible to any observer held the promise of reducing the growing confusion over the "pervasiveness" standard. In the long tradition of jurists who have sought procedural answers to festering substantive disputes, proponents of the "reasonable person" test appealed to perspective—in this case, a kind of universal common sense—to mitigate controversy over "pervasiveness."

> *"The assertion of a single valid perspective on sexual harassment belied the gender differentiation that many kinds of research were beginning to reveal."*

Challenges to the Reasonable Person Standard

But as feminist advocates soon made clear, the "reasonable person" standard only complicated the controversy. Their challenge to this standard reflected the confluence of two intellectual movements within feminist theory. The first was a tendency toward gender differentiation, characteristic of both cultural and radical feminisms. These movements resisted the gender-neutrality characteristic of equality theories, which had described women as substantially similar to men. Cultural feminists argued that this move understated and undervalued the biological and social ways in which women differed from men. Radical feminists charged that the focus on women's conformity to male norms diverted attention from a system of power relations through which male characteristics become normative. Both groups bridled at the possibility that women's perspectives would be described in terms simultaneously applicable to men.

The second influential movement was the challenge to objectivist accounts of knowledge. Feminist writers assailed the notion of "truth" as something "out there," external to the position of the observer, accessible by certain neutral observational methods. The status of legal norms or social understandings as "true" or "neutral," and the legitimation of certain methods for gaining access to them, are incidents of power, they argued. Resisting such power meant exposing the extent to which understandings of social relations are shaped by social location. And it meant exposing those viewpoints considered to be neutral or true as another example of a partial perspective, distinguished only by the ability of its adherents to make their vision normative.

Resistance also required a challenge to objectivist modes of knowledge production. One important strategy in this effort has been a re-valuation of nondominant ways of knowing about the world. Some scholars, influenced by cultural feminism, have valorized "ways of knowing" they describe as characteristic of women: reasoning from personal experience is one example; choosing contextual reasoning over abstract principle is another. Other scholars, retaining a focus on the power dimension, have claimed an "epistemic advantage" for those at the bottom of reigning hierarchies. The oppressed, in this view, enjoy a double source of knowledge: their experience in a society built around the understandings of the privileged familiarizes them with those perspectives, but gives them a view from a subordinated social location that the privileged lack.

Differences in Perception

These diverse insights combined to fuel a critique of the "reasonable person" standard. Feminist advocates pointed first to the gendered origins of the standard. The "reasonable person" had its beginnings in the "reasonable man," a fellow who "takes the magazines at home and in the evening pushes the lawn mower in his shirtsleeves." (*Hall v. Brooklands Auto Racing Club*, 1933, quoting "unnamed American author.") As this early twentieth century elaboration reveals, what was being presented as universal common sense was in fact the sense of a particular, socially located person: one whose perspective was shaped by his freedom to relax with his magazines at home, and to enjoy sovereignty over his physical—and familial—domain. Moreover, the assertion of a single valid perspective on sexual harassment belied the gender differentiation that many kinds of research were beginning to reveal. Social scientists like Barbara Gutek pointed to a sharp divergence in the way men and women view sexualized conduct in the workplace. Men were likely to see sexualized words or gestures as flattering, indicative of long-term interest, and not threatening to professional progress; women were likely to associate them with manipulation, exploitation, or threat, and to see them as imperiling their professional prospects. Analyses like that of Catharine MacKinnon offered an explanatory social context for these

> *"'Women's ways of knowing' could be used to reinforce stereotypes of the intuitive or irrational woman."*

differences. Women workers' experience of marginality within the workplace, and sexual vulnerability in and outside it, caused them to view the sexual inflection of work relations with a fearfulness unlikely to be shared by their male counterparts. Finally, feminists worried that the "reasonable person" standard might confirm the (largely male) judiciary in its unreflective assurance that it understood the phenomenon of sexual harassment. Judges might view it as authorizing them to decide cases on the basis of their own intuition: the same "common sense" that had marked the administration of the "reasonable person" standard in tort law—and the same "common sense" that had normalized the practice of sexual harassment in the first place.

All of these factors suggested the preferability of a "reasonable woman" standard. This formulation would explicitly challenge notions of a universal perspective. It would characterize the evaluation of harassment, like the experience of harassment itself, as a phenomenon strongly differentiated on the basis of gender. The gender-specific language would place male judges on alert that they could no longer rely on their unexamined intuitions. The "reasonable woman" standard would replace those intuitions with a perspective that promised a radical revision of workplace conditions. Yet beyond the notion that such a perspective would "take harassment seriously"—viewing it neither as a right of the employer, nor as a harmless, if vulgar, form of male amusement—there was little explicit discussion of what insights or sensibilities it entailed.

As the eighties closed, this approach began to be embraced by the federal courts. In a landmark case called *Ellison v. Brady,* the Ninth Circuit Court of Appeals held that sexual harassment should be evaluated from the perspective of the "reasonable woman." In *Ellison* a woman received a series of letters from a colleague she barely knew, describing his love for and continuous surveillance of her. The trial court had shrugged off the behavior as a "pathetic attempt at courtship," but the Court of Appeals disagreed. It stressed the importance of considering the conduct from the standpoint of a "reasonable woman": "a sex-blind reasonable person standard," the court noted, "tends to be male biased and tends to systematically ignore the experiences of women." It held that, viewed from the perspective of a "reasonable woman," receiving "long, passionate, disturbing" letters from a person one barely knew represented sufficiently pervasive and severe harassment to create a hostile environment.

The court recognized the need, in such a context, to elaborate the differences in perspective between men and women. And it took a few steps in that direction, noting that conduct considered unobjectionable by men might be offensive to women, and stating that women's vulnerability to sexual assault gave them a "stronger incentive" to be concerned about sexual behavior in the workplace. But the largely passive stance of the *Ellison* court toward the elaboration of perspectival differences is expressed in its "hope that over time men and women will learn what conduct offends reasonable members of the opposite sex."

Focusing on Differences

Both the strengths and the drawbacks of the *Ellison* opinion were underscored in the revolution catalyzed by Anita Hill. Women's denunciation of senators who failed to "get it" stressed the gendered character of perceptions of sexual harassment, and the need for a gendered standard of evaluation. The "reasonable woman" standard was, in fact, adopted by several additional courts in the wake of the Senate hearings. But the growing concern of even well-intentioned men with the "new rules of engagement" pointed to the need for explicit discussion of the determinants of gender difference in this area. Both men and women sought greater clarity about the ways in which their perceptions of sexual harassment diverged, and the "hope" for mutual understanding expressed by *Ellison* failed to fill the bill.

As the call for a fuller elaboration of women's perspectives continued, the "reasonable woman" standard began to be challenged from an unexpected quarter: the feminist movement itself. There were several sources of this attitudinal sea change. Some feminists worried that unitary images of female difference could be manipulated by hostile forces. Images of women that emphasized care or connection could be used to explain the absence of women from more competitive jobs—a link that was made in the notorious *Sears* litigation. "Women's ways of knowing" could be used to reinforce stereotypes of the intuitive or irrational woman. Others challenged accounts of strong gender differentiation as essentialist and potentially oppressive.

> *"Reasonableness . . . could be interpreted to mean not the average person, but the person enlightened concerning the barriers to women's equality in the workplace."*

A range of "anti-essentialist" feminists, led by lesbians and women of color, argued that unitary depictions of women replicated the false and exclusory universalism of the gender-neutral approach. Some asked whether the divergent social circumstances of women could possibly yield the same knowledge: how could modes of reasoning shaped by the domestic context, for example, apply to women who did not remain in the home or live within conventional families? Others argued that the unity presented in depictions of "women's experience" derived not from homogeneity but from erasure. Comparatively privileged white middle class women—through solipsism or strategic exclusion—had eclipsed the experiences of less privileged subgroups.

Feminists Question the New Standard

These insights made many feminists wary of the gathering momentum behind the "reasonable woman" standard. They worried that the "reasonable woman," like other paradigmatic "women" of feminist theory, would turn out to be white, middle class, and heterosexual. Others asked whether simply living as a woman assured a particular perspective on sexual harassment. The disparagement of sexual harassment claims by female "mavericks" like Judge Maryanne Trump Berry gave some advocates pause. The "reasonable woman" might simply free women judges to resort to *their* intuitions, in ways that were not uniformly promising to female claimants. Moreover, the standard might fail to prompt the desired response from male judges—permitting them to indulge their own, biologized visions of female difference. So there was a growing division among feminist advocates over the "reasonable woman" standard, with some calling for a further elaboration or differentiation of the standard, and others seeking a return to gender neutrality or a rejection of all "reasonableness" criteria.

These differences among feminists were brought to the fore by the Supreme Court's second case on hostile environment sexual harassment: *Harris v. Forklift Systems*. That case presented the question of whether plaintiffs must demonstrate "serious psychological injury" in order to win their cases. But the court also agreed to consider whether hostile environment claims should be reviewed under a gendered or gender-neutral standard. Those feminist advocates who filed amicus briefs with the court were frankly divided on the question of the standard: the Employment Law Center and Equal Rights Advocates endorsed a "reasonable woman" standard, while Catharine MacKinnon and the Women's Legal Defense and Education Fund argued that "reasonableness" standards, whether gender-specific or gender-neutral, reinforce stereotypes and distract the court from the primary issue—the conduct of the defendant. The decision, when it came, was anticlimactic. Although the court resoundingly rejected the psychological injury requirement, it resolved the question of standard in less than a sentence, stating that the court should review plaintiff's claim according to the perspective of the "reasonable person," with no elaboration and no explanation of its decision.

It is hard to know what conclusions to draw from this cryptic affirmation of gender-neutrality. It suggests that a court that has displayed studied disinterest in group-based distinctions is not prepared to embrace a standard that underscores—and perhaps risks instantiating—gender difference. Some subset of male judges will now, no doubt, resort to their own, unschooled intuitions in evaluating sexual harassment cases. But has the court scuttled the entire project of introducing a new, non-dominant sensibility about sexual harassment into adjudication? I see no reason to draw so negative a conclusion. The first goal of the "reasonable woman" standard was to emphasize the gendered character of sexual harassment and prevent resort to a "common sense" that was likely to preserve the status quo. The second goal was to permit access to a distinct set of perspectives that would open the way for a transformation of workplace norms. Though the courts have made only limited progress in fleshing out these perspectives, their elaboration is essential to reshaping the perceptions of judges, and ultimately of those who structure the workplace. This second, and arguably more important, task can still be performed under a "reasonable person" standard.

A Neutral Standard

My own argument begins with the anti-essentialist insight that neither modes of knowing nor particular bodies of knowledge are inextricably linked to biological set or social gender. There are things that women are more likely to know by virtue of having lived as women. There are practices—such as those involving devaluation or sexualization—to which they are likely to have a heightened sensitivity by virtue of having experienced them, heard about them repeatedly, or seen them applied to other women. But this likelihood cannot be collapsed into inevitability: some women have had few of the experiences that produce such sensitivity; others respond with indifference or denial; women who are aware of discriminatory practices may perceive them in different ways. Just as being female does not guarantee transformative perceptions of sexual conduct in the workplace, being male does not exclude the possibility of having, or developing, them. If perceptions of sexual harassment do not depend solely on biology, life experience, or gender-specific modes of knowing, but rather on varied sources of information regarding women's inequality—if such perceptions, in other words, are a matter not of innate common sense but of informed sensibility—then they can be cultivated in a range of women and men. The "reasonable person" standard, properly elaborated, might be a vehicle for the courts to play a role in this educative process. The reasonableness term, as Martha Chamallas has suggested, could be interpreted to mean not the average person, but the person enlightened concerning the barriers to women's equality in the workplace.

Bibliography

Books

Elizabeth Bouchard — *Everything You Need to Know About Sexual Harassment*. New York: Rosen, 1997.

Ellen Bravo and Ellen Cassedy — *The 9 to 5 Guide to Combating Sexual Harassment*. New York: John Wiley & Sons, 1992.

David M. Buss and Neil M. Malamuth — *Sex, Power, Conflict: Evolutionary and Feminist Perspectives*. New York: Oxford University Press, 1997.

Lois Copeland and Leslie R. Wolfe — *Violence Against Women as Bias Motivated Hate Crime: Defining the Issues*. Washington, DC: Center for Women Policy Studies, 1991.

Barry M. Dank and Robert Refinetti, eds. — *Sexual Harassment and Sexual Consent*. New Brunswick, NJ: Transaction, 1997.

Richard Dooling — *Blue Streak: Swearing, Free Speech, and Sexual Harassment*. New York: Random House, 1996.

Billie Wright Dziech and Linda Weiner — *The Lecherous Professor: Sexual Harassment on Campus*. Champaign: University of Illinois Press, 1992.

Elizabeth Fried — *Sex, Laws, and Stereotypes*. Shawnee Mission, KS: National Press, 1995.

Anita Hill — *Speaking Truth to Power*. New York: Doubleday, 1997.

June Larkin — *Sexual Harassment: High School Girls Speak Out*. Toronto: Second Story Press, 1994.

Virginia A. Lathan — *Preventing Sexual Harassment*. Sacramento: Curry-Co, 1997.

Anne Levy and Michele Antoinette Paludi — *Workplace Sexual Harassment*. New York: Prentice Hall, 1996.

Catharine A. MacKinnon — *Sexual Harassment of Working Women: A Case of Sex Discrimination*. New Haven: Yale University Press, 1979.

Susan Gluck Mezey — *In Pursuit of Equality*, New York: St. Martin's Press, 1991.

Celia Morris — *Bearing Witness: Sexual Harassment and Beyond: Everywoman's Story*. New York: Little, Brown, 1994.

Michele A. Paludi and Richard B. Barickman	*Academic and Workplace Sexual Harassment: A Resource Manual*. Ithaca: State University of New York Press, 1992.
Michele A. Paludi	*Sexual Harassment on College Campuses: Abusing the Ivory Power*. Albany: State University of New York Press, 1996.
Barbara Kate Repa and William Petrocelli	*Sexual Harassment on the Job*. Berkeley, CA: Nolo Press, 1992.
Carol R. Ronai, ed.	*Everyday Sexism: In the Third Millennium*. New York: Routledge, 1997.
Peter Rutter	*Sex, Power, and Boundaries*. New York: Bantam Books, 1996.
Peter Rutter	*Understanding and Preventing Sexual Harassment: The Complete Guide*. New York: Bantam Books, 1997.
Rosemarie Skaine	*Power and Gender: Issues in Sexual Dominance and Harassment*. Jefferson, NC: McFarland, 1996.
Margaret S. Stockdale, ed.	*Sexual Harassment in the Workplace: Perspectives, Frontiers, and Response Strategies*. Thousand Oaks, CA: Sage, 1996.
Amber Coverdale Sunrall and Dena Taylor, eds.	*Sexual Harassment: Women Speak Out*. Freedom, CA: The Crossing Press, 1992.
Susan L. Webb	*Step Forward: Sexual Harassment in the Workplace*. New York: Mastermedia, 1991.

Periodicals

Alexandra Alger and William G. Flanagan	"Sexual Politics," *Forbes*, May 6, 1996.
Cheryl L. Anderson	"'Nothing Personal': Individual Liability Under 42 U.S.C. 1983 for Sexual Harassment as an Equal Protection Claim," *Berkeley Journal of Employment and Labor Law*, Summer 1998.
Helen Benedict	"Fear of Feminism," *Nation*, May 11, 1998.
Ron Berenbeim	"The Politics of Sexual Harassment," *Across the Board*, April 1996. Available from 845 Third Ave., New York, NY 10022-6679.
Angela Bonavoglia	"The Sacred Secret," *Ms.*, March/April 1992.
Jerry Buckley et al.	"Watershed? Not Quite," *U.S. News & World Report*, October 28, 1991.
Deborah Epstein	"Can a 'Dumb Ass Woman' Achieve Equality in the Workplace? Running the Gauntlet of Hostile Environment Harassing Speech," *Georgetown Law Journal*, 1996.
Cynthia Estlund	"Freedom of Speech in the Workplace and the Problem of Discriminatory Harassment," *Texas Law Review*, 1997.

Bibliography

Susan Faludi   "Sex and the Times," *Nation*, April 20, 1998.

Suzanne Fields   "Is It Really Harassment?" *Insight*, December 9, 1991. Available from 3600 New York Ave. NE, Washington, DC 20002.

Ted Gest and Amy Saltzman   "Harassment: Men on Trial," *U.S. News & World Report*, October 21, 1991.

Marcia Ann Gillespie   "We Speak in Tongues," *Ms.*, January/February 1992.

Ellen Goodman   "Powerful Men and Vulnerable Women," *Boston Globe*, November 15, 1996. Available from the Globe Store, 1 School St., Boston, MA 02108.

Juliana Gruenwald   "Call for Separate Training Reignites War of Words," *Congressional Quarterly*, December 20, 1997. Available from 1414 22nd St. NW, Washington, DC 20037.

Mark Hansen   "Love's Labor Laws," *ABA Journal*, June 1998.

Lewis Kamb   "Sexual Harassment and Beetle Bailey," *Gauntlet*, vol. I, 1997. Available from 309 Powell Rd., Springfield, PA 19064.

Elizabeth Kolbert   "Sexual Harassment at Work Is Pervasive, Survey Suggests," *The New York Times*, October 11, 1991.

Elizabeth Larson   "Shrinking Violets at the Office," *Women's Quarterly*, Spring 1996. Available from 2111 Wilshire Blvd., Suite 550, Arlington, VA 22201-3057.

Marianne Lavelle   "The New Rules of Sexual Harassment," *U.S. New & World Report*, July 6, 1998.

Brian Mitchell   "Sex Scandal du Jour," *Chronicles*, May 1997. Available from the Rockford Institute, 934 N. Main St., Rockford, IL 61103.

Naomi Munson   "Harassment Blues," *Commentary*, February 1992.

David Niven   "The Case of the Hidden Harassment," *Harvard Business Review*, March-April 1992.

Jonathan Rauch   "Offices and Gentleman," *New Republic*, June 23, 1997.

Stephen F. Rohde   "Outspoken Professor Wins Victory in Academic Freedom Case," *Gauntlet*, vol. I, 1997.

Hanna Rosin   "Sleeping with the Enemy," *New Republic*, June 23, 1997.

David G. Savage   "Signs of Disagreement," *ABA Journal*, May 1998.

Vicki Schultz   "Reconceptualizing Sexual Harassment," *Yale Law Journal*, April 1998.

Charlene Marmer Solomon   "The Secret's Out," *Workforce*, July 1998. Available from PO Box 55695, Boulder, CO 80322-5695.

Susan Brooks Thistlewaite   "Sexual Harassment: To Protect, Empower," *Christianity and Crisis*, October 21, 1991. Available from 537 W. 121st St., New York, NY 10027.

David Wagner   "Workplace Laws and Conduct Unbecoming," *Insight*, February 23, 1998. Available from 3600 New York Ave. NE, Washington, DC 20002.

Philip Weiss   "Don't Even Think About It. (The Cupid Cops Are Watching)," *New York Times Magazine*, May 3, 1998.

Naomi Wolf   "Sex with the Boss: Why Not?" *George*, April 1, 1998. Available from ISI/*George* magazine, 30 Montgomery Street, Jersey City, NJ 07032.

Cathy Young   "Groping Toward Sanity," *Reason*, August/September 1998.

Organizations to Contact

The editors have compiled the following list of organizations concerned with the issues debated in this book. The descriptions are derived from materials provided by the organizations. All have publications or information available for interested readers. The list was compiled on the date of publication of the present volume; the information provided here may change. Be aware that many organizations take several weeks or longer to respond to inquiries, so allow as much time as possible.

Center for Women's Policy Studies (CWPS)
2000 P St. NW, Suite 508, Washington, DC 20036
(202) 872-1770

Established in 1972, CWPS is an independent feminist policy research and advocacy institution. The center studies policies affecting the social, legal, health, and economic status of women. It publishes reports on a variety of topics related to women's equality and empowerment, including sexual harassment, campus rape, and violence against women.

Concerned Women for America (CWA)
370 L'Enfant Promenade SW, Suite 800, Washington, DC 20024
(800) 323-2200
website: http://www.cwfa.org

CWA's purpose is to preserve, protect, and promote traditional Judeo-Christian values through education, legislative action, and other activities. Its members believe that feminism has harmed society by encouraging women's participation in the workforce, promoting divorce as a symbol of freedom, and endorsing the use of child day care. CWA publishes the monthly *Family Voice* in addition to brochures, booklets, and manuals on numerous issues, including feminism and working women.

Department of Defense
Office of the Assistant Secretary of Defense for Public Affairs/Directorate for Public Communication
1400 Defense Pentagon, Room 1E757, Washington, DC 20301-1400
(703) 697-5737
e-mail: dpcintrn@osd.pentagon.mil • website: http://www.defenselink.mil

The office is responsible for presenting the official positions of the military on current issues, including sexual harassment. It maintains one officer responsible for information on women in the military and publishes a brochure that discusses sexual harassment in the military.

Equal Employment Opportunity Commission (EEOC)
1801 L St. NW, Washington, DC 20507
(202) 663-4900

The purpose of the EEOC is to eliminate discrimination in the workplace. To achieve this purpose, the commission investigates cases of alleged discrimination, including cases of sexual harassment; helps victims prosecute cases; and offers educational programs for employers and community organizations. The EEOC publishes a packet of information about sexual harassment.

The Feminist Majority Foundation

1600 Wilson Blvd., Suite 801, Arlington, VA 22209
(703) 522-2214 • fax: (703) 522-2219 • hot line: (703) 522-2501
e-mail: femmaj@feminist.org • website: http://www.feminist.org

The foundation researches ways to empower women. It maintains a hot line that provides information, resources, and strategies for dealing with sexual harassment. The foundation publishes a report that includes an overview and critical analysis of sexual harassment laws and an examination of women's experiences of being sexually harassed. It also publishes the quarterly *Feminist Majority Report* as well as a newsletter, fact sheets, books, and videos.

Feminists for Free Expression (FFE)

2525 Times Square Station, New York, NY 10108-2525
(212) 702-6292
e-mail: freedom@well.com • website: http://www.well.com/user/freedom

FFE was founded in 1992 by a diverse group of feminists devoted to preserving a woman's right and responsibility to read, listen to, view, and produce materials of her choice without the intervention of the state on her behalf. FFE advocates the freedom to express all messages, and its Internet website provides information on sexual harassment, pornography, art, and the Internet as well as a bibliography of books and articles by FFE members.

Foundation for Economic Education (FEE)

39 S. Broadway, Irvington-on-Hudson, NY 10533
(914) 591-7230 • fax: (914) 591-8910
e-mail: freeman@fee.org • website: http://www.fee.org

FEE studies and promotes capitalism, free trade, and limited government. It occasionally publishes articles opposing government solutions to the problem of sexual harassment in its monthly magazine the *Freeman*.

The Heritage Foundation

214 Massachusetts Ave. NE, Washington, DC 20002-4999
(202) 546-4400 • fax: (202) 546-8328
e-mail: info@heritage.org • website: http://www.heritage.org

The foundation is a conservative public policy institute dedicated to the principles of free competitive enterprise, limited government, individual liberty, and a strong national defense. It believes that national security concerns justify limiting the media and that pornography should be censored. It publishes the monthly *Policy Review*, the periodic *Backgrounder*, and the *Heritage Lecture* series, all of which sometimes address issues of violence and pornography.

National Coalition Against Censorship (NCAC)

275 Seventh Ave., New York, NY 10001
(212) 807-6222 • fax: (212) 807-6245
e-mail: ncac@ncac.org • website: http://www.ncac.org

NCAC is an alliance of organizations committed to defending freedom of thought, inquiry, and expression by engaging in public education and advocacy on national and local levels. It believes censorship of violent materials is dangerous because it represses intellectual and artistic freedom. NCAC maintains a library of information dealing with First Amendment issues and publishes the quarterly *Censorship News*.

National Coalition of Free Men

PO Box 129, Manhasset, NY 11030
(516) 482-6378
e-mail: ncfm@ncfm.org • website: http://www.ncfm.org

The coalition's members include men seeking a "fair and balanced perspective on gender issues." The organization promotes the legal rights of men in issues of abortion, divorce, false accusation of rape, sexual harassment, and sexual abuse. It conducts research, sponsors education programs, maintains a database on men's issues, and publishes the bimonthly *Transitions*.

National Council for Research on Women (NCRW)

11 Hanover Sq., New York, NY 10005
(212) 785-7335 • fax: (212) 785-7350
e-mail: ncrw@ncrw.org • website: http://www.ncrw.org

NCRW promotes and generates research that encourages policy and action on feminist issues. The council publishes the periodical *IQ*, which focuses on topics of concern to women and girls; the newsletter *Women's Research Network News;* and reports, including *Sexual Harassment: Research and Resources*.

National Organization for Women (NOW)

1000 16th St. NW, Suite 700, Washington, DC 20036
(202) 331-0066 • fax: (202) 785-8576
e-mail: now@now.org • website: http://www.now.org

NOW is one of the largest women's organizations in the nation. The group works for political change through legal action and within the electoral system. NOW supports economic and social equality for women and utilizes class-action lawsuits and public-information campaigns to achieve change on issues, including discrimination against pregnant women, sexual harassment in the workplace, and pay equity.

National Organization for Women Legal Defense and Education Fund

99 Hudson St., New York, NY 10013
(212) 925-6635 • fax: (212) 226-1066
website: http://www.nowldef.org

The fund provides legal referrals and conducts research on a broad range of issues concerning women and the law. It offers a comprehensive list of publications, including testimony on sexual harassment, books, articles, reports, and briefs.

9to5, National Association of Working Women

231 W. Wisconsin Ave., Suite 900, Milwaukee, WI 53203-2308
(414) 274-0925 • fax: (414) 272-2879 • hot line: (800) 522-0925
e-mail: NAWW9to5@execpc.com

The association is the leading membership organization for working women. It utilizes class-action lawsuits and public-information campaigns to achieve change on issues including discrimination against pregnant women, sexual harassment in the workplace, and pay equity. 9to5 counselors communicate with working women in the United States and Canada through the Job Problem Hotline and publishes books and reports, including *The 9to5 Guide to Combating Sexual Harassment*.

Office for Victims of Crime Resource Center (OVCRC)
Box 6000, Rockville, MD 20849-6000
(800) 627-6872
website: http://www.ncjrs.org

Established in 1983 by the U.S. Department of Justice's Office for Victims of Crime, OVCRC is crime victims' primary source of information. The center answers questions by using national and regional statistics, a comprehensive collection of research findings, and a well-established network of victim advocates and organizations. OVCRC distributes all Office of Justice Programs (OJP) publications on victim-related issues, including *Female Victims of Violent Crime* and *Sexual Assault: An Overview*.

Rockford Institute
934 Main St., Rockford, IL 61103-7061
(815) 964-5053 • fax: (815) 965-1826
e-mail: rkfdinst@bossnt.com

The institute seeks to return America to Judeo-Christian and traditional family values by educating the public on religious and social issues. It promotes the view that day care is harmful to children and that every effort should be made to allow mothers to raise their children at home. The organization advocates home-based business as one way of allowing mothers to stay at home. Rockford publishes the monthly monograph *The Family in America* and its supplement *New Research,* the monthly magazine *Chronicles*, and the newsletter *Mainstreet Memorandum.*

Index